T0315108

THE

PUBLICATIONS

OF THE

SURTEES SOCIETY

VOL. 204

THE

PUBLICATIONS

OF THE

SURTEES SOCIETY

ESTABLISHED IN THE YEAR
M.DCCC.XXXIV

VOL. CCIV

At a MEETING of the SURTEES SOCIETY, held on 10 June 1999, it was ORDERED —

'That the volume of pitmen's songs, complied and edited by Dr Dave Harker, should be printed as a volume of the Society's publications'

SONGS AND VERSE
OF THE
NORTH-EAST
PITMEN
c.1780–1844

EDITED
BY
DAVE HARKER

TYPESET FROM DISC BY
ROGER BOOTH ASSOCIATES, HASSOCKS, WEST SUSSEX

PRINTED FOR THE SOCIETY
ATHENÆUM PRESS LIMITED, GATESHEAD
1999

ISBN 0–85444–061–5

CONTENTS

Acknowledgements viii
Abbreviations ix
Bibliography x
Introduction: Print, Verse and the Pit Villages 1
    1662–1830 2
    1831–1832 9
    1833–1840 16
    1841–1843 18
    January-March 1844 34
    April–May 1844 41
    June 1844 50
    July–August 1844 58
    Aftermaths 63
Chief Sources of the Manuscript and Broadside Texts 68
Principles of Selection and Arrangement 76
Editorial Conventions 77
Texts 79
Appendices 317
Index of Places, Persons and Institutions 325
Index of Titles and First Lines 332

ACKNOWLEDGEMENTS

The editor thanks the Librarians and staff of Cambridge University Library, Glasgow University Library, Newcastle Central Reference Library, Newcastle Literary and Philosophical Society, Northumberland County Record Office, the Picton Library, Liverpool, the Robinson Library, University of Newcastle, the Vaughan Williams Memorial Library, London, and the Wigan Archives, Leigh Town Hall.

Particular thanks for advice and support – some of it stretching over a quarter of a century – are offered to Owen Ashton, Douglas Bond, David Craig, Linda Duncan, Alastair Elliot, Kenneth Goldstein, Lesley Gordon, Derek Hatton, Matt Kelly, Annie Makepeace, Margaret Norwell, Stephen Roberts, Ian Russell, Frank Rutherford, Elaine Scanlan, John Smethurst and Malcolm Taylor.

Once again it is pleasant to thank the President, Secretary and Council of the Surtees Society for their willingness to publish such 'unofficial' material and especially for their flexibility in allowing me to include a somewhat longer Introduction than has been traditional, because of the special issues raised by attempting to use songs, verse and associated material as legitimate historical evidence.

This work is dedicated to all those men, women and children from the pit-villages who were and are determined to be free, and in particular to the memory, friends and comrades of Roger Pearce.

ABBREVIATIONS

Allan	Thomas Allan Collection, Newcastle Central Library (Allan: SL 427.52).
Bell	Northumberland Record Office, Bell Mining Collection, NRO/3410/Bell.
B/W2	'A Collection of local songs and poems which have appeared in print in Newcastle-upon-Tyne and its neighbourhood. By John Bell, Landsurveyor, Gateshead. Gateshead. 1800', Newcastle University Library (Bell/White 2; 821.04).
B/W13	'A Poetic Selection', Newcastle University Library (Bell/White 13; W821.04 – POE).
C & R	Raymond Challinor & Brian Ripley.
CUL	Cambridge University Library.
CULM	Cambridge University Library Madden Collection, Volume M16, 'Country Printers' (Northumberland and Durham).
Goldstein	Professor Kenneth S. Goldstein's private collection of broadsides.
NCL	Newcastle Central Library.
NCL 1844	'Pitman's Strike 1844' volume, Newcastle Central Library (Pitman 1844: SL 331.89 Cr 31306).
NEIMME	North of England Institute of Mining and Mechanical Engineers.
NRO	Northumberland Record Office.
NUL	Newcastle University Library.
NUL Loose	Loose broadsides, Newcastle University Library ('Broadside Collection').
Picton	Picton Library, Liverpool, 'History of the Coal Trade' collection (Kf3), 'Workmen's Strikes' Volumes I and II.
Wigan	Wigan Archives, Leigh Town Hall, 'Pitmen's Strike Collection' (D/DZ A31).

x

BIBLIOGRAPHY

Periodicals
The Miners' Advocate.
The Miners' Journal.
The Miners' Monthly Magazine.
The Monthly Chronicle.
The Newcastle Weekly Chronicle.

Secondary sources
Allan, Thomas, *A Choice Collection of Tyneside Songs* (Newcastle, 1863).
Allan, Thomas, *Tyneside Songs* (Newcastle, 1972 [1891]).
Allen, Edward, et al, *The North-East Engineers' Strikes of 1871* (Newcastle, 1971).
Anon, *Address of the Reformers of Fawdon* (Newcastle, 1819).
Anon, *A Voice from the Coal Mines* (South Shields, 1825).
Anon, *Rules and Regulations...of...The United Association of Colliers* (Newcastle, 1825).
Anon, *A Candid Appeal to the Coal Owners and Viewers...* (Newcastle, 1826).
Anon, *Tyneside Songster* (Alnwick, ND [?1840]).
Ashton, T.S., & Sykes, Joseph, *The Coal Industry of the Eighteenth Century* (Manchester, 1929).
Bell, John, *Rhymes of Northern Bards* (Newcastle, 1971 [1812]).
Burt, Thomas, 'Methodism and the Northern Miners', *The Primitive Methodist Quarterly Review*, (July 1882), pp. 385–97.
Burt, Thomas, *An Autobiography* (London, 1924).
Callcott, Maureeen, & Challinor, Raymond, eds, *Working Class Politics in North East England* (Newcastle, 1983).
Callinicos, Alex, *The Revenge of History. Marxism and the East European Revolutions* (Cambridge, 1991).
Callinicos, Alex, & Simons, Mike, *The Great Strike* (London, 1985).
Catcheside-Warrington, C.E., *Tyneside Songs* (Newcastle, ND [?1911– ?][four volumes]).
Challinor, Raymond, *The Lancashire and Cheshire Miners* (Newcastle, 1972).
Challinor, Raymond, *A Radical Lawyer in Victorian England* (London, 1990).
Challinor, Raymond, & Ripley, Brian, *The Miners' Association – A Trade Union in the Age of the Chartists* (London, 1968).
Chicken, Edward, *The Collier's Wedding* (Newcastle, 1764 [?1720s]).
Colls, Robert, *The Collier's Rant* (London, 1977).
Colls, Robert, *The Pitmen of the Northern Coalfield* (Manchester, 1987).
Douglass, Dave, *Pit Life in County Durham* (Oxford, 1972).
Flett, Keith, *The Language and Vision of post-1848 Chartism* (London, 1996).
Fordyce, William & Thomas, *Catalogue of 4to. Slip Songs* (Newcastle, ?1841). [CULM]
Fordyce, William & Thomas, eds, *Newcastle Song Book* (Newcastle, 1842).
Fordyce, William & Thomas, *The History...of Durham* (Newcastle, 1857).
Fynes, Richard, *A Review of the Real and Sham Reformers who have been amongst the miners for the last ten years* (1872) [NCL].

Fynes, Richard, *The Miners of Northumberland and Durham* (East Ardsley, 1971 [1873]).

Galloway, Robert, *Annals of Coal Mining and the Coal Trade* (London, 1898, 1904).

Gittings, Clare, *Death, Burial and the Individual in Early Modern England* (London, 1988).

Green, William, 'Chronicle and Records of the Coal Trade', *Transactions of the NEIMME*, Volume 15, (1865–66), pp. 175–281.

Greenwell, George, *Glossary of Term. used in the Coal Trade* (London, 1888).

Hair, P.E.H., 'The Social History of British Coal-Miners, 1800–45', unpublished D.Phil. dissertation, University of Oxford (1955).

Hair, Thomas, *Sketches of the Coal Mines in Northumberland and Durham* (Newcastle, 1969 [1844]).

Hammond, John & Barbara, *The Skilled Labourer* (London, 1919).

Handle, Johnny, 'Industrial Folk Music and Regional Music Hall in the North East', *English Dance and Song*, (August 1965), pp. 106–8; (October 1965), pp. 138–41; (New Year 1966), pp. 6–9.

Harker, Dave, 'John Bell, the "Great Collector"', (1971), pp. iii–liii in Bell, *Rhymes*.

Harker, Dave, 'Thomas Allan and "Tyneside Song"', (1972), pp. vii–xxviii in Allan, *Tyneside Songs*.

Harker, Dave, 'Popular Song and Working-Class Consciousness in North-East England', unpublished PhD dissertation, University of Cambridge (1976).

Harker, Dave, *One for the Money: politics and popular song* (London, 1980).

Harker, Dave, 'The Original Bob Cranky?', *Folk Music Journal*, Volume 5, Number 1, (1985), pp. 48–82.

Harker, Dave, *Fakesong: the manufacture of British 'folksong', 1700 to the present day* (Milton Keynes, 1985).

Harker, Dave, & Rutherford, Frank, eds, *Songs from the Manuscript Collection of John Bell* (Durham, 1985).

Harker, Dave, 'Taking fun seriously', *Popular Music*, Volume 15, Part 1, (1996), pp. 108–21.

Harrison, Brian, & Hollis, Patricia, *Robert Lowery, Radical and Chartist* (London, 1979).

Hunt, Christopher, *The Book Trade in Northumberland and Durham to 1860* (Newcastle, 1975).

Jenkins, Mick, *The General Strike of 1842* (London, 1980).

Jones, Carol, 'Experience of a strike. The North East Coalowners and the pitmen, 1831–1832', (1986), pp. 27–54 in Sturgess, *Pitmen*.

Korson, George, *Coal Dust on the Fiddle* (Philadelphia, 1943).

Kovalev, Y.V., ed., *An Anthology of Chartist Literature* (Moscow, 1960).

Lloyd, Albert, ed., *Come all ye bold miners* (London, 1952, 1978).

Lloyd, Albert, ed., *Coal Dust Ballads* (London, ND [?1952]).

Lloyd, Albert, *Folk Song in England* (London, 1967).

Lockey, Liz, 'The Bell Family', unpublished dissertation, BA Library Studies, Newcastle upon Tyne Polytechnic, (ND [?1979]).

Londonderry, Edith, *Lady Anne* (London, 1958).

Mackenzie, Eneas, *An Historical...View of...Durham* (Newcastle, 1834).

Maehl, W.H., 'Chartist Disturbances in Northeastern England, 1839', *International Review of Social History*, Volume VIII, Number 3, (1963), pp. 389–414.

Maehl, W.H., 'Augustus Hardin Beaumont: Anglo-American Radical, 1798–1838', *International Review of Social History*, Volume XIV, Part 2, (1969), pp. 237–50.

Manders, F.W.D., *A History of Gateshead* (Gateshead, 1973).

Marat, Jean, *The Chains of Slavery* (London, 1774).

Marshall, John, ed., *A Collection of Songs...* (Newcastle, 1827).

Marx, Karl, & Engels, Frederick, *Collected Works* (London, 1975–).

McCord, Norman, 'The Murder of Nicholas Fairles, Esq., J.P.', *South Shields Archaeological and Historical Society Papers*, Volume 1, Number VI, (1958), pp. 12–19.

Meech, Thomas, *From Mine to Ministry; the Life and Times of Thomas Burt* (Darlington, ND).

Middlebrook, Sydney, *Newcastle-upon-Tyne: Its Growth and Achievement* (Newcastle, 1968).

Mitford, William, *The Budget; or, Newcastle Songster* (Newcastle, 1816).

Moyes, W.A., *The Banner Book* (Newcastle, 1974).

Neale, Jonathan, *The Cutlass and the Lash* (London, 1985).

Raven, Michael & Jon, eds, *Folk-lore and Songs of the Black Country and the West Midlands* (Wolverhampton, 1965–67[three volumes]).

Richardson, R., 'Primitive Methodism: Its Influence on the Working Classes', *Primitive Methodist Review*, Volume 25, (1883), pp. 261–73.

Ritson, Joseph, *The Northumberland Garland* (Newcastle, 1793).

Roberts, Stephen, *Radical Politicians and Poets in early Victorian Britain. The Voices of Six Chartist Leaders* (Lampeter, 1993).

Robson, Joseph, *The Monomaniac and Minor Poems* (Newcastle, 1848).

Robson, Joseph, ed., *Songs of the Bards of the Tyne* (Newcastle, 1849).

Robson, Joseph, *The Autobiography of Joseph Philip Robson* (Newcastle, 1870) .

Ross, John, *Catalogue of Slip Songs...* (Newcastle, 1849). [NUL]

Rowe, David J., 'Some Aspects of Chartism on Tyneside', *International Review of Social History*, Volume 16, Part 1, (1971), pp. 17–39.

Selkirk, James, ed., *Selkirk's Collection of Songs and Ballads for the People* (Newcastle, 1851).

Sharp, Cuthbert, ed., *The Bishoprick Garland* (London, 1834).

Siegel, Paul, *The Meek and the Militant: Religion and Power Across the World* (London, 1986).

Sill, Michael, 'The Journal of Matthias Dunn, 1831–1836: Some Observations of a Colliery Viewer', (1986), pp. 55–80 in Sturgess, *Pitmen.*

Stokoe, John, & Reay, Samuel, eds, *Songs and Ballads of Northern England* (Newcastle, 1893).

Sturgess, R.W., ed., *Pitmen, Viewers and Coalmasters: Essays on North East England Coalmining in the Nineteenth Century* (Newcastle, 1986).

Thompson, Dorothy, ed., *Early Chartists* (Columbia, South Carolina, 1971).

Thompson, Dorothy, *The Chartists* (New York, 1984).

Thomson, Frances, *Newcastle Chapbooks in Newcastle-upon-Tyne University Library* (Newcastle, 1969).

Vicinus, Martha, ed., *Broadsides of the Industrial North* (Newcastle, 1975).

Walker, George, *List of Songs...* (Durham, ND [?1837]). [CULM]

Walters, W., *The History of the Newcastle on Tyne Sunday School Union* (Newcastle, 1869).

Wearmouth, Robert, *Methodism and the Working Class Movements of England, 1800–1850* (London, 1947).

Wearmouth, Robert, *Some Working-Class Movements of the Nineteenth Century* (London, 1948).

Webb, Sidney, *The Story of the Durham Miners (1662–1921)* (London, 1921).

Welbourne, E., *The Miners' Unions of Northumberland and Durham* (Cambridge, 1923).

Welford, Richard, *Men of Mark Twixt Tyne and Tweed* (Newcastle, 1895 [three volumes]).

Wilson, Keith, '"Whole Hogs" and "Sucking Pigs" – Chartism and the Complete Suffrage Union in Sunderland', (1983), pp. 17–22 in Callcott & Challinor, *Working Class Politics.*

Wilson, Keith, 'Chartism and the North East Miners: a Reappraisal', (1986), pp. 81–104 in Sturgess, *Pitmen.*

Wilson, Thomas, *The Pitman's Pay and Other Poems* (Gateshead, 1843).

INTRODUCTION

PRINT, VERSE AND THE PIT VILLAGES

Traditional historians tend to ignore what they still term 'literary' evidence, or to relegate it to epigraphs and footnotes, probably because they have yet to develop an appropriate methodology for dealing with it.[1] This is particularly true of material deriving from the labouring poor and the working class, which is also, usually, either ignored or patronised by traditional literary critics on account of its perceived lack of (usually, undefined) 'literary quality'. When such materials as songs and verse are used by academic historians, all too often highly mediated texts are quoted selectively in order to support analyses based on 'official' sources. Worker-authors are made to speak *for*, or *on behalf of*, other workers, so as to lend 'authenticity' to a particular interpretation of events, though their texts are rarely treated as an integral part of the available body of evidence or even quoted with perfect accuracy. It is not surprising, then, that scholars trying to understand the thoughts and feelings of the vast majority of the population in history have felt frustrated:

> We cannot really be sure that the vision which rank-and-file Chartists had in their heads of what society could be like, and how it could be achieved, was the same as that found in the Chartist press, or given verbal expression on platforms by Chartist leaders.[2]

The texts which form the body of this book represent what may be a unique opportunity to test this pessimistic thesis, since they represent a coherent body of material current in Northumberland and Durham in the period c.1780 to 1844, and particularly during the Great Strike of 1844.

---

1. For a critique of a recent unhappy attempt, see Harker (1996).
2. Flett (1996), 13.

However, there are two preliminary problems. Firstly, these materials have not previously been subjected to careful scholarly analysis in order to establish which derive from worker-writers and which do not. Secondly, many texts have been *mediated*, some of them more than once. Consequently the use of these and other worker-made materials by activist-historians such as Richard Fynes and Thomas Burt, by optimistic academic historians such as Raymond Challinor and Brian Ripley and by pessimistic ones like Robert Colls, is supplementary to an analysis based on traditional sources, such as those produced by the union bureaucracy or by agents of the state. However, once the song, verse and associated materials come fully into play a notably different understanding of the dynamics of the Great Strike becomes both possible and necessary, so it is necessary to begin by giving a brief and factual account of the events in which these texts played an important role, and of how they came to be written, edited for publication and published. Every effort has been made to present empirical information as fully and as accurately as possible and to avoid unnecessary interpretation.[3] Considerable care has also been taken to suggest how and why this propaganda varied and to underline the importance of differentiating between material made *by, for, on behalf of* or *about* pit-village people, a project which has necessitated including an analytical account of the various forms of mediation of texts which derived from working class writers, whether done by union officials, folklorists or traditional historians of both left and right.

1662–1830

The Great Strike of 1844 was not the first dispute in the Northumberland and Durham coalfield. In 1662, two thousand colliers petitioned the king, asking him to intervene between themselves and their employers. In the later 1730s, industrial action won piecemeal gains. In 1740, a year of dearth and high prices,

---

3. Some interpretation is unavoidable, and since no historian or editor is innocent, all that can be done here is to make the writer's perspective and methods as transparent and, hopefully, as consistent and self-reflexive as possible. The tradition at work here, then, is that of classical marxism, as outlined in Callinicos, *The Revenge of History* – a perspective which is not, of course, to be mistaken for the Stalinist distortion which caused so much confusion during the Cold War, and which sadly still does in some sheltered and unscholarly quarters.

pitmen joined other coal trade workers to 'regulate' the price of grain in Newcastle market and won a thirty per cent rise in basic pay. The first North East coalfield strike took place in 1765, when four thousand pit-workers struck against the attempt to impose leaving certificates, (formal release documents without which a pit-worker could not start at another colliery), designed to restrict the mobility of labour in an increasingly class-divided society. One hundred thousand people were 'out of bread' for six weeks. In 1785 the Sunderland magistrates felt obliged to ask for a barracks in order to cope with the restive pitmen and keelmen.[4] Yet every versified story concerning pit-villagers in this period is written about them and not by them, including the only two songs which predate 1800.

Call the Horse, Marrow (1)[5] is the oldest surviving song to attempt to render pit-village speech phonetically and to use specialised coal-working terminology, and while it could have functioned as a rhyme to accompany a dance, there is no hard evidence that it was produced by pit-village people. More likely it was put together by an outsider for the consumption of other outsiders, a poetical practice dating back to Edward Chicken's *The Collier's Wedding*, which probably appeared in print in the 1720s.[6] After all, only those who did not already speak idiomatically would need printed guidance. Similarly, there is no evidence that *The Colliers Rant* (2) derives from the labouring population. William Brockie noted that it 'was a rare treat to hear Topliff sing it', yet Robert Topliff was an organist at Trinity Church, London, and entertained petit-bourgeoise audiences during holidays in his native North East during the 1840s.[7]

The first years of the nineteenth century produced a brief spell of prosperity in North East pit-villages, largely because the state needed thousands of sailors and soldiers. Taking advantage of this tightening

4. Harker, 'Popular Song', pp. 54–100; Fynes, *The Miners*, pp. 9–10; Hammond, *The Skilled Labourer*, pp. 19–20.
5. Numbers in bold type (sometimes in brackets and with letters) refer to texts in the body of this volume. Additional information relating to publication is to be found in the accompanying notes.
6. Harker, 'Popular Song', pp. 41–45.
7. *Newcastle Weekly Chronicle*, 31.7.1875, 19.8.1876. In December 1844, 'Topliff's New Musical Entertainment' was advertised by a poster for the Assembly Room, Sun Inn, Darlington. Prices ranged from one shilling for children at the back to half a crown for adults at the front, and in the final 'Local melange' was to be Mr. Topliff's rendition of a 'Local song', *'As me and maw Marrow.'* See below, p. 311.

of the labour market, pit-workers formed an illegal union or 'combination' and gradually forced higher levels of binding money – cash given at the signing of the Yearly Bond or contract – reaching a peak level in 1804.[8] During this period, young, unmarried pitmen spent their spare cash not only on the annual Binding Day in Newcastle but also on the fortnightly Pay Saturday trips to the town, and this led to a number of anti-pitman satires in song, constructed around the stereotyped figure of 'Bob Cranky'. Bob Cranky's 'Size Sunday (3) was probably the first. It was written in 1803 by John Selkirk, a Quayside clerk, and was published in 1804 by Margaret Angus, widow of Thomas Angus, who from 1800 until 1812 ran her late husband's business in the Side, Newcastle, specialising in chapbooks, slip songs, battledores and school books.[9] Margaret Angus and Son also catered for the local pianoforte-owning market, and this is why they published another version of Bob Cranky's 'Size Sunday, as 'A Favourite Comic Song' made by 'a Gentleman of Newcastle'.[10]

As yet, there seem to have been no creative links between the region's pit-workers and the urban print-trade; but when an employers' offensive drove down binding money and wage-rates from 1805 to 1810, the Methodist pitman, Ben Embleton, and people like him, organised a union or 'Brotherhood' and led a strike which brought out thirty-one collieries, using what we now know as flying pickets. Coalowners who were also magistrates were allowed by the state to use troops to break a strike. They arrested the Methodist union leadership and housed them in stables kindly loaned by the Christian Bishop of Durham. All this took place in seven weeks, starting in October 1810. In subsequent years there was a change of attitude towards pit-village people amongst some local petit-bourgeois songwiters. A New Song, on XYZ; or, Pitmen's Luck (4), by the cordwainer William Mitford,[11] seems much more sympathetic to pit-village people than the last of the 'Bob Cranky' pieces, Bob Cranky's

---

8. Fynes, The Miners, pp. 15–16; Colls, The Pitmen, pp. 77–78.
9. Hunt, The Book Trade, pp. 3–4.
10. Harker, 'The original Bob Cranky?', (1985).
11. Mitford became a singing-landlord in the 1820s (Allan, Tyneside Songs, pp. 132–36; Newcastle Weekly Chronicle, 4.10.1879, 4.10.1884). This piece articulates an urban artisan's perspective on pitmen's alleged hedonism, but it does so with less venom than earlier examples of the genre.

Account of the Ascent of Mr Sadler's Balloon **(5)**. John Marshall[12] printed a broadside of Mitford's song, and soon afterwards the Tyneside print-trade was caught up in the political repercussions of the economic crisis which took hold after the end of the wars with France in 1815.[13] For a while Marshall published versified material aimed at labouring communities, such as *A Curious Dialogue* **(6)**, while continuing to produce Mitford's[14] *Cappy; or the Pitman's Dog* **(7)**, a satire of a Newcastle roughneck, and *The Pitman's Courtship* **(8)**,[15] a piece about the merits of private enterprise and primitive accumulation, dressed up as a song about a pit-village couple. But in 1817 Marshall was sacked as Librarian of the Literary and Philosophical Society for publishing (presumably, William Hone's) *Political Litany*.[16]

---

12. John Marshall was the son of Betty Marshall, who 'used to make a livelihood for many years by hawking numbers of periodical publications for the different booksellers' in Newcastle, and of John Marshall senior, a Unitarian Baptist. In 1799, John Junior was already a printer when he was elected Librarian at the Literary and Philosophical Society, and by 1801 he was also a bookseller and had a circulating library in Gateshead (Hunt, *The Book Trade*, p. 65). He published broadside songs, chapbooks and songbooks, and followed up *The Northern minstrel, or Gateshead Songster* of 1806–7 with a series of chapbook collections including 'local' songs using Tyneside settings and phonetic spelling. In February 1810, Marshall's Gateshead shop was burned out, but on the basis of a subscription he re-established himself in the Old Flesh Market, Newcastle (Harker, (1971), xli–xlii).
13. Harker, 'Popular Song', pp. 266–347.
14. Manuscript notes indicate that it was 'Wrote by William Mitford Shoemaker in the Back Row Newcastle' and identify 'Cappy' as 'Ernshaw, a Constable in Newcastle.' The latter was a 'gross, vulgar fellow' (Allan, *Tyneside Songs*, p. 141).
15. The phoneticising of the diction is more muted here, perhaps because there is little humour in the story.
16. This was evidently a political watershed for Marshall. In 1818 he published an account of Hone's three trials, followed, in 1819, by the *Extraordinary Red Book*. In 1820, he issued the *Radical Reformer's New Song Book* and *The Wreath of Freedom or Patriot's Songbook*: in 1821, the *Christian Reformer's Monthly Tract*; and in 1823 a collection of *Coronation Songs*, satirising George IV, plus the *Northern Reformers' Monthly Magazine and Political Register*. He also spoke at the Newcastle meeting to celebrate the release of Henry Hunt, the radical reformer. Interestingly, James Pollock – who published a close variant of 6, and may have had a connection with Marshall – was bankrupted in 1817, again in 1828 and once more between 1834 and 1844 (Hunt, *The Book Trade*, pp. 65, 73–74).

Whether John Marshall's radical printed material was produced on a commercial or a political basis is unclear, but there was evidently a growing market for printed matter of all kinds amongst urban radicals and pit-village activists. In October 1819, political 'classes' began to be formed on the Wear and quickly spread to the colliery villages along the Tyne. Pit-workers at Percy Main, for example, had a fund and furnished a room in which to meet, argue, organise and read. Colliery Viewer[17] John Buddle asserted that Thomas Wooler's radical paper, the *Black Dwarf*, was 'to be found in the Hat Crown of almost every pitman you meet' on Tyneside before the end of 1819.[18] Certainly, the 'Reformers of Fawdon' felt it worthwhile to get John Marshall to print an *Address* specifically aimed at pit-village people, though one which preached peaceful reform. Also in 1819, the religious element in the pit-villages was already coming to be sharply polarised and thereafter many of the urban and pit-village radicals entered the 'democratic and progressive' Primitive Methodists.[19] According to a Methodist historian,[20] by 1821 there was open talk of an alliance between the urban radicals and the Primitive or Ranter Methodist organisations. One of the two ejected Methodist preachers after the 1819 Newcastle Town Moor meeting to protest at the Peterloo Massacre was William Stephenson Junior, the printer who had been happy enough to produce John Adley's rather conservative *The Coal Trade* (9) only a year before, but who later became 'an ardent reformer, nay a staunch republican'.[21]

During the 1820s the links between radical printers and trade union and Ranter organisations became stronger. The Ranters built chapels for meetings and Sunday Schools, taught children and adults to read, write and speak in public, and to value themselves as the spiritual equals of magistrates, coalowners and aristocrats, thereby adding to the demand for cheap printed material like *The Bold Collier* (10), which may have been an early example of versified trade union propaganda. There is certainly a note of class-based confidence in this story, even though the rival is characterised as a foreigner. *The*

17. A Viewer was a senior manager in charge of one or more collieries.
18. Colls, *The Pitmen*, pp. 85, 243-45.
19. Burt (1882), 391.
20. Wearmouth, *Methodism*, pp. 67, 70.
21. Hunt, *The Book Trade*, p. 85; Allan, *Tyneside Songs*, pp. 313–14.

Miner's Binding (11), published in 1822 by Pollock, was more openly pro-union,[22] and reinforces the theory (believed by the coalowners) that the 'Brotherhood' of 1810 and its system of delegates survived into the early 1820s. The text has clear political attitudes towards those who would 'make themselves gentlemen' at the expense of the 'we' who had been 'all brought to nothing on both Wear and Tyne' – in other words, to those workers who broke the agreement to bind collectively, rather than pit by pit. Of course, the appeal to some 'Great Ruler' suggests a degree of economic and political quietism which fitted in with the Ranter Methodist ideology that was coming to be hegemonic in several collieries, but it is interesting that there is no suggestion of phoneticised diction here, and that wider (if sometimes tentative) links with sympathetic printers were being forged. *Hetton Coals* (12), however, shows that even a radical printer like Stephenson could not afford to turn down pro-coalowner material.

Much of the radical printed material from the mid-1820s took the form of prose. The repeal of the Combination Acts in 1825 led very quickly to the foundation of the United Association of Colliers with its own *Rules and Regulations*, printed for the Society by John Marshall. By 1826 the Hetton Colliery Association had its own purpose-built hall,[23] and, following the example of the Tyne seamen in 1825, the better-organised colliery-based trade union branches began to develop their own printed propaganda, like *A Voice from the Coal Mines*, hoping to influence 'Coal Owners – their Head Agents – and a Sympathizing Public'. They sought out printers like Marshall, Stephenson and also Joseph Clark Junior [24] in South Shields Market Place, though this was evidently not a risk-free business, since Clark may have been 'engaged in some of the principal Printing Houses of London' but his printing career in South Shields was rather brief.

---

22. According to Hair, 'Social History', p. 39, Hetton Colliery attracted 'all the "disorderly characters" and "scum of the others"' during the 1820s. The putative author, Jowsey, seems to have been in a position of some authority, but his 'phonetic' diction suggests an improbable level of familiarity between the owner, the sinkers and the pitmen.
23. Colls, *The Pitmen*, p. 247.
24. Hunt, *The Book Trade*, p. 25. Hunt was wrong to believe that Clark printed only one broadside, though his involvement with the United Association of Colliers at Hilda Pit may have discouraged work coming in from local employers and their supporters.

Consequently, when the Association wished to have printed *A Candid Appeal to the Coal Owners and Viewers of Collieries on the Tyne and Wear* in 1826, they turned once again to John Marshall in the Old Flesh Market, Newcastle, which was not very far away from their headquarters at the Cock Inn, Head of the Side. This document was directed at economic issues, but it also addressed questions of safety; and while the seven-week strike which took place after Binding Day, April 5th 1826, went down to defeat, and the leaders were victimised, even in defeat it remained possible to agitate on the issue of pit-explosions.[25]

Anxieties about safety were directly connected to agitation against the Bond, since the annual contract tied a pit-worker to one pit whatever its safety record, so it is particularly interesting that Stephenson printed *On the Sufferings of the Pitmen* and *The Widows' Lamentation* (**13 & 14**), a double broadside possibly commissioned by widows and dependents in order to help raise the cost of funeral expenses. This seems to have been the first locally-produced broadside to have this specific function, though the narrator's use of 'they' and 'their' suggests an author not necessarily part of the pit-workforce. The self-conscious use of the first person and the inclusion of thoughts and even hesitations – and, of course, the exclusion of phonetic diction and even of localised idiom – underline both the horror of the situation and the personal involvement which the piece is intended to generalise to potential financial supporters. Both texts are dignified, circumstantial and orthodoxly (but not overly) God-fearing, presumably to minimise any possible sectarian religious or political offence and so help to maximise donations. [26] The contrast with the double broadside (**15 & 16**) *Come, Lay Down Yor Picks* and *The Pitman's Surprise*, written (possibly by Robert Emery[27]) for the Newcastle Freemen, could hardly be greater; though

---

25. Multiple deaths underground became common in the 1820s. Officially, one pit-worker was killed on average every ten days, but the death-toll was probably ten times that rate (Galloway, *Annals*, Volume 1, p. 465; Fynes, *The Miners*, pp. 16–17, 149–51.

26. William Stephenson wrote verse, as well as 'supplying hawkers with songs, slips, last dying confessions, etc' (Allan, *Tyneside Songs*, pp. 313–14). Verse like this contrasted sharply with the smug romanticism of Thomas Wilson's *The Pitman's Pay*. For the use and abuse of this poem by historians, see Harker, 'Popular Song', pp. 350ff.

27. For Emery, see Allan, *Tyneside Songs*, pp. 284–90.

the fact that John Marshall maintained a commercial link with this body so late as 1828 suggests that political polarisation within the Tyneside petit-bourgeoisie was still far from complete.

1831–1832

The later 1820s and early 1830s saw the tightening of links between the leading coalfield Primitive Methodist trade unionist, Thomas Hepburn,[28] and a Newcastle radical like John Marshall, both of whom were part of the radical coterie which met regularly in the back of Emerson Charnley's bookshop in Newcastle. By February 26th 1831, the pitmen's union was sufficiently rooted to have two hundred delegates capable of bringing ten thousand colliery workers to the Black Fell, a hill east of Birtley, where they decided collectively to refuse to sign the offered Bond. The delegates' headquarters at the Cock Inn, Newcastle, housed what Viewer Buddle sarcastically called the 'Cock Parliament',[29] yet this organisation brought an 'immense number' of pit-workers to the Black Fell a fortnight after the initial meeting, and subsequently assembled twenty thousand colliery workers – the overwhelming majority of the coalfield's workforce – to march through Newcastle to the Town Moor on March 21st, to the undisguised terror of the shopkeepers.

It seems highly likely that the laconic *First Drest Man of Seghill* (17) was a key component in this campaign, given that the events referred to took place on March 19th 1831. The broadside may well have been sold or distributed on the Town Moor before the traditional binding day of April 5th. (The owners' lock-out began on April 6th.) Publicly, Hepburn threatened to hand over to the magistrates anyone who disciplined blacklegs in the traditional manner, yet this song indicates that on such questions there were very deep disagreements at the heart of the union.[30] Its 'hero' was Willie Dawson, who had

---

28. Hepburn, born in 1795, learned how to organise in the Ranter Methodists after 1822, as did the former Wesleyan preacher, William Hammond, and Ben Embleton, a veteran of 1810 and 1811. 'Hepburn's Union' began at Hetton Colliery where, since 1829, he had worked alongside future union leaders such as Charles Parkinson (also a Ranter Methodist) and Robert and Christopher Haswell. Another key activist, Sam Wardle of Backworth, was a Ranter, too (Welbourne, *The Miners' Unions*, p. 30; Richardson (1883), 264; see also Burt (1882), 393).
29. Jones (1986), 33.
30. Compare Colls, *The Pitmen*, p. 253.

been unwise enough to agree in advance to be bound under the previous conditions, and the prospect of sharing Willie's fate – being stripped naked and chased across the moors, with only a hat to hide both your embarassment and an erection brought on by cold and fear – might well (so to speak) have stiffened-up other potential waverers. Moreover, the reprinting of the piece by Marshall (to produce a print-run of at least fifteen hundred copies) suggests that such material was judged to be necessary, popular and likely to be effective. Willie Dawson was also celebrated in *The Oppressions of the Pitmen* (18). The author for whom this broadside was printed [31] – Joseph Hall, a Sherriff Hill collier – was probably acting on behalf of the union, since he is concerned not only to rally union members behind Hepburn and the union officials, but also to put a wedge between the coalowners and their Viewers.[32] *Grievances of the Pitmen* (19) was evidently intended both to raise the strikers' morale and to inform other people of the details of the union's case,[33] and the warning reference to state force is particularly interesting, as is the hint at a generational gap in some families over the propriety of a political escalation of an economic dispute.[34]

The most effective strikers' tactics in 1831 involved direct action, and though General Bouverie used troops on April 7th to reopen one colliery, he declined to do so a second time. So, while *The Pitman's Complaint* (20) relates to what we know of Hepburn's preferred rhetoric, it contrasts sharply with the language of the famous note left behind at a Viewer's house by strikers.[35] By early May the

---

31. The printers were Douglas and Kent of Drury Lane, Newcastle, though the radical connection was still in place, since Douglas had been William Stephenson Junior's apprentice. There may also have been a radical connection to the printer of *Grievances of the Pitmen* (19), James Beckwith, who is believed to have started business in Houghton-le-Spring in 1833 before moving to Sunderland in 1841, where he quickly went out of business and sold his press, types and printing materials to John R. Williams (Hunt, *The Book Trade*, pp. 9, 32, 96).
32. Sherriff Hill banner showed a rat eating a pit-worker's bait-poke – the rat symbolising a colliery official.
33. The reference to 'Our children' and the formality of the language suggest there is some doubt as to whether the author really was a Newbottle Colliery putter boy, especially since John Adley, author of 9, also worked there.
34. See Colls, *The Pitmen*, 250; Fynes, *The Miners*, p. 20; Walters, *Sunday School Union*, p. 205.

employers' side began to crumble.[36] May 13th, the date of this broadside, was also the day on which the coalowners met union officials in the Coal Trade Office at Newcastle. The piece was printed 'for the Author' by William Fordyce at his shop in Newcastle's fashionable Dean Street.[37] At this time of economic and political crisis a respectable, commercially-minded printer evidently had no qualms about printing strikers' propaganda, and may even have had some sympathy with the political aims of the workers' petit-bourgeois allies, given the song's reference to Parliamentary Reform.

The union's use of other printers may have been unavoidable, since John Marshall's leftward move in politics had its consequences for the state of his business. In 1830 the traveller for the *Encyclopaedia Britannica* wrote that Marshall was 'A dirty man with a dirty family and a dirty stock. Suspended my lists outside his door, which gave them a better chance of being kept clean'. He was still ready to print strike-related material in the early summer of 1831, as is demonstrated by *The Pitmen's Complaint* (21), but this piece was probably by an outsider since it addresses strikers, their (male) supporters and the employers from a populist and moral perspective. Its author, Jeremiah Knox, is an enigmatic figure, and the name may have been a pseudonym,[38] but the piece suggests that Hepburn and the petit-bourgeois Reformers were anxious about confrontation with the forces of the state and about the effects on trade.[39] However, as the strike drew to a close, John Marshall was in no position to help. In the summer of 1831, John Bell Junior noted:

---

35. See Fynes, *The Miners*, p. 21.
36. Colls, *The Pitmen*, p. 250; Fynes, *The Miners*, pp. 18, 20–21; Meech, *From Mine to Ministry*, p. 6; Jones (1986), 35–36; Welbourne, *The Miners' Unions*, p. 31; Wearmouth, *Methodism*, p. 218.
37. For William and Thomas Fordyce, see Hunt, *The Book Trade*, p. 36, and their c.1841 *Catalogue of 4to. Slip Songs* (Madden 16/401).
38. Knox, writing as from Winlaton, wrote a song on *The Keelman's Stick* in March 1823 and had it printed by John Marshall in Newcastle (B/W2). He also wrote a versified protest against *Short-Weight Butter*, possibly in the 1820s (*Newcastle Weekly Chronicle*, 14.12.1889), and a broadside publicising a higher-paying employer, *The Nailors' Advanced Prices*, three hundred copies of which were printed by Marshall on April 12th 1825 (Madden 16/440). Owen Ashton suggests he may have been related to the known Chartist, Robert Knox.
39. Compare Fynes, *The Miners*, pp. 23–24; Challinor, *A Radical Lawyer*, p. 75.

> Marshall still continuing in difficulties, he gave Bond in judgment to the friend who had become security for his Rent; and one of his Creditors having made a fresh seizure, Miles (the friend and relative before named) also seized and he was wholly sold off, his Printing Presses, Types and other Printing Materials being sold on Monday June 13th 1831 (the best press being sold to John Clarke, Printer) and the Stock in Trade on the following day: – and the library consisting of [6,000] volumes by private contract to Eneas Mackenzie Junior for 130£. This business had latterly been badly managed and his stock was in the dirtiest nay filthiest state imaginable. It generally produced very low prices. the quantity of Lumber and Waste Paper was immense.[40]

John Marshall then disappeared.

Probably from mid-June 1831, printed songs and verse concerning pitmen seem to have been written to or about them, rather than by one of their own number. *The Pitmen's Agreement* (22), for example, dates from mid-June 1831 when the strike was won in Durham,[41] but to clinch victory in Northumberland those still on strike required financial support from Durham pitmen back at work, and this piece advocates such tactics. On the other hand, *The Pitmen's Stick* (23), also by Jeremiah Knox, stresses the petit-bourgeoisie's economic dependence on pit-workers' spending-power and praises the union leadership's quietist strategy, so as to focus on the political agenda of the Parliamentary Reformers. The same goes for *The Pitmen's Union* (24) and *The Total Banishment of Self-Tyranny & Oppression* (25), published by Stephenson and Eneas Mackenzie, respectively,[42] and from the autumn of 1831 the petit-bourgeois

---

40. This sale included Marshall's Stanhope and Minerva presses, his three hundred Bewick woodcuts, his collection of children's books, and, presumably, his other chapbooks and broadsides (NCL & NUL Bell Book Trade Ephemera; Hunt, *The Book Trade*, p. 65; Harker (1972), xiii–xiv; Harker, 'Popular Song', p. 364). For John Clarke, who printed the Marshall sale notices, see Hunt, *The Book Trade*, p. 25.
41. Burt (1882), 392; Galloway, *Annals*, Volume 1, p. 466. The strike secured the abolition of Tommy Shops, payment in ready money, a limit of twelve hours on the working day for boys and an estimated thirty per cent rise in wage rates. At Hetton, the men came out again until the principal Viewer and all the blacklegs were sacked (Welbourne, *The Miners' Unions*, p. 32; Colls, *The Pitmen*, p. 91).

reformers concentrated on political rather than on trade union activity.

After the success of the 1831 strike, the pitmen's union employed methods formerly used by their employers. One of their rules was

> That if any member of this society have a desire to leave his colliery to go to any other, he be required to get a certificate from the colliery he belongs to and lay it before the committee of the colliery he intends to go to, before he goes to make a bargain or agreement with the master he intends to agree with, or be excluded from the society.[43]

Hepburn, meanwhile, was organising union members to go to Reformers' demonstrations, where the 'banners were numerous, and of the gayest description, nearly all being embellished with a painted design, and with a motto more or less connected with the recent struggle between the miners and the employers'. Pitmen were also useful as signatories for the Reformers' petition to the King, though Hepburn clearly had illusions in the powers of parliamentary reform: '"Only get the bill," he is reported to have said at a Reform meeting, "and every working man will have rum in his coffee every morning"'. Yet when it came to the question of direct action in an industrial dispute, Hepburn steadfastly sided with the *Durham Chronicle* and the state. Meanwhile, the most intransigent coalowners threatened to have a 'sweep' of the 'ungovernable' delegates, 'cost what it will!', by not binding any union members in April 1832.[44]

The strike of 1832 began with Hepburn criticising union members for the tactics which had won in 1831. So while the Ranter 'cadre' preached non-violence and held out the long-term perspective of

---

42. Eneas Mackenzie Senior, 'a strong Radical' and Secretary of the Northern Political Union, died in February 1832 from cholera. The unreformed Newcastle Corporation had been pumping drinking water from the tidal part of the Tyne, to save money, at a period when that river was already an open sewer (Welford, *Men of Mark*, Volume 3, pp. 117–18; Hunt, *The Book Trade*, pp. 63–64).

43. Galloway, *Annals*, Volume 1, p. 467.

44. Fynes, *The Miners*, pp. 24–25, 33; Hammond, *The Skilled Labourer*, p. 39; Welbourne, *The Miners' Unions*, pp. 33–34; Jones (1986), 41. See also Jones (1986), 59; Sill (1986), 59.

building libraries, General Bouverie was extremely anxious about possible solidarity action by keelmen and seamen. JPs used police to help lock out the men, protect blacklegs, break up strikers' meetings and arrest and evict union activists, the very people who were responsible for the 'widespread tranquility' that prevailed. Two hundred men – the same number as attended some union delegate meetings at Newcastle – were picked out as 'marked men', arrested for 'conspiracy' and locked up in Durham Gaol, where, true to form, they organised a choir. But whereas the owners' case was well-publicised through newspapers, posters, leaflets – including what looks like 'black' propaganda – and in letters to the Home Office, the union's case hardly got into print.[45]

The Pitman's Union (26) may have been intended as a morale-booster immediately before the strike, since it seeks to associate union membership with sexual gratification in a traditionally sexist single-entendre: the supposedly female narrator will 'for ever take your part'. *A New Song* (27), on the other hand, not only summarised the union position for members and potential supporters but also lined up God on the union's side, since "tis only he,/ Your enemies can subdue'. Others – and especially pit-village women – felt and acted rather differently.[46] *A Copy of Verses Written on the Pitmen being turned out from their Houses* (28) evidently refers to the events of June 2nd 1832, when over a thousand families were evicted in Coxlodge and Kenton from tied houses owned by the Brandling family, whose head was a Church of England vicar. In this operation, troops and police were deployed as though they were a private army.[47] Yet the tone of this text is both quietist and bitter, with the Bible being used as ammunition against 'Judas' blacklegs;[48] and the author makes connections between the pitmen and other members of their own class, the 'Mechanics' who 'feel the pain' 'When times are with the

---

45. Colls, *The Pitmen*, pp. 191, 251; Manders, *A History of Gateshead*, pp. 311–12; Fynes, *The Miners*, pp. 28–29; Richardson (1883), 264–66; Hair, *Sketches*, p. 44 note; Hammond, *The Skilled Labourer*, p. 42; Webb, *Durham Miners*, p. 34.

46. Fynes, *The Miners*, p. 31; Allen et al, *The North-East Engineers' Strikes*, p. 73; Manders, *A History of Gateshead*, p. 93.

47. Sill (1986), 59; Welbourne, *The Miners' Unions*, pp. 36,38; Manders, *A History of Gateshead*, pp. 311–12.

48. Men driven to work as blacklegs had to pledge never to rejoin the union (Jones (1986), 43; Fynes, *The Miners*, p. 35).

pitmen hard', rather than, as in 1831, with the petit-bourgeois Parliamentary Reformers.

Moral force proved ineffective as a union strategy and so the issue of leadership came into question. This may explain the appearance of *The Pitmen's Union* (29), which retains the faith in 'Christ, the Pitmen's friend' and calls on help from that quarter in opposition to the 'Tyrant's hand'. The ideological link between God, 'our Union' and Hepburn is made perfectly explicit: they stood or fell together, and in the end, they fell. Perhaps nowhere is this made more clear than in the events surrounding the death of Nicholas Fairles, a South Shields JP who had tried to intervene in the strike of 1831. On June 11th 1832, four days after the Reform Act passed into law, Fairles was found near to death at Jarrow Slake. His assailant was never caught, but William Jobling was hanged, his body taken from Durham Gaol accompanied by a troop of cavalry and then gibbeted in a grotesque iron cage near his home at Jarrow Slake, all for having held Fairles' horse's head. Yet when a policeman shot and killed a miner in an unprovoked attack early in July 1832 he was sentenced to six months in prison on the very day that Jobling was executed.[49] A commercial broadside was produced to cash in on the interest in Jobling's execution, but neither the author nor publisher of *Lamentation of William Jobling* (30) had the courage to attach their names.

From this point, other counsels prevailed in the pit-villages, and though in August 1832 Hepburn belatedly and rhetorically proposed a general strike, the union was beaten. Most colliery workforces had admitted defeat by September 1832, but the union was formally dissolved only in February 1833. Hepburn was spurned by union members for his ineffective leadership, tried unsuccessfully to sell tea around the region and, like many other activists of 1831 and 1832, spent the rest of the 1830s rethinking his position. Though he had formerly 'never entered upon the consideration of important matters' without 'first praying to God', he had left the Primitive Methodists before the year was out.[50]

49. Fynes, *The Miners*, pp. 22–23, 32–33; Colls, *The Collier's Rant*, pp. 107–8; 257. Compare McCord (1958).
50. Colls, *The Collier's Rant*, pp. 107–8; Jones (1986), 43, 49; Fynes, *The Miners*, pp. 35–36, 244; Richardson (1883), 264; Colls, *The Pitmen*, pp. 97–98, 114, 191, 199, 257, 352 note 29; Welbourne, *The Miners' Unions*, p. 42; Sill (1986), 68.

1833–1840

According to Thomas Burt's parents, 'For the next ten or twelve years the mining districts of the North were in a condition of more or less disturbance. It was a time of transition, of battle, and revolution' with enormous implications for the relations of nonconformity to politics.[51] Former blacklegs, such as the one-time lead-miner, Mark Dent, experienced the same worsened working conditions as ex-strikers, whilst being more likely to face dismissal, so there was continuous pressure to rebuild the union and support for the new general unions also grew. In 1834, after the across-the-board pay cut of 1833, Viewer Buddle opined that 'Nothing but poverty...prevents a general strike', though there were rumblings about a coalfield strike in 1836.[52] There was also a renewed need for printed propaganda,[53] which may have occasioned *A New Song* (31), though its

---

51. Burt (1882), 392.
52. Sill (1986), 71–73, 77; Colls, *The Pitmen*, pp. 219–20; Maehl (1963), 393.
53. There had been a hiatus in radical song- and verse-publishing during the mid-1830s. Angus was out of the trade by 1829: Marshall and Mackenzie followed in 1832; Stephenson worked as a printer only between 1834 and 1838; Douglas and Kent split up in 1836, and the former concentrated on publishing the *Gateshead Observer* until he shot himself in 1854. In the middle and late 1830s, the brothers Fordyce enjoyed a commanding position in the North East market for broadsides and chapbooks, with outlying shops in both Hull and Carlisle. Only a few socially-aware broadside songs came from the Fordyces in the 1830s, but one was a satire on *The Teetotal Society Leaders* (B/W13), which supports Tory drink trade interests. The Newcastle branch of the Society had been formed in 1835, and that in Gateshead by 1836, but the Ranters in the pit villages had opened their chapel doors to temperance propagandists long before. By 1833 all of their Sunderland Circuit preachers were teetotalers, partly because they wished to counteract the payment of pit-workers' wages in pubs. This influence later embraced the Chartists – the Durham Charter Association was founded in a Sunderland Coffee House, for example, and the 'Female Democratic Tea' became an institution (*The Monthly Chronicle* 1899: 44; Manders, *A History of Gateshead*, pp. 158–59; Colls, *The Pitmen*, pp. 131–32, 187, 198–99, 267, 275–76; Burt (1882), 391–92). There were probably connections between some of the militant pitmen and the first Secretary of the Newcastle Society, James Rewcastle, who printed the *Northern District Temperance Record* in 1837 and who had a shop specialising in Nonconformist and Temperance literature at 103 Side, Newcastle from 1834 to 1838, and at 11 Dean Street between 1841 and 1847 (Hunt, *The Book Trade*, p. 77). Rewcastle also printed slip-songs – see 110.

sentimentality about the outcome of the 1832 strike suggests that this piece was written from other than a pit-worker's perspective.

The effects of the economic crisis of the mid-1830s forced pit-men into activity, and there was a six- or seven-week strike in 1837.[54] *A New Song, Called the Haswell Binding* (32) seems to date from around that period, though its authorship may not have been as proletarian as the 'Coal-Hewer' attribution suggests, given the uncritical praise for untried new technology and for the colliery management.[55] *The Pitmen's Union* (33) may also date from 1837. It mentions the lead-miners who had been used to break the strike of 1832, but 'the Union' was not represented as the membership so much as a centre of moral authority and power which would sort things out on their behalf – 'The Union, my lads, will soon put us all right'. Moreover, the doubling of this text with the lugubrious *Remember the Poor* and its publication by the brothers Fordyce suggest that not only a working class audience was being targetted here. However, some commercial publishers' attitudes towards pit-village people were changing a little, if only because of market pressures. *A New Song in praise of Willington Colliery* (34) is more even-handed as between employers and employees than some earlier Fordyce broadsides, though this was not true of George Walker at Durham, whose *The Collier Swell* (35A) was a very crude satire on pit-village pretentiousness.[56] Similarly, Walker's *Haswell Cages* (36) was evidently not for pit-village consumption, given its complacently assumed knowledge of the inside of railway carriages and its absurdly optimistic view of pit-management benevolence and safety-consciousness. In fact such a piece chimed in with the lies that Viewer Buddle reportedly told to a House of Commons committee investigating the question of pit-safety.[57]

Such one-sided publicity underlined the need for pit-workers to have direct access to print in order to disabuse the public, seek support from other workers and inform and support each other. Once again the initiative seems to have been political rather than

54. Wearmouth, *Methodism*, p. 187.
55. Fynes, *The Miners*, pp. 149–50, records almost four hundred deaths in North East collieries during the 1830s, including 102 at Wallsend Colliery in 1835, with more at Haswell in 1840 and 1841 and nine at Thornley in 1841.
56. Thomas Dodds later set this piece in type as *The Pitman Turned Swell* (35B) but may not have published it.
57. Fynes, *The Miners*, pp. 152–53.

economic. At precisely this period the Chartist leader Feargus O'Connor was constructing new political networks amongst disillusioned petit-bourgeois Radicals and working-class militants, amongst whom were recently-politicised activists such as Hepburn, who re-emerged in 1837 as first president of the Newcastle Working Men's Association.[58] And yet, while the Sunderland booksellers and publishers George Binns and John Williams were particularly influential until 1842, throughout the first period of Chartist agitation, working-class activists in the North East had little unmediated access to printers,[59] since locally-produced printed propaganda was largely restricted to Augustus Beaumont's *Northern Liberator* and the Leeds-based *Northern Star*.[60]

1841–1843

The early history of the brothers Thomas and Henry Dodds remains obscure. The first local directory entry for them as 'Printers, Head of the Side' was in 1841, but where they got the training and the capital for their venture is not known.[61] The fact that Henry soon left to set up his own business suggests that they had some money of their own; and they probably had links to Chartist politics and to the market for political literature. For example, the type-face and layout of *O'Conner's Visit to Newcastle* (37) are very reminiscent of some of their later work, though the colophon-less text was, of course, illegal. The somewhat

---

58. For Hepburn in 1832–1837, see Fynes, *The Miners*, pp. 36, 244; Rowe (1971), 22; Richardson (1883), 264. In 1838, Hepburn publicly defied the Mayor of Newcastle, ex-Radical John Fife, who was knighted in July 1840 (Thompson, *Early Chartists*, p. 176).
59. Roberts, *Radical Politicians*, pp. 39–57.
60. For verse published by the Chartist organs, especially the *Northern Star*, see Kovalev, *Chartist Literature*.
61. A Robert Dodds had been a printer, bookseller and stationer in South Shields c.1811–1838 (and possibly so late as 1841), and he was in partnership with Alfred Johnson in 1833. Another Robert Dodds operated as a bookseller and bookbinder in Newcastle between 1811 and 1837. Matthew Stephenson Dodds was the 'most important nautical book supplier in Newcastle', as well as a printer, stationer and map-seller from 1834 until 1870 or even later (Hunt, *The Book Trade*, p. 31). Whether these three men were related to each other, or to Thomas and Henry Dodds, is not clear. Electoral lists for Newcastle indicate that a Thomas Dodds lived at St.Ann's Row between 1836 and 1838, another had a house and a shop at Ouseburn, and a Freeman of that name was listed at 21 St Martin's Court for 1836–37.

peremptory tone of this production is reminiscent of the language of the 'old Reform Bill alliance',[62] though stripped of the defectors to Whigs and Whiggery. There is also a Hepburnian ring to the idea that if 'all the poor men of the North' will put their faith in one man he will go and get their political rights for them. But there is clear local knowledge at work in this text, since the communities listed had pits within their boundaries or close to them.[63]

The Dodds brothers began issuing a series of broadside songs, No.3 of which, *Future Prospects of Taxation*, was later republished by Thomas alone as No.38 (NUL Loose; CULM 16/36). This was a hard-hitting attack on the Tory government's increases in indirect taxation, which were announced in the summer of 1841, but the text may have been imported from London and re-set over the Dodds' colophon, a common enough practice amongst provincial printers for over a century by this date,[64] though its language was as unlocalised as the effects of the taxation. There is some chariness about Chartist politics in the piece, as though its author and printers wanted to target as big a market as possible, as they did with No.7, *The Drunkard Reformed* (CULM 16/23), which dealt with the anti-Tory politics of sobriety and moderation but stopped short of teetotalism. Occasionally, the politics of the early Dodds pieces was less than progressive, as in No.9, *State of the Times* (**38**), which articulates a sad nationalism in the reference to 'German beggars' and, in *Man Little Thinks*, a noted ambivalence on the drink question, since it was followed by four *Toasts*. The main piece links up 'collier men' with other labouring groups, rhetorically, addressing 'all you working people' and posing the key political question, 'what shall we do now', but in a language, tone and manner which suggest non-proletarian authorship.[65] In No.11 in what was now Thomas Dodds' numbered series, *The*

---

62. Thompson, *The Chartists*, p. 33.
63. O'Connor was in Newcastle in November 1836, in Summer 1837 and in January and June 1838. In 1840 he spent time in prison (Thompson, *The Chartists*, p. 156); so 1841 seems the most likely date for this broadside. It may have been written by George Binns, who was probably the best-known local Chartist versifier before he emigrated to New Zealand (Roberts, *Radical Politicians*, pp. 9–57).
64. Harker, 'Popular Song', p. 37.
65. At some point before the appearance of this text, Henry slipped out of the business. He appears to have set up a 'New Grocery Warehouse', leaving the printing to Thomas. However, Henry retained his politics and advertised his establishment in the *Miners' Advocate* of May 18th 1844.

Blooming Young Prince (CULM 16/25), the cost to the poor of the royal family is hammered home relentlessly, and the interestingly mis-spelt Mr 'Doods' advertised himself as someone 'who has always on hand a large assortment of Book and Sheet Songs.' No.16 was a double broadside, featuring *William of a Man of War* and *The Holy Friar* (NUL Loose), the first of which points up the folly of believing Navy recruitment propaganda while the latter attacks the hypocrisy of the clergy and the church, at a period when many North East people were reduced to a diet of potatoes.[66] No.17 featured *Rory O'More Turned Teetotal* – a pro-temperance piece which drew on a long tradition of patronising the Irish – with a conventional celebration of martial bravery, *With a Helmet on his Brow*, and two verses of love-poetry, *A Captive thus to thee* (CULM 16/26).

But the world around Dodds' business was not standing still. By 1842, politics and economics were once more beginning to come together. In the later 1830s and early 1840s, coinciding with the Chartist agitation, there had been a massive expansion of coal-mining investment, employment and production in the North East, and above all in County Durham.[67] There were strikes, as in 1837, but politicised miners were routinely blacklisted. Ironically, the resulting enforced movement by victimised militants helped to spread one version or another of the Chartist message – as well as trade union ideas – across the coalfield. Some of the developing cadre, like the Rechabite Peter Burt, were also religious men and pacifists, but others, including Peter's brothers, had espoused physical force politics. From the point of view of rank and file pit-workers such distinctions mattered little at bargaining time, since what they needed were articulate, literate and brave individuals to focus their hopes – the kind known to Viewers and Owners for what they called their 'great skill, and cunning and circumvention'.[68] Gradually, union organisation came to be generalised. Late in 1841, a Law Fund was

---

66. Challinor, A Radical Lawyer, p. 32.
67. Green (1865–66), 238, 240, 243; Ashton & Sykes, *The Coal Industry*, p. 298; Mackenzie, *Durham*, pp. cv–cvi; Hair, *Sketches*, p. 6; Colls, *The Pitmen*, pp. 6, 7, 61, 62, 308 note 3; Fordyce, *Durham*, Volume 1, p. 571, 2: 631note; Galloway, *Annals*, Volume 1, pp. 451–52, 470, 472, 2: pp. 6–11, 178; Middlebrook, *Newcastle-upon-Tyne*, p. 186; Hair, 'Social History', pp. 19–20, 22–23, 262,Table 3.
68. Meech, From *Mine to Ministry*, pp. 2–8; Green (1865–66), 236; Wearmouth, *Methodism*, p. 187.

established to help fight Owners' attacks on pay, conditions and security of employment, and in January 1842 the Sunderland Chartist, George Binns, placed an advertisement in the *Northern Star*, calling on local pit-workers to 'adopt measures for resistance to the tyranny of the coal owners and their Viewers' by sending a delegate to a meeting at Chester-le-Street organised by the workers at Thornley Colliery. The aims of this meeting were economic and defensive rather than political and offensive, but the network which drew the delegates together was basically the readership of the Chartist newspaper overlapping with the network of practising or lapsed Ranter Methodists.[69] The delegates met again at Monkwearmouth in early February to report on colliery soundings on restricting the working day to one of eight hours. Effectively, they had begun to re-form the union, and the agitation for the Philanthropical Society in Summer 1842 was conducted using a mixture of Chartist and Ranter tactics, including the Camp Meeting.[70]

At precisely this time, Thomas Dodds began to intervene politically in the commercial market for songs which had been dominated for so long by Walker and, especially, Fordyce.[71] In June 1842, for example, Dodds issued a piece celebrating the locally-owned racehorse, *Beeswing* (No.22: NUL Loose).[72] No.23 was *My Grandmother's Days* (CULM 16/28, paired with the sentimental *Fair Eliza*), which invokes a mythical golden age, harking back to the 1790s 'tree of liberty', but which also lambastes the parasitism of Prince Albert and sympathises with the Lancashire unemployed. No. 24 was the 'west-country' *Sary Sykes* plus the self-consciously formal *Death of the Sailor Boy* (CULM 16/27).[73] In July he published No. 25, *Newcastle & London Boat Match, For £100 Aside* **(39)**, from 'Head of the Side', but given the realities of the Navy from the sailors' point-of-view, and the fact that it had been used in industrial

---

69. Ben Embleton took the chair and Thomas Hall of Thornley Colliery was elected Secretary. Martin Jude and John Hall had been delegates from Byker Hill to Chartist meetings .

70. C & R, *The Miners' Association*, pp. 11, 60–61.

71. The Fordyces moved to 15 Grey Street in 1841, but Thomas left in 1842 to be an auctioneer (Hunt, *The Book Trade*, p. 36).

72. See *The Monthly Chronicle* (1890), 270.

73. The address was given as 77 Side, so unless Dodds had two working addresses at the same time, which is unlikely, this may be a reprinting, since No.39 is said to have been published from 43 Side.

disputes on the Tyne in both 1815 and 1825, there is a naive tendency here to appeal to an alleged cultural homogeneity in an ever more class-divided society.[74] More interesting, therefore, in terms of the later decisive shift in focus of Dodds' business, was that this piece was replaced at No.25, probably in 1842 or 1843, by *The Bonnie Pit Lads* (**40B**), and was subsequently reissued in a different format, perhaps late in 1843 (**40C**).[75]

Dodds kept an eye open for versified material about political events which had a commercial appeal, and his output of songs and verse appears to have quickened as the economic crisis deepened during the summer of 1842.[76] In July 1842 he published as No.26 *Farewell Address To their Countrymen and Friends, Of all those unfortunate Men who received their several Sentences, of Transportation, at the Summer Assizes for the year 1842, by the Judges on the Northern Circuit*, which appears both with and without a series number (NUL Loose; CULM 16/29). This text sympathises with the poor but stops short of justifying the expropriation of the rich, and advocates strictly Parliamentary and reformist politics. So do other numbered broadsides issued from 43 Side, including No.28, *Peel's Income Tax, or a miss at popularity!!* and the satire on the birth of *The Prince of Wales* (which bore no series number), both of which repeat familiar themes, but which also contain a sharper critique of royalty, Parliament and rulers in general. Such material may by now have been targetted at a market somewhat distinct from the straightforwardly commercial one, though No.31, *The Lass of N———— Town* and *Alice Gray* had a note stating 'Hawkers and others supplied'. This was followed by more traditional fare such as No.33, *Jemie Forest* and *Jem Forester, My Jo*, No.34, *A New Song called The Fiddler of this Town* and *Tom Tack*, and No.35, *Doncaster Races, or a new song on Bluebonnet and Beeswing* together with *The Pilot* (CULM 16/30–34).

What indicates a shift towards a class-based and clearly political market, at a time when a local worker found reading the *Northern Star* could be sacked,[77] is No.37, *The Weaver's Lamentation* (**41**), which was

---

74. Neale, *The Cutlass*; Harker, 'Popular Song', pp. 267–80, 316–38.

75. There had been a song called *The Bonny Pit Lad* (sometimes *The Canny Pit Lad*) since before 1800. John Bell noted in his manuscript tune-book that the tune had new words 'added to it, as a song' 'about Ritson's time'.

76. Middlebrook, *Newcasle-upon-Tyne*, p. 178; Manders, *A History of Gateshead*, p. 232; Wilson (1983), 22 note 26.

77. Wilson (1986), 98.

evidently intended to raise cash for unemployed weavers visiting the region. A simple piety is linked to a shared sense of community – 'our case', 'our trade', 'our families' – and then to an expectation that other workers would respond positively, on a class basis. In *The Poor Tradesmen's Lamentation* (42) the appeal is widened so as to highlight the insecurities of the self-employed, and to stress the interdependence of such people with the major groups of labouring people within the context of an assumed nonconformist ideology. (The piece also employs the common Chartist form of a supposed dialogue with a member of the bourgeoisie.) *The cries of the poor* (43) celebrates the Chartist heroes of the Newport Rising, and is an unapologetic appeal to Chartist history and principles, class-based internationalism and the hatred of a clearly-identified ruling class.[78] *The state of the times and their causes* (44) was perhaps an example of 'niche' marketing, aimed at the religiously cynical, but it represented a brave gesture, given the politicisation of religion at this period of ideological and economic crisis, when many were trying to separate respect for the Bible from an adherence to any particular church.[79] None of these four overtly political pieces appeared in Dodds' numbered series. Presumably, he was still trying to keep both political and traditional commercial markets supplied, but separately, and this may explain why *The Roving Ploughboy* (Appendix 1)[80] was spiked. At this point, the reissued *The Future Prospects of Taxation* (CULM 16/36) indicates Dodds had moved to '77, Side, a little above Dean street', and wished his regular customers to find him there. As we shall see, this move coincided with a much sharper political and trade union focus in Dodds' printed songs and verse, when the majority of respectable reformers had split from the Chartists.[81]

There was no mechanical link between low Chartist morale after the General Strike of 1842, state repression and the agitation for the Philanthropical Society. Some colliery workforces were more militant

---

78. Jones, Williams and Frost were transported in 1840 for their part in the Newport Rising. The Irish parliament was abolished in 1801 'forty years since'. Who Wilson, Hardie and Baird and the forty-five others transported to Botany Bay were is unclear, but there were large-scale transportations after the General Strike of 1842 in Lancashire.
79. Thompson, *The Chartists*, pp. 116–17.
80. *The Blacklegs* (90) mentions a scab who had formerly been a ploughboy.
81. Challinor, *A Radical Lawyer*, pp. 55–56, 63, 67, 86, 89.

than others. At places like West Houghton and South Shields, openly Chartist meetings could be held. At other places, even more was possible, as owners like Lord Londonderry kept up the pressure. When Ben Embleton gave a rousing speech at Thornley Colliery in Autumn 1842 on the issue of Viewers instructing men and boys to use open candles in gassy pits, the entire workforce came out on strike the next day. By November 1842, there were sufficient colliery delegates at a Wakefield meeting organised through the *Northern Star* to establish not only a national Miners' Philanthropical Society but also a trade union, the Miners' Association. The North East delegates came from collieries which had been highly active throughout the period of Chartist activity since at least 1839, and they brought with them the records of the deaths, maimings and harassment which made them determined to get rid of the hated yearly Bond. Appropriately, David Swallow, the newly-appointed Miners' Association full-time official, was taken around the North East coalfield by the veteran Ben Embleton.[82]

The tensions between economics and politics, and those between Ranter Methodism and Chartism, were built into the Miners' Association. In March 1843, for example, the chairman of a meeting of 20,000 pitworkers on Scaffold Hill was reminded that 'Providence was not the author of their distress but class legislation'; and when a rising demand for steam coal helped change the balance of forces the men at Tyneside collieries 'exuded militant confidence', whether O'Connor showed up or not. Twenty travelling agitators – politely referred to as 'lecturers' – were appointed by the Association in the North East, to help organise restriction of output and the run-down of stockpiles. In the Summer of 1843, mass meetings and other forms of agitation took place at collieries, at Shadon's Hill and at other traditional meeting-places, sometimes drawing crowds of more than 20,000; but the tensions between the Association's leadership, its lecturers and the rank-and-file activists continued. Struggles broke out in individual collieries as the union grew and this in turn gave workers confidence. Association officers spoke at Newcastle Chartist Hall, Chartist camp meetings and other places, as well as at collieries like Thornley and Bishop Auckland. Pit-workers joined the union in

82. Jenkins, *The General Strike*, pp. 191–239; Wearmouth, *Some Working-Class Movements*, p. 151; C & R, *The Miners' Association*, pp. 14, 44, 47, 61, 210–12; Wilson (1986), 89; Colls, *The Pitmen*, p. 282.

their thousands, and by June 1st 1843 almost every Durham colliery sent its delegate to the Northumberland and Durham meeting at the Black Swan, Newcastle, where it was agreed to approach the Bath Chartist lawyer, William Prowting Roberts, with a view to securing his services on a full-time basis.[83]

The problem of communicating large amounts of fairly complex argument and information to thousands of pit-workers in dozens of North East collieries could not be left to the Leeds-based *Northern Star*. What the Northumberland and Durham District needed was a sympathetic printer who would obviate the need to make a significant amount of capital investment in a press and print-shop technology, not to mention having to hire a competent pressman. Thomas Dodds was the obvious choice, since he had a successful commercial business which seems to have kept him free of the kind of pressure which helped sink John Marshall in 1832. Dodds had been doing jobbing work for the Association from early 1843 (and perhaps since November 1842), and he may well have been appointed or engaged along with (or soon after by) the committee

---

83. Galloway, *Annals*, Volume 2, p. 174; C & R, *The Miners' Association*, pp. 13, 14, 16, 19, 64–66, 74–75, 88, 94–96, 111; Welbourne, *The Miners' Unions*, pp. 65–66. Several officers were appointed on the basis of their political experience alone. John Hall, the Secretary, had been a Chartist flax-dresser in South Shields. Beesley, a Physical Force Chartist and a chair-maker in Accrington in 1842, argued successfully for the Association Law Fund and was sent off to recruit Roberts. Roberts, the son of a vicar-turned-schoolteacher, had gone to Charterhouse School and on to a London solicitor's office – all the while retaining his Church of England Toryism – and then set up as a solicitor in Bath. When the government transported some Tolpuddle labourers in 1834 for swearing an illegal oath in order to form a trade union, Roberts moved left. By 1837 he was a leading figure in Bath's Working Men's Association. In 1839 he was taken to court for 'seditious libel', and like many leading Chartists he spent part of 1840 in gaol. His appointment was secured on August 11th 1843, but his request that William Beesley be his assistant (which was granted over the claims of a victimised ex-pitman, 'brother Smith' of Auckland Distict) gave great offence and added to the tensions which already existed inside the Association. Roberts' success in winning the hearts and minds of many of the Association's members simply made matters more tense, and this was particularly true, apparently, at North Elswick. Thomas Dodds printed a leaflet for that colliery's union officials against Beesley's appointment (Colls, *The Pitmen*, pp. 282–83; C & R, *The Miners' Association*, pp. 15, 19–21; Challinor, *A Radical Lawyer*, pp. 3–6).

elected in May 1843, since the moving of Dodds' business from 43
Side to 77 Side probably took place in May or June 1843, and
certainly by July. It may be that the embarrassment caused by a
pitman being convicted of murder was the last straw, especially
after the publication of *Copy of Verses on the Castle Eden Tragedy*
(45).[84] By late Spring 1843 Dodds was entrusted with the printing of
letter-heads, posters, certificates, leaflets, receipt books, rules and
balance-sheets for the Northumberland and Durham District and
for the Association nationally. His political reliability, local roots
and a readiness to give access to print for both Chartists and those
interested in 'the promotion of union for Trades purposes alone' –
as the North Elswick *Address* (published on July 10th 1843) puts it –
gave him a virtual monopoly. But it also placed him right at the
heart of the various tensions within the Association, especially

---

84. A Dodds leaflet (possibly a broadside) containing the verse and a prose
text apparently once existed, but the Wigan broadside *Wilful Murder of M.
Pearson at Castle Eden* appears to come from a Durham newspaper.
Thomas Dodds was probably at 77 Side by the time of the Pearson court
case and execution (C & R, *The Miners' Association*, pp. 63, 65, 79–80, 98).
Up to mid-1843, Dodds seems to have kept his openly Chartist and trade
union broadside-printing separate from his numbered series, and he
often published politically-sensitive material without a colophon. The
Balance-Sheets at Wigan throw some important light on the national
Miners' Association's relationship with Dodds. Between September 30th
and November 11th 1843, Dodds' bill was little more than £18 – or
around £3 per week – out of a total expenditure of £230, and most of that
was for printing the *Journal*. But other printers were used, including a Mr
Dent – possibly the Roger Dent of Pilgrim Streeet, Newcastle, who was the
son of the late Eneas Mackenzie's former partner (Hunt, *The Book Trade*,
p. 30) – and even Messrs Fordyce. Someone else (presumably Martin Jude)
was paid £3 for the 'loan of a room', so the Association was probably still
based at Jude's Three Tuns ale-house in Manor Street, which offered bed
and board, and probably acted as the delegates' main port-of-call in
Newcastle – compare Harrison & Hollis, *Robert Lowery*, p. 82. The next
Association Balance Sheet, covering the period from November 11th to
December 16th 1843, shows Dodds receiving £100 (at an average of £40
per week) or almost half the total expenditure of £202. It is possible,
then, that he remained an independent printer throughout 1843 and
1844, though concentrating (especially after December 1843 and up until
the end of the strike) on Association business. No wages for him are
recorded in the Balance Sheets, though they go into great detail (down to
one penny) on other expenditures.

when 'Brother Unionists on the Tyne, Wear, & Tees' used his printshop to get in touch with each other independently of national or District officers, or even of the General Delegate meetings.

The Chartists, and especially Roberts and Beesley, also needed some regular way of communicating with rank-and-file activists on both trade union and political issues, in order to try to weld the two overlapping constituencies together and to win hegemony within the union. Their solution was the *Miners' Journal*, which was advertised in a flier printed by Dodds on October 4th 1843. The first edition was printed and sold by Dodds 'for the Society' in the Side on October 21st,[85] but in spite of this being a Society publication, all communications were to be sent, post-paid, to William Beesley at William Prowting Roberts' Law Offices at No 11 Royal Arcade. The *Miners' Journal* was, therefore, under their editorial control, and it promised to be a 'chronicle of sufferings' for the members, 'an almanack of all their law trials and victories' and, in general, 'the DESPOT'S PLAGUE'. Distribution, on the other hand, was a Society matter and involved rank and file activists in using a trade union network for what was also political propaganda; yet the mixture of class-conscious politics and militant trade unionism struck a chord. Roberts' articles exuded cheery contempt for all deference or unthinking piety, equated profits with robbery and insisted that pit-workers would never get a 'fair wage' until they enjoyed the full fruits of their labours.[86] The general strike, then, was an 'inevitable step in

---

85. Dodds' flier suggests that each colliery 'will take one for every four of its members once every fortnight, making one-halfpenny per month each man' (Wigan 86). It had an initial print-run of 6,000 copies at a cost price of around one farthing apiece, though it was apparently not an organ of the Association. 6,000 copies of issues number 2 and 3 were published. By February 1844, all but 2,000 of all these 18,000 copies had already been sold (Balance-sheets, Wigan). Quite how the Ranter leadership of the Association viewed such politics in a periodical advertised as having been printed 'for the Society' is unclear, but there had been a cautious welcome in the address 'to the members' on November 18th 1843. Subsequent events suggest that Association leadership came to hate it.
86. Helen Macfarlane's English translation of the *Communist Manifesto* was first published in the Chartist journal, *The Red Republican*, edited by Julian Harney, between June and November 1850 – compare Challinor, *A Radical Lawyer*, p. 109.

social emancipation' while partial struggles 'weaken us and thus postpone the hour of our social emancipation'.[87]

The first *Journal* of October 21st 1843 contained a bland, untitled piece of verse about 'Mother', immediately above Beesley's editorial request for 'communications' from readers, indicating a willingness (as in other Chartist-inspired periodicals) to encourage readers' compositional skills. Yet as songs and verse made by pit-village people came in it seems to have been taken for granted that this material had to be edited for the press. One of the first to arrive was William Roxby's *A New Song* (46A), which also survives in an edited form (46B) in what turned out to be the hand of William Daniells.[88] Both texts have a hole where they were evidently 'spiked', and though the piece may not have been printed, the changes thought appropriate tell us a good deal about Daniells' literary and political preferences. Some changes were clearly necessary, since Roxby was thinking in terms of a male monarch six years after Victoria ascended the throne; but Daniells' mediated text is unimpeachably loyal and seeks to reinforce the separation of politics and economics: 'All party disputes shall be banished from hence/ The bane of good feelings the foe to Good Sense'. In addition, 'Union' had become nothing less than a 'Science', and Daniells substitutes human agency ('we') for that of God ('He'). Taken one text at a time such detailed changes might be regarded as accidental, but taken cumulatively Daniells' mediations were as least as much political as literary.

The first-known surviving manuscript text which went into print was not Roxby's piece but another text with a similar title, and it is interesting to consider why this version of *A New Song* (47A) was preferred and why it was printed not in the *Journal* but as a small broadside. The author, probably J. Matthews of Wingate, sees the role of rank and file pitmen as being to 'blend in UNION', but the edited text (47B) makes this a relationship based rather more on dependence on the bureaucracy than on workers' self-activity – 'To Union st[ill?] blending, for Union's our all'. True, the Old Testament

---

87. From almost the first day of Roberts' appointment as the Miners' Attorney-General, Home Office files contain reports about meetings he addressed (Challinor, *A Radical Lawyer*, pp. 25, 112, 121).

88. For Daniells, see below, footnote 95. All surviving mediated manuscript texts which can be dated appear to derive from after the demise of the *Miners' Journal*.

God of Battles is retained, as is the (apparently uncontradictory) appeal to Reason and the stress on a version of the labour theory of value. But while the original text accepts the rights of capital, unlike in Daniells' mediation, it does so without equivocation:

> We Want not A Sword we want not to fight
> But peace and contentment possessing our right
> But Should we be Branded and forced to the field
> We'll glory in death that Scorns Ere to Yield.

Daniells' mediations were evidently intended to have an effect on the rank-and-file solidarity work throughout the coalfield.[89] So was James Wardhaugh's *The Miners' Philanthropical Society* **(48)**. This text is important because it shows that not all versified propaganda used in the North East was of local origin: what linguistic clues there are suggest that the author may have come from Yorkshire or Lancashire. The tone of the printed version is optimistic and damns 'Coal-pit Kings' in this world and (as 'the devil's own') in the next; but while he clearly believed that such class hatred would appeal to a wide audience amongst pit-workers – those who have already 'let the Tyrants know their tricks are at an end' – Wardhaugh is openly anxious 'not to offend' any potential member or supporter in an organisation which, as yet, was not 'rightly form'd'.

Some writers of manuscript texts were even more cautious and conciliatory. Nicholas Cowey's piece on ventilation at Shotton Moor Colliery **(49)** is full of flowery diction, eccentric punctuation and general pretentiousness, plus lavish praise for lesser colliery officials and even for Viewer Brown, and for Mr Foster (a coalowner, or possibly a Senior Viewer). Cowey may even have been one of the 'Noble Clan' he sets out to praise for being 'Strong in disjudication' and of a 'Virtuous inclineation'.[90] Of course, it may be that Viewer Brown was conscientious in his inspections, and such men had to face the same dangers as other pitmen and pit-boys underground, and so were 'wo[r]thy of their station', but quite why Daniells put so

---

89. The small broadside version of this piece, retitled *Union and Liberty* **(47C & 47D)**, was apparently used later in 1844 for agitational purposes, but Daniells (or perhaps Dodds) tinkered with the text once again.
90. Cowey also wrote **101**. 'Hornby' could possibly have been William Hornsby who wrote **57**, **89** and, probably, **107**.

much effort into editing (in fact, largely rewriting) this piece is unclear, especially since it seems not to have got into print. Perhaps Cowey felt that by praising good colliery officials and a good owner he might exhort, shame or atomise the rest, but, possibly on account of the implied class-collaboration, Daniells left the rewritten verse on the spike throughout 1844.

There seems to have been a clear and public alignment of the union and the union printer in late 1843, signalled by the appearance of *The Pitman's Union* (50) as part of Dodds' numbered series and published over his colophon. (The short 'filler' piece is sexist material, but serves to emphasise the transitional nature of this broadside.) Harking back to the Reform Act betrayal of 1832 and to the transportation of the Newport Chartists in 1840, and pointing up splits inside both the ruling class and the middle class, this piece bridges the gap between Dodds' previous Chartist-oriented songs and those issuing the specific call for trade unionism. According to the lead song, the gap between rich and poor, the immiseration of the weakest, the futility of argument or even of 'talk', point towards the need for union; and while it is no revolutionary clarion-call and it has no conception of a society free from booms and slumps, it does advocate the elimination of 'oppression' by making 'tyrants with us bend' through trade union measures alone. Rather different in tone and content is *The Madman of Wingate* (51), which probably appeared in summer 1843, when there had been a serious dispute at Wingate Colliery about the arbitrary introduction of a wire rope in the pit-shaft.[91] This song uses a contemporary, commercially-successful tune, *Betsy Baker*, and it probably refers to a blackleg. The piece would probably have been used only at a local level, as would *The Wingate Grange Blue Hounds in Pursuit of a Fox* (52), whose otherwise obscure story is evidently satirical of the New Police. Unless the extant copy is a printer's proof, this text seems to have appeared illegally without an imprint, and so activists would have understood that Thomas Dodds would risk prosecution.

---

91. Every pit-worker's life depended on this untried technology so there was understandable anxiety. The Wingate men refused to trust a wire rope which had twenty-two out of its ninety-six strands severed, and one of their number, John Barkhouse, was prosecuted for breaking the conditions of the Bond. He was found a lawyer, but an unsympathetic local bench sent him to prison in July (C & R, *The Miners' Association*, p. 96. Compare Fynes, *The Miners*, p. 37; Colls, *The Pitmen*, p. 26).

The attraction of this illegal option to activists is underlined by what happened when Beesley received the original manuscript of *Union* (53). He decided to give it a place in the *Journal* for November 4th 1843, but the editing process was substantial.[92] The first verse becomes a chorus: seven quatrains are amalgamated into four eight-line stanzas; two quatrains are transposed, and there are many minor changes to grammar, spelling, punctuation and capitalisation. Idiom is excised and a stilted, unlocalised, would-be 'standard' diction imposed. Personality is minimised, and the Old Testament God of Battles is secularised. There are abstract rhetorical appeals to ideas like 'liberty' and 'union', but crucially not only the hate but also the stress on activity is mellowed – 'Union' itself was going to do the struggling, not the flesh and blood members who formed it. That said, the *Journal* and its politics probably forced the issue in the long-running battle inside the Association between the 'moderates' and the Chartists. In November 1843 the former won the vote that no lecturer should stay in one place longer than six months and none of them should mix business with politics.[93] Then, in a situation where Roberts' popularity was rising sharply after his victory in the Thornley case, the national leadership of the Association decided to have its own periodical, *The Miners' Advocate*.[94] The editorship went to William Daniells, the Chartist candidate of the 'moderates' –

---

92. The manuscript of *Union* seems to have found its way to 77 Side, where it was re-edited but not printed in the *Advocate* until July 1844. Daniells preferred some unusual readings from I.N.'s manuscript. Above all, I.N.'s narrative voice – which has an air of one person speaking to equals, perhaps in a chapel context, about collective oppression and the need for collective activity – is rendered bland, banal, pompous and almost entirely passive.

93. The editorial of the last *Journal* denounced 'partial strikes', but looked forward to a 'universal' strike when that became practicable. It contained neither a song nor any coherent verse, but only a series of moralising couplets.

94. Notice was given in the second issue of the *Journal* (4.11.1843, p. 16) that it would 'be considerably enlarged'. Dodds had ordered 'a new assortment of type...for the express purpose'. In the third and last issue (18.11.1843, p. 18), Roberts informed readers that he had asked Beesley to resign as editor because of the pressure of legal work. All communications for the *Advocate* were to be sent to the Editor at 77 Side, but the first issue of the paper made it clear that all correspondence was to be sent to the Editor at 4 Picton Terrace, Newcastle, and not to Dodds' printshop.

largely non-Chartist trade unionists[95] – and the first number of the paper appeared on December 2nd 1843, with the editor installed at the same address as the printer, Thomas Dodds.[96] An editorial announcement in the *Advocate* on January 13th 1844 shows that relations between the editor and Roberts and Beesley were already strained, probably on political grounds. This was clear even to outsiders, like the government agent, Tremenheere, who declared a strong preference for the *Advocate* over the then defunct *Journal*, on account of the latter's agitation for a general strike as opposed to the former's reassuringly 'temperate' perspective.[97]

---

95. Daniells had been a carpet-weaver in Lasswade near Edinburgh, and Secretary of the Mental Improvement Society. He became a Chartist and wrote occasional pieces for the *Northern Star*. On July 1st 1843 he became a Miners' Association lecturer for Scotland. Daniells 'quickly became secretary of the Fifeshire miners', and then moved south to take up the twenty-one shillings a week post of Editor of the new *Miners' Advocate*. The other candidates were William Thomason – an Edinburgh Chartist who was 'a fierce opponent of strikes', but who later became an Association lecturer – and William Dixon, an ex-weaver who was a political supporter of Roberts and who had faced a cavalry charge in 1842, and had seen his brother slashed four times. Dixon became a lecturer for the Association in Staffordshire. Overall, then, the 'left' did better than the 'right', but the man of the 'centre' got the job plus a seat on the Executive Committee, which gave him the opportunity to speak frequently at mass meetings.

96. The *Advocate* had a print-run of 8,000 copies, at a unit cost price of almost one penny, or slightly more if Daniells' wages and expenses were taken into account. It sold at three-halfpence. By the time of the second fortnightly issue, the print run was raised to 10,000, and stayed at that level until No 10 (except for a slight increase to 11,000 for No 5). But there were still 7,500 copies of previous issues 'on hand' on February 10th 1844, so the paid sale was just over 8,000 an issue amongst a membership of over 50,000 (and possibly as high as 80,000). This was despite the efforts of some forty full-time lecturers, and the availability of the periodical from Chartist-influenced shops, like those of David France and Thomas Horn in Newcastle, and James Williams in Sunderland, plus the Newcastle shops of James Sinclair and James Edgar. The paper was also to be had from the Association Treasurer and from the printer, Thomas Dodds (C & R, *The Miners' Association*, pp. 16, 66, 69–73, 75, 117, 219–20; Colls, *The Pitmen*, pp. 282–85. See also Challinor, *A Radical Lawyer*, pp. 75, 84, 141; *Miners' Advocate*, 10.2.1844, p. 42; Harrison & Hollis, *Robert Lowery*, p. 94; *Advocate*, 2.12.1843, p. 8).

97. C & R, *The Miners' Association*, pp. 75–76, 100, 106, 122; Fynes, *The Miners*, pp. 38–39, 49.

In the very first issue of the *Advocate* Daniells had a clear idea of what kind of versified material he required. The author of 'lines from Haswell' is told firmly that they 'will not suit', though no reason is given. The 'Poetry from R.H.Fawcett' (56, presumably) would appear in 'our next', which it did, but the sender of 'The brave lads of the Tees, Wear and Tyne' (probably Hornsby's 57) is informed that his offering is 'under consideration'. *The Union Knot*, sent in by 'our friend W.S.N. of East Holywell' but signed by Thomas Nicholson (63), did not appear until February 1844. The first verses to be published were both by William Hammond, a 'veteran miner from Sunderland' who was a full-time lecturer for the Association in Scotland, having been appointed along with William Daniells in July 1843.[98] *An Address to the Miners of Scotland* (54) and *Union!* (55) seem sincere, but they are also for the most part abstract rhetoric. For example, 'unity' is posed as a total cure for 'slavery', and the former will work to help pit-workers 'bask as freemen bright'. According to Hammond, 'Union' is an almost autonomous force, and those who were 'determined to be free' had only to join and then leave matters in the hands of the officials.

This emphasis is reinforced by the verse published in the second issue of the *Advocate*. R.H.Fawcett, a member of the Durham and Northumberland District Committee of the Association, probably intended *The Miner's Complaint* (56) for the *Journal*, since it bears a date of November 6th 1843. The verse's regular metre, stanza form and religious ideology set the pattern for what Daniells felt appropriate. In the published version,[99] with the narrator's wife dead, their children destitute, and the narrator on the point of death,

---

98. Probably, like Hepburn, Hammond got politically active after the failure of the nonconformist leadership's tactics in the strike of 1832. One of his former pupils recalled that he had been a Wesleyan local preacher, but
   the 'preacher' thought Willy wrong in taking public part in the union, and he became a Primitive. He was a grand old man when I knew him in 1842 or '3. He had been unable to secure employment in the mines, and travelled with 'numbers'; had read much, and remembered it. He spent much time in drilling me into and imbuing me with an intense love of liberty and an undying hatred of oppression (Richardson (1883), 264).
   Hammond was one of the four full-timers left in July 1845, when coalowners were sacking miners simply for attending Association meetings.
99. No manuscript versions of any of the pieces first published in the *Advocate* seem to have survived.

Fawcett offers a moral and personal critique of capitalist social relations, with fairness abandoned on this earth and justice (albeit reluctantly) postponed to the next. Such angry quietism was not hegemonic amongst Association activists and is not to be found in *An Address to the Miners of Britain* (57),which appeared in the *Advocate* on December 30th 1843. William Hornsby[100] of Shotton Moor Colliery was evidently a veteran of 1831 and 1832 – 'for ten years we've carried the yoke' – but his hope lay in the 'Goddess of Conquest' rather than the 'Heaven' he mentions only in passing. Like Hammond, he is keen to build a national union, so that one coalfield workforce could not be set off against another; but while he is swayed by moral force arguments he reminds Association members of their own power, as well as their moral superiority, in verse which is direct, confident, determined and articulated in a swinging metre. Evidently, in the verse submitted to the Association there existed the same political tensions we have noted at work elsewhere.

January–March 1844

Tensions within the Association over strategy and tactics were evident at the start of 1844, and relations between Daniells and the Law Office seem to have been particularly strained.[101] This helps explain the publication in the first *Advocate* of 1844 of the acrostic on James Smith (58), a member of the Executive since at least November 1843. His flatterer was keen to keep the union free of those who, like the Chartists, wished to 'intrude'. And as if to hammer home the

---

100. Hornsby also wrote 89 and probably 107. A 'Hornby' is a minor colliery official at Shotton in 49.
101. C & R, *The Miners' Association*, pp. 113–25. In the *Advocate* (31.1.1844) Daniells denied receiving a report of the December trial from Beesley, who was all but called a liar. In his defence, the Editor recounts how 'Mr. Roberts sent for us to his office and wished us to insert a report taken from the "Durham Advertiser, "' but since 'this day was the day before we went to press, when nearly all the form was set up for the paper, and when, indeed 6,000 of one side was actually printed, the report would have taken near five columns, consequently, we had no room'. He needed a week's notice, since 'we are compelled to go to press on the Tuesday before the day of publishing, in order to allow proper time to forward the Advocate to distant places by the Saturday'. In an apparent compromise, Daniells suggested that an account of the Thornley trials should be printed separately from the paper, 'but of the same size, so that they may bind together'.

point, this piece was accompanied by the verse of another official, William Thomason. *The Workhouse Boy* (59) stresses self-help, application to work – at a time when official union policy was to restrict output to allow all miners to find work – Sunday clothes and blameless courtship, followed by decent marriage in a rural setting, and underlines the hegemony of bourgeois values amongst Association officers, at a time when there was pressure for a national strike from the radical Chartists and sections of the rank and file.[102] Perhaps this is why Daniells decided to go outside the Association for versified material. In the *Advocate* for January 27th there appeared Joseph Philip Robson's *The Miner's Doom* (60A).[103] Whether Robson was personally known to any of the Association officials isn't clear,[104] but he had produced slim volumes of technically competent, slightly pompous and unimaginative verse. Daniells' anxiety to encourage this contributor with coy anonymity, special notices, flattery and, as the year wore on, regular publication, indicates his own literary preferences and ideological perspective very clearly, as does his claim that the Association 'intended to take no power from honest and upright employers,' though he did not say where such paragons were likely to be found.[105]

However, the appearance of *The Miners' Complaint* (61) indicates that those critical of 'class-made laws' and in favour of the Chartist

---

102. Thomason had Chartist associations (Roberts, *Radical Politicians*, p. 72 note 10). He was a recently-appointed Association lecturer for South Wales, and one of the defeated candidates for the *Advocate* Editorship. He later wrote a 'scandalous handbill' attacking the Executive and Roberts which the *Advocate* (27.7.1844, pp. 144–45) noted was also 'quite illegal, it not bearing the printer's name'.

103. This piece had been mentioned in the *Advocate* of January 13th 1844, with a promise that it would appear in the next issue, which it duly did, as by the 'Author of *The Tyne Exile's Return*'.

104. Owen Ashton points out that Robson was a member of the Oddfellows' Friendly Society and that he mentions Martin Jude in *The Monomaniac*.

105. 60B was published months later, to help raise funds at the 'Musical Melange' at the Lecture Room, Nelson Street, Newcastle on August 13th 1844. A poster announced that Mr Joseph Fawcett would sing *The Battle of Minden* and (probably Robson's version of) *The Miner's Doom*, dressed in his pit clothes, and to the accompaniment of Mr Sessford – see Robson, *Autobiography*, p. 15; Harker (1972), xiii–xv. This text was also used in the December 1845 issue of the *Advocate*. No manuscript version

Continued

lawyer could still get their verse into print on broadsides, though without Dodds' colophon. Its subject is the eventual acquittal of the strikers from Thornley Colliery, but for all its secular and militant tone this piece tends to minimise the role played by the rank-and-file at places like Thornley, a community which refused to be intimidated by police. Many were prepared to go to jail or even to emigrate rather than give in to tyranny, and they were the 'we' who did the essential groundwork before 'Mr. Roberts', 'the Miner's friend' could 'set our brother free'. Thornley Colliery's workforce also seems to have been well-organised in terms of printed propaganda. *A New Song, Called the Wonderful Shaver, or Tom R—d—n's Life* (62A), was probably published in early February, when blacklegs had their windows stoned and gardens wrecked and heard 'rough music' and shotgun blasts. One such, Thomas Richardson, had collected money for the strikers and then gambled it away, and this song was obviously made in his honour, then printed without colophon by Thomas Dodds and used to discourage similar behaviour. A fortnightly paper which reached perhaps only one in ten of the Association membership simply wasn't geared up to act swiftly and firmly on such matters, so access to the medium of print remained of strategic importance to both factions within the Association.[106]

On February 2nd 1844 an anonymous leaflet was printed in Dodds' shop and sent out with all the bundles of the latest issue of the *Advocate*. Apparently it was written by a pitman called Antony Stove, who was close to the Association's Executive Committee and who signed himself 'An unsophisticated unionist and hater of humbug'. He accused Roberts of trying to incite local strikes and

Continued from p 35

---

of **60C** or any other Robson piece can be traced, but the author was still tinkering with it for *The Monomaniac* in 1848. Robson noted that *The Miner's Doom, The Trapper Boy's Dream* (68), *The Miner's Motto* (84) and *The Song of the Coal Mine Sprite* (which appeared in the *Advocate* for January 1846, p. 144) 'were written for the "Miners Advocate", a weekly [sic] paper in the interests of the colliers of the mining districts, then edited by Mr. William Darnells [sic], and printed by Mr. Thomas Dodds' (Robson, *Autobiography*, p. 16).

106. When the piece was republished (**62B**) as part of a double broadside with *The Miner's Complaint* (61), Daniells (or possibly Dodds) tinkered with it a little, since its last line now secularised the villain's fate.

Beesley of once having been found drunk.[107] But since Roberts had repeatedly written and spoken against local and sectional disputes and Beesley was an almost fanatical teetotaller this was particularly strange. The issue was resolved by colliery votes of confidence in Roberts and a call to the Executive to resign, which found an abrasive echo in the *Northern Star*. Yet though Jude, Hall and the rest were let off with a reprimand by the delegates, the Executive had to pay Dodds to print a thousand copies of a disclaimer of any involvement and one hundred and fifty copies of Roberts' rejoinder, all of which were distributed with the paper.[108] Thereafter, the District officers busied themselves with an unsuccessful campaign to appeal to local 'tradesmen' to form a 'Miners' Friendly Protection Society' and other cross-class initiatives. The address for the *Advocate's* Editor shifted once again, this time to 4 Castle Street, Newcastle.

Daniells' verse-publishing policy in the *Advocate* remained conservative. Thomas Nicholson's *The Union Knot* (63), for all its bland and pompous sentiments, was published two months after it had arrived from 'our friend W.S.N. of East Holywell', due to 'unavoidable causes' and in spite of a reminder. However, Robson's acrostic on John Hall (64), a stilted wedding congratulation to the Association Secretary, received immediate attention. In the next issue, what was probably Robson's vaguely utopian *The Coal King!* (65) was preferred to the acrostic by William of Cassop Colliery, who was told baldly by Daniells that it 'will not do'.[109] What would do, evidently, was Robson's *Lines to the Memory of Mr. B. Pyle* (66). Pyle was 'long an

---

107. Wigan. An NCL leaflet addressed 'To the Pitmen of Thornley Colliery' and deriving from the *Durham Chronicle*, allegedly by 'One who is tiring of the Union' at Shiney Row, is more honest about its anti-union perspective.
108. Challinor, *A Radical Lawyer*, pp. 114–16, 136–37. Hall was nominated for the Chartist General Council in 1842 by Byker Hill Chartists, but he often opposed Roberts and once had his pay called into question by delegates. He thought the Association should form schools, reading rooms and cooperative libraries, and he exhorted pitmen to 'Know Thyself' by 'the queenly power of reason', since 'only the provident portion' of pitmen could save the rest of their class (C & R, *The Miners' Association*, pp. 11, 16, 75, 92; Colls, *The Pitmen*, pp. 193, 194).
109. *Advocate*, 27.1.1844, p. 40. Notes that 'The poetry from East Holywell shall appear' and that 'The lines from East Holywell entitled "The Union Knot" shall most certainly appear' are in the *Advocate*, 16.12.1843, p. 13. Nicholson may also have written 53 and he certainly wrote 78.

accredited and talented lecturer of the Miners' Association, and throughout his life was an ardent advocate of the rights of his fellow-men'. He had been 'one of Hepburn's cadre' and was well known for his opposition to violence and to mixing political and economic questions, having once been condemned at a mass meeting for attacking Chartism.[110] The appearance of John Wall's orthodoxly pious *Lines, Written on Seeing the West Moor Explosion in the 'Miner's Advocate'* (67)[111] indicates that colliery village poets were still active, but not enough worker-writers shared the *Advocate* Editor's sentiments on poetic as well as economic and political matters.

In the *Advocate* of March 9th, Daniells tried to keep some of his poetical correspondents happy, telling one from Seaton Delaval that his verses were 'under consideration, but we fear they cannot be inserted in their present form'. A 'Brother Miner, from Kimbley, Nottinghamshire', also had to wait, while a writer from East Holywell (possibly Thomas Nicholson) is told that the editor will 'try to find room' in the next issue. Instead, *The Trapper-Boy's Dream* (68), yet another Robson piece, jumped the queue,[112] though pit-village people did not need reminding that they were poor, or that they had 'better feelings'. The melodramatic image of the narrator having his brains 'mingled with the clay' suggests another audience, one which would approve the bourgeois sentiment that *'For 'tis alone by sacrifice affection we can prove'*, and so would feel inclined to make charitable donations.*The Pitman's Hymn* (69) also celebrates the 'christian collier' and hints at his common interest with his atheist fellow-pitmen. Interestingly, the companion text, *The Ranter's Ship* (70) – which side-steps the class issue and calls on both rich and poor to undergo a moral conversion – also bore a colophon, making it possible for whoever sold the two separable pieces to suit the

---

110. C & R, *The Miners' Association*, p. 19; Colls, *The Pitmen*, p. 383; *Advocate*, 24.2.1844. Medical assistance paid for by his employers could save not his life (Wigan Balance Sheet). According to the *Advocate*, (24.2.1844), Pyle had been appointed as one of the lecturers for Scotland in January 1844. It is unclear whether Robson volunteered this verse, but Pyle died on February 12th and Robson dated his elegy on February 19th.

111. Fynes, *The Miners*, p. 150, lists yet another disaster at the same colliery on July 18th 1844, when five more miners were killed.

112. The author, coyly identified as 'the Author of the "Miner's Doom"' on this occasion, dated his piece February 27th – and had it in print by March 23rd.

propaganda to the audience, though either song would have been serviceable at any point for cash-collecting and propaganda purposes.[113]

The moral argument was evidently felt to be crucial in winning support from people outside the pit-villages, so *The Collier Boy* **(71)**, with its orphan's mother's narrative voice, can be seen as part of a moral struggle against owners' greed and Viewers' bullying. For once, 'Heaven's laws' are taken to be on the side of this-worldly retribution – as against the other side's worship at 'Their Baal shrine' – but only after the righteous 'see the foe in death laid low'. There is more dignified rage and political quietism in *The Explosion* **(72)**, by William Hammond, but it is notable how Daniells loses the narrative 'I' after the second edited line and retells the tale in an impersonal, almost passive narrative voice. Daniells' distance from local idiom and local experience is also underlined by his failure to understand why the fiancee's sobbing was appropriately rendered as 'sab sab sabbath next for wedding day'. Hammond would probably have experienced the scene at a newly-widowed woman's house, down to the macabre details of having to wash a smashed face and the rescue of a lock of the dead pitman's hair. He would also have been down a pit after an explosion, locating the 'putrid bodys' and helping see them 'coffind close and sent away', and he would have been at inquests to hear a Coroner pronounce all that death, mutilation and misery was the result of an 'accident'. Daniells and Dodds, probably, had not. Yet there is no evidence that this moral propaganda shifted the owners one jot. A printed *Address* to the Owners from the Executive met with silent contempt.[114] Printed verse like *The Pitmen's Disgust to the Monthly Bond*

---

113. The Balance Sheet for December 16th 1843 to February 10th 1844 indicates payments to Dodds of £134 out of a grand total of £405, all but £17 for printing the *Advocate*. (Dodds also paid eleven shillings for advertising space for his business.) Between February 10th and April 13th 1844, he received £218 – though £190 was for printing five numbers of the *Advocate* – out of a grand total of £278. On March 12th 1844, Daniells was reimbursed £1 for office-rent, so he may have been sharing 77 Side with Dodds since the previous December. Indeed, this Balance Sheet was published from (as well as printed in) the Miners' Advocate Office. Dodds had no national monopoly, however: he did not print the minutes of the Glasgow conference of late March 1844 – that was done by a Mr Robertson, of whom there is no trace in Hunt, *The Book Trade* – and there is no evidence that the Association was ever his sole source of income.

114. Fynes, *The Miners*, pp. 49–51.

(73) could, however, serve other than moral functions.[115] This piece evidently contained the Association's response to the Owners' efforts in March 1844 to divide the union's membership, and its stiltedness suggests it may have been put together quickly, so as to get to the various collieries before the *Advocate*. Roberts argued that leaflets should be printed on this question and sent to other working-class organisations.[116] Versified argument is easier to remember, and the arguments about the vulnerability of the activists was a very important one to win, whatever their politics, as Daniells emphasised in the *Advocate* of March 23rd.

Matters were quickly coming to a head during March 1844. Roberts had already begun publishing *The Miners' Monthly Magazine*.[117] In it he argued for a general strike by a 'universal combination', but also, no doubt sensing the mood, for the need for stocking up for a confrontation which he foresaw beginning nearer October 5th than April 5th. The 'moderates', on the other hand, had Dodds print five hundred copies of a Parliamentary petition which begged that mines should be properly inspected, wire ropes removed, wages paid weekly and coal weighed accurately.[118] (The owners, meanwhile, met on March 16th to organise resistance to any attempts to raise wages or to alter their Monthly Bond.) At the Glasgow delegate conference of the Association, efforts were made to prevent Roberts from speaking, and he and Beesley were smeared in anonymous leaflets purporting to advertise a Chartist meeting, much to the delegates' disgust.[119] The conference narrowly voted not to call a national strike and the North East representatives split on the question of a regional strike, but permission was given for that District to go it alone.[120]

---

115. A much scrawled-over copy of the 'Monthly Monster' is at Wigan.
116. Challinor, *A Radical Lawyer*, p. 145.
117. It was edited from Roberts' office at 11 Royal Arcade, published as from London and Manchester, and printed by Michael Benson at 3, Dean Street, Newcastle. Benson had been apprenticed to the liberal Hodgson family and had taken over William Boag's business in 1838 (Hunt, *The Book Trade*, p. 13). Monthly publication allowed Roberts to print news items from the previous 28 days without incurring stamp duty.
118. There is a copy at Wigan. See also Fynes, *The Miners*, pp. 51–52.
119. Roberts' *Magazine*, No 1, p. 7, noted the Executive reminder that his brief was limited to North East England.
120. Burt, *An Autobiography*, p. 156; Fynes, *The Miners*, pp. 49–53, 55–56; C & R, *The Miners' Association*, pp. 88–92, 123–25; Challinor, *A Radical Lawyer*, pp. 117–19.

The divisions between ex-Chartists, non-Chartists, anti-Chartists, 'moderate' Chartists and Roberts' and Beesley's radical Chartists had rarely been clearer,[121] and the economic and political arguments which divided the North East Association leadership are in some ways evident in what happened to the original manuscript of *A Call to the Miners of Great Britain* (**74**) at Daniells' hands. Every line is altered: many are rendered unintelligible, and many more are completely changed in letter and in spirit. Even more significantly, the apparent echoes of an older radical tradition – stretching from praise for F.O'Connor, J.Frost and W.P.Roberts, perhaps as far back as Jean-Paul Marat's *Chains of Slavery*, and referring not just to 'Freedom' but to a 'Republick' – are mediated almost out of existence. The author's passionate politics, hatred and contempt for the state and its agents and his evident determination to be free are all diluted into bland, passive and often nonsensical rhyme. The contrast between the written feelings which went into 77 Side, Newcastle, based on the rough justice currently being handed out in the pit-villages, and those of the printed material sent out from there by William Daniells, could hardly have been greater.

April-May 1844

The Great Strike of 1844 began on April 5th with a march of 35,000 pitmen and their supporters to Shadon's Hill behind the music of 'various bands' and with flags and banners 'flying in every direction'. There were only 34,000 North East pit-workers altogether, so the degree of unanimity was remarkable, but their aims were clear: a return to customary rates of pay, the end of the Bond, the abolition of unjust fines, no more than a ten-hour day for boys and some sort of negotiating procedure to settle disputes. However, the Association was split on political lines, so it had to be a broad church, but though there was a public renunciation of hostilities between Roberts and the

---

121. There were clear divisions at some collieries between 'moderates' and Chartists. The *Advocate* (23.3.1844) condemned the 'Intolerance' shown to a pitman living 'not 20 miles from Chester-le-Street', who 'used to play an instrument in the colliery band; lately this man has changed his course of life, he having joined the Methodist body, consequently he gave up playing in the band; after this he could do nothing right, and ultimately he was discharged from the colliery! This is a most disgraceful business, and reflects precious little credit on the party or parties who turned the poor fellow from his employ because he became religious!'

Newcastle Executive, the Ranter leadership monopolised the platform at Shadon's Hill. Daniells strove to take up Hepburn's mantle with an urgent appeal to 'keep the peace and use no violence', as this would 'give them great moral power and would be to them a shield of defence', and this policy was pushed at every meeting and in every official publication throughout April. As in 1832, 1831 and 1810, the owners, led by Lord Londonderry (who also acted as Lord Lieutenant of County Durham), were not equally quietist: they had no problems with the use of state-approved violence in a trade dispute, though General Arbuthnot had his doubts.[122]

There were also doubts about the Association's financial strength, given that union funds were just about breaking even. It cost sixpence to join the union, membership cards cost a penny and there was a penny weekly subscription, so raising cash from sympathisers was crucial, as was the active cooperative of sympathetic (or long-sighted) shopkeepers and farmers. Consequently, Dodds was called upon to prepare a steady stream of posters, leaflets, credentials and receipt books for collectors of money for 'Unemployed Miners' and for the Law Fund. Some documents had blank spaces for adaptation by individual colliery committees, but for the most part financial control was concentrated at the centre. Dodds also printed songs and verse designed to help raise funds, and this was particularly appropriate not only because of the trade union tradition of fund-raising by singing in groups, but because music, songs and singing formed an integral part of Ranter religion and both Chartist and Association mass-meetings.[123] This does not mean, of course, that there was no atheist tradition. Thomas Binney recalled the 'awful swearing, obscene conversation and filthy songs' of at least one pit-village during this period,[124] and though none of these songs survived, the roseate picture of Ranters who 'gave' pitmen 'hymns for his public-house ditties'[125] needs to be

---

122. Fynes, *The Miners*, pp. 55–56, 60–61, 63; Richardson (1883), 265; Burt (1882), 391; Galloway, *Annals*, Volume 2, p. 176; Colls, *The Pitmen*, pp. 297–99; Challinor, *A Radical Lawyer*, pp. 121–23; C & R, *The Miners' Association*, pp. 129–30.

123. Colls, *The Collier's Rant*, pp. 138–39.

124. Thomas Burt, *An Autobiography*, p. 60, recollected how he and other pit-boys used to swear violently, but one of the most gifted swearers, Peter Mackenzie, was later a famous Methodist preacher.

125. C & R, *The Miners' Association*, p. 48; Welbourne, *The Miners' Unions*, p. 57.

viewed with some scepticism. A manuscript note on **85A**, possibly in Dodds' handwriting, suggests 'The writer was brought up a collier & i think he has done it well', but others felt differently:

> The pretended Sanctified Rhyme on this and the succeeding half a Dozen pages were said to have been written by the Travelling Methodist Preachers and Class Leaders, or at least they got the blame of doing them. they were hawked about and sold at one penny each.[126]

Political tensions were likely to be found not only between Ranters and Chartists, then, but inside each body, too; and so when we examine the songs and verse produced by such people we should look for (and expect) a considerable amount of ideological struggle and contradiction.[127]

There was an obvious need to publicise the Association's case as quickly as possible amongst actual and potential supporters and to strengthen the strikers' morale. These were the functions of *The Coal Owners' Vend, and the Miners' Union* (75), originally published by William Ainsley, a printer, bookseller and mustard manufacturer in the heart of Durham City. His text, neatly folded into eight, was set up by Dodds at least as far as proof stage without any major mediations, though no finished Dodds broadside seems to exist. Printing and publishing pro-union and pro-strike material was, therefore, not Dodds' monopoly, but the language of this piece is far more confident than other Dodds publications: it is firmly in support of Roberts' radical Chartism and against the hypocrisy of owners who had had their 'union', the Vend, for twenty-seven years. The reference to 'each Blackleg, our greatest enemy' also suggests that Ainsley may have had a connection with the pitmen of Thornley Colliery, who had been coping with blacklegs for months before

---

126. This note appears in manuscript on the NRO exemplar of Robert Holder's *The Colliers' Appeal to the Country* (85B) but, unfortunately, several of the texts referred to are not now to be found in the collection.

127. Tremenheere noted the strike 'had a religious feeling to it', 'mixed up in a strange and striking manner with this movement'. Pit-villagers met in chapels, 'when prayers were publicly offered up for the successful result of the strike', and went to Prayer Meetings '"to get their faith strengthened"' (Wearmouth, *Some Working-Class Movements*, p. 188. Compare Siegel, *The Meek and the Militant*).

April 5th 1844, but whether his broadside was mainly politically or economically motivated is not clear.[128]

The Miners' Friend (76) by William Johnson of Framwellgate Moor, is rather more contradictory. Judging by this piece (albeit almost certainly mediated by Daniells), Johnson evidently believed that God's will was linked to the 'voice of a Nation' as a whole, irrespective of social class, and he accepted labour as a necessary 'curse'; but he also resented the fact that some people appeared undamned and he wanted a less unequal society. So while his verse is generally quietist and dogged, the contradictions within his own perspective are left unresolved in a passionate outburst of willingness to face martyrdom. Quietism is to some extent challenged within Johnson's text – blows are to be returned, and evils have to be grappled with – but then 'victory' looms in the distance as an apparently autonomous consequence, ready to 'crown us in this our just cause'. Another Johnson piece, *The Miners' Grievances* (77A), was probably intended primarily as a morale-booster in pit-villages and working-class communities.[129] Yet while leaving most pathos and jargon alone, it is possible to see precisely how Daniells rewrote more and more of each line as he got towards the end of the piece and carried on tinkering with details at the proof stage. In some verses, this meant that only the rhyming end-words were retained, while the rest were re-cast or completely replaced.

In spite of the public show of solidarity between the rival factions in the Association, there was a political censorship at work in the *Advocate* which became more obvious towards the end of April 1844. Daniells was empowered to 'refuse the insertion of all *sectarian politics* and sectarian religion', and to 'insert and draw the attention of the Miners, and the productive classes generally, to all important Parliamentary proceedings'. Yet he could not have a weekly paper without having to pay the government's newspaper tax, which would

---

128. Colls, *The Collier's Rant*, pp. 104–5; Fynes, *The Miners*, pp. 60–61; Challinor, *A Radical Lawyer*, p. 121; C & R, *The Miners' Association*, pp. 129–30.

129. Not many outsiders would know that 'splent' was coarse grey coal, that 'foul coal' was the unsaleable stuff, that 'separation' referred to the owners' insistence that only large, 'round' coals should be filled by face-workers, and that a 'neuk' was a passing-place undergound; though most northeasterners would understand that 'mence' was to do with decency and dignity.

push up the price of each issue to threepence-halfpenny and require a guaranteed circulation of five thousand copies, plus advanced subscriptions and a levy to cover the government's insistence on a £600 security deposit, all from strikers who were beginning to feel the pinch. He also needed access to printing machinery – another indication that Dodds was operating on a commercial basis – if he was to compete with Roberts' *Miners' Monthly Magazine*, let alone with the well-established and well-respected *Northern Star*, the paper which even the Executive assumed all activists subscribed to and read, and to which reports of the strike were sent.[130]

How the political tensions within the Association worked through into the *Advocate* is well exampled by the fact that Thomas Nicholson's acrostic on *The Miners' Advocate* (78), with its moral force perspective, was preferred in the issue of April 20th to a prose piece from Thornley which Daniells stressed 'cannot be inserted' since 'it would subject us to an action for libel'. Even so, Nicholson's piece had taken seven weeks to get into print, and Daniells insisted that 'Our poetical friends must have patience, we are in possession of a great number of poetical epistles, many of which, we fear, it will be impossible to prune into shape so as to appear in the "Advocate"'.[131] What did get through were verses from conventionally literary non-combatants and from some Association officers. Anything sent in anonymously was automatically rejected, and only occasionally was a striking rank-and-file versifier encouraged to revise their work – 'The Notes of the Union Trumpeter, New Trimdon, are discordant, he must sound again'. Yet 'The poem entitled "Let us Live by our Labour", by the writer of "The Miner's Doom" [ie J.P.Robson], shall be inserted in No.12, the talented author has our thanks, we trust he will continue his favours. The poetry from Bo'ness in type.' Suitable verse from strikers was evidently not forthcoming.

130. C & R, *The Miners' Association*, p. 40–41. Compare Colls, *The Pitmen*, p. 192. Later, copies of the *Northern Star* were sent to strikers free of charge (Wilson (1986), 86).
131. *Advocate*, 20.4.1844, p. 88. Compare the *Northern Star*, 27.11.1841, in which the Editor, William Hill, pleaded with the poets to 'give us a little respite', since he had 'loads of their obliging communications unlooked at', and on December 18th 1841 he proclaimed that 'Fifty poets must wait their turn'. Roberts believes that there were 'very probably, thousands of Chartist poets' and that Hill 'clearly threw away far more than he ever read or published' (Roberts, *Radical Politicians*, pp. 4, 8 note 12).

Only two weeks into the strike, the Association Executive was by no means happy with the degree of autonomy allegedly enjoyed by the colliery-based committees, but the need for considerable amounts of income from sympathisers worked to undermine attempts at centralisation. However, on April 20th Daniells warned his readers against fraudulent collectors – 'All persons seeking contributions not provided with such certificates are imposters' – and on the same day Martin Jude was nominated as the official receiver of donations from tradespeople, all of whom were to be acknowledged in the *Advocate*. On April 25th a hundred small posters were produced, possibly for display in shopkeepers' windows, and on April 27th a thousand collecting certificates were printed, together with five hundred copies of a notice warning 'The Benevolent and Sympathising Public, of Newcastle and Vicinity'

> against certain parties going about endeavouring to collect Subscriptions for the Unemployed Miners of Northmberland and Durham without being authorised to do so, and thereby injuring the said Miners. Any individual feeling desirous of assisting us, will be kind enough to forward what they choose to give to the Committee at the Three Tuns, Manor street, or to pay it to none but persons bearing a Printed Certificate, signed by the underneath Committee, and stamped with the District Seal.[132]

Yet with twelve hundred certificates in operation, with perhaps half a dozen people in some of the 'musical bands' and with open access to the printed songs and verse in Dodds' shop, this collecting activity must have been quite hard to control from the centre.[133] Besides, activists had other printing resources than Dodds, and, while we do not know whether print-runs were in their hundreds or their

---

132. Wigan.

133. A surviving Northumberland and Durham District Balance Sheet for April 23rd to May 20th 1844 (Wigan) shows Dodds being paid £8 13s out of a total expenditure of £16 8s 11d. He made a donation of £1 to the hardship fund in the *Advocate* for May 4th, while Mrs Thomas Dodds gave a further ten shillings. The sheet for the period from September 6th to October 12th 1844 seems to indicate that Dodds received about half the District's total expenditure, but that for October 12th to November 13th 1844 shows him receiving only £2.9s.0d out of a total of over £49.

thousands, the style and content of broadside songs and verse tended to be quite different from those of the material allowed into the 'Poetry' section of the *Advocate*, like George Cowie of Bo'ness' lines on *Patriotism* (79), which appeared on May 4th 1844.[134]

Also in early May, Daniells seems very concerned about strikers' self-activity in another matter:

> a few unthinking individuals have lately committed breaches of the peace; we are mortified at this, because we know that the great body of the Miners strongly repudiate such rash, mad conduct – because we know that the delegates, committees, and indeed all the offical men in the association are opposed, from principle, to violence or intimidation of any description – and because we know that the enemies of the association and the public press (with a few honourable exceptions) will charge the blame on the whole Association which has only been committed by rash unthinking men.[135]

Quite how far Daniells was out of touch with local activists is underlined by his uncritical quotation from the Combination Act and by the fact that strikers' patience was being praised by the bourgeois papers at the same time as they suppressed or radically marginalised any other perspectives on the dispute. In fact it was not striking pitmen, by and large, who were involved in most direct action: instead, it was women, youths and children who took the initiative in confronting blacklegs, since all the Association leadership could offer were abortive attempts to talk to the owners, more mass meetings and the consistent exclusion of other people's politics.[136] In the coalfield, the situation was already becoming critical. By May 11th, the *Newcastle Journal* admitted that there was 'great distress', with some people already too weak to leave their beds. The owners acted: women, children, the sick and the elderly were targets of a campaign of evictions, which seem to have begun in

---

134. Cowie chaired an Association meeting in his home town, and so was probably a union official of some sort (*Advocate*, 24.2.1844, p. 53).
135. *Advocate*, 4.5.1844.
136. *Durham Chronicle*, 26.4.1844; C & R, *The Miners' Association*, p. 130; Colls, *The Collier's Rant*, pp. 106–7; Colls, *The Pitmen*, pp. 297–99; Galloway, *Annals*, Volume 2, pp. 176–77; Burt, *An Autobiography*, pp. 33–34; Fynes, *The Miners*, pp. 64–71, 137.

the second week in May.[137] But all the Association leadership could do was to counsel moral force and martyrdom.

James Purdy's *The Miners Rights* (80A) was treated as grist to this ideological mill. The author seems to have lifted several lines from William Johnson's *The Miners' Grievances* (77), but his moral outrage and the assumed agreement amongst 'frinds' override any concern to produce standard poetry. This anger is, however, flattened by Daniells' habit of tidying up spelling, syntax and verse-structure, so what had been a dignified appeal reads more like a pious whinge. Somewhat different, however, was Jane Knight's *A New Song on the Pitmen's Grievances* (81). This too was an insider's song, done by one of only two known women writers from the coalfield, but it was published on a colophonless broadside. She writes of the Wingate community as 'us', and seems confident enough not only of a general condemnation of blacklegs (not least for their hypocrisy) but also of their fate, whether the strike was successful or not. She also implies that at least some of those who were compelled to 'wander' in search of support were female, but she evidently wrote her song for male voices – it is 'Our wives and children' who 'are turned out'. She understood that women like her were as much a part of the strike, and of the union, with the same hero, 'Mr. Roberts', as the most militant activists, and she preferred emigration to going back beaten. Of course, not every striker agreed, and others were undecided. In John Atkinson's *A New Song* (82), for example, there is an underlining for italics in Daniells' manuscript revision (82B) about Roberts – 'He never led us yet to wrong', implying, perhaps, that he still needed watching – but this slight qualification does not appear in the colophonless printed version, suggesting that the person paying for the printing wasn't prepared to accept any bending of the political content.[138]

Daniells' attitude to blacklegs was to have their names sent to General and Delegate meetings 'so that they may be shown up',[139] but in this context George Patterson's apparently lapidary *Lines on the Death of Robert Carr* (83) from Framwellgate Moor Colliery appear

---

137. Burt, *An Autobiography*, pp. 34, 36, 37; Meech, *From Mine to Ministry*, pp. 1, 18; Fynes, *The Miners*, pp. 62, 72, 74, 108; Burt (1882), 393; Colls, *The Pitmen*, p. 300. See also 107.

138. Thornley Colliery officials described their tactics for combatting attrition in the *Advocate*, 18.5.1844.

139. *Advocate*, 18.5.1844.

somewhat ambiguous. Carr was reported as having been 'killed by being blown over the gangway on returning from his work', and so he may have been a blackleg. Exclamations about 'Uncertain life!' and the pious-sounding advice – 'oh, may we ready stand/ For death prepared to sit at God's right hand' – may, then, have been ironic, and the piece's insertion may have been a concession to the more militantly-inclined activists. What is certain is that one piece mentioned in the *Advocate* on May 4th 1844, but not written by a striker, was printed as soon as Daniells could manage. Using his full name for the first time – and following those few shopkeepers and others who had taken this step some time before, some of whom may have attended the various public meetings organised to win Odd Fellows', 'Tradesmen' and in fact any petit-bourgeois support[140] – Joseph Philip Robson offered more bland and moralistic verse in the shape of *The Miner's Motto* **(84)**.

Robert Holder's *The Colliers' Appeal to the Country* **(85)** also followed the Executive's line of patiently explaining. In reality, however, the problem was that 'the Country' was characterised by sharp class divisions, even amongst those 'good Christians' he addresses as a monolithic (and morally unimpeachable) unity. This was precisely the fissuring which the abruptly-named *Song* **(86)**, allegedly written by 'An Old Pitman', sought to exploit.[141] The verses appear to have come from a newspaper, and appear under a sub-heading, 'PRIZE POETRY', with the following note:

The following production has been forwarded to us, in consequence of Mr Roberts, the Pitmen's Attorney-General, having, with equal liberality and good feeling, offered, through the medium of his *Magazine*, a prize of Two Guineas for the best, and ten shillings for the second best, Parody on the song of "The brave old Oak" – the subject to be "The Strike." The writer says, "he has not tried his hand much at verse, being more accustomed to handle the pick than the pen."

---

140. The Executive asked Dodds to produce two hundred copies of a highly-coloured poster (Editor's collection) for a meeting on May 22nd which may have helped launch the pamphlet, *The Question Answered: "What do the Pitmen want"*, written by an Ouston Colliery pitman, William Mitchell. It sold over six thousand copies by the middle of June.

141. The author's sobriquet was often used (eg, *Advocate*, 13.1.1844). See also *Tommy Wiseacre's Farewell to the Union and the men at the heed on't* (NCL 1844) and *A New Song* **(116)**.

However, we claim for him a fair field; and if Mr Roberts do not award
him the higher premium, we trust he will deem him worthy of the
lesser – which may be left at our office till called for. The "Old Pitman"
informs us that the money would be very acceptable, as he has now
been seven weeks on strike, and has had nothing, during that period,
but "hungry guts," and fourpence from the Union.

The anonymity of this piece speaks volumes, but whether the poet
had ever been near a coal-face is questionable, given his Golden
Ageism about happy times. However, both he and the editor
understood that the political cleavage within the Association was
their best hope of dividing the strikers ideologically. At the end of
May 1844 Londonderry complained to the Home Office that 'not a
man is to be seen, not an engine in operation, not a curl of smoke
from any pit'.[142] The strike remained solid.

June 1844

After two months on strike, what Roberts called the 'trial between the
long purses of the owners and the hungry guts of the pitmen'
sharpened, not least because 'as yet the amount of subscriptions' to
the official funds 'was trifling', and most of that went on intercepting
blacklegs and paying their train fares home. Total strike pay per man
for the whole dispute amounted to sevenpence-halfpenny, so people
made their own arrangements with sympathetic shopkeepers or
farmers, depending on figures like Peter Burt to stand as security for
their credit, or relied on the efforts of colliery-based union committees. Even so, morale was high at the June 11th mass meeting at
Tantobie near Tanfield. Up to fifty thousand people 'came from their
respective districts in procession, with music, flags, &c,' to reaffirm
their solidarity, and the approach of two local JPs caused no alarm.
John Tulip, 'that quiet man', 'rejoiced with tears, regarding it as a
moral victory' that the JPs avoided the reckless use of troops which
characterised Londonderry's tactics in 1832 on Shadon's Hill. With
such an effective internal moral hegemony there was, of course, little
need of state force to ensure that many pit-village people tolerated
eviction, intimidation, blacklegging and hunger in silence, but as
June wore on the material pressures on the communities began to

---

142. Challinor, *A Radical Lawyer*, p. 122.

test the Association leaders' moral and political strategy and tactics severely.[143]

What was at stake here was the validity of the ideology of Ranter Methodism, quietist trade unionism, faith in the law of the land and belief in the state's fairness. Even after the strike, Tremenheere remained puzzled by an apparent contradiction within Primitive Methodist practice:

> The owners of this colliery lent a house to the primitive Methodists, for their religious meetings. At the time of the strike, one of the preachers preached in it in favour of the strike. Another of them took in the 'Northern Star', and regularly every week read it to a meeting of the men.
>
> I asked, during the strike, several of the local preachers, why they did not show the men that they were wrong, which as reasonable men themselves, they must know they were; but if they interfered at all, it was against us.[144]

Tremenheere did not understand the extent of the ideological polarisation in the pit-villages, any more than did an editor of a bourgeois newspaper:

> Among the pitmen in this neighbourhood are many of the religious sects termed Ranters and Latter-day Saints, and these men, it is stated, believe poor, deluded creatures – that Mr Roberts, the Pitmen's Attorney-General, is a second Moses sent for their deliverance.[145]

The reality was probably rather more rational, complex and political:

> Revd Spoor spoke for the union in Mr Dobson's long room at Willington; a preacher who opposed the union was dragged from his pulpit at Wingate; other preachers who opposed were obliged to leave their congregations; the Wesleyan ministers who stood aside were jeered: 'the Ranters used their influence to disaffect our members'.[146]

143. Welbourne, *The Miners' Unions*, pp. 75, 78; Fynes, *The Miners*, pp. 72–73, 75–77; Colls, *The Pitmen*, p. 285; Burt, *An Autobiography*, pp. 38–42; Richardson (1883), 267–68.
144. Colls, *The Pitmen*, p. 196.
145. C & R, *The Miners' Association*, p. 134 note, quoting a newspaper cutting dated June 1st 1844.
146. Colls, *The Pitmen*, p. 191.

Then, even Primitive Methodist congregations split on the rock of material hardship: all South Shields circuit went into decline, and for three societies this proved terminal.[147]

This ideological polarisation can be seen in the verse produced in June. What appeared in the *Advocate* was very different to what Dodds was prepared to print for strikers on broadsides. From the distance of Stobhill, near Dalkieth, David Moffat felt confident in the abstract power of 'Union' to slay the 'Philistine' with a 'single stone', and he had his verse published in the *Advocate* within one week of sending it. However, *An Address to the Miners* (87) offered no concrete, active strategy to 'lay our proud Goliath low', when strikers' families were down to hand-to-mouth foraging. Similarly, James Gordon of Spital Tongues had his lugubrious verse printed in the *Advocate* of June 15th, not far from advertisements for 'Fancy Silk Handkerchiefs and Stocks' and 'Best Sweet Wines' at 15d a bottle. *The Famishing Miner* (88) recognised the immediate material difficulty, but elsewhere in the same issue Daniells – who spent three weeks of June in Scotland – complained about people collecting money when they were 'not duly authorized' but paid none of it 'into the General Board'. None of the Newcastle-based leadership had a complete grasp of (let alone any effective strategy to end) the desperation in the pit villages, at a time when the owners were making the most of the rise in the number of blacklegs and the high level of their alleged earnings.[148]

It wasn't that rank and file strikers failed to produce what they thought was appropriate versified propaganda. Daniells reported that he had 'a vast number of poetical pieces on hand', amongst which 'those found worthy of insertion will be published in regular

---

147. Colls, *The Pitmen*, p. 160.
148. Cramlington owners produced a leaflet claiming pay was ten shillings a shift. Within a week Dodds printed a refutation by the 'Late Workmen of East Cramlington Colliery' (NCL; Wigan). There was even a poster warning Carlisle citizens against accepting the owners' propaganda (NCL). Londonderry had been warned by his Viewer on April 24th that 'a cessation of the Strike in less than three weeks would be positively injurious to your Lordship's interests', since stockpiled coal could be sold off at 'excellent prices'. However, once those super-profits had been made, Londonderry needed blacklegs in order to produce coal, and higher wages could be offset against much higher market prices. By June 14th, even so, the dispute had become 'very disagreeable' to him, both as a coalowner and as Lord Lieutenant in charge of the Durham County magistrates (Colls, *The Pitmen*, pp. 293–94, 300).

succession'. This included 'the poetry by W.M. Hunter, of Stevenson Colliery, Scotland', which was 'under consideration' but 'must be revised prior to insertion',[149] though it seems not to have been published. The *Advocate* remained strangely reticent about blacklegs, above all in its 'Poetry' section, so it is interesting to speculate as to whether William Hornsby's manuscript of *A New Song* (89A) was ever intended to go in the paper or whether the broadside form (89B) was felt to be more appropriate. Whoever took this decision, the manuscript text is stripped of blacklegs' full names – and those of bosses' men, religious hypocrites, thieves, cowards and the workshy – by Daniells. Rather more focussed was John Henderson's manuscript, *The Blacklegs* (90A), which deals with an individual from Hebburn who broke ranks with the strikers and with the Rechabites. Henderson seeks to associate economic treachery with moral degeneration, but his text also points to the ideological crisis within pit-village institutions and makes no bones about blacklegs getting their reward when striking pitmen 'get their due'.[150]

The union's economic and political crisis came to a head in late June, when two hundred men were said to be leaving the Association each week.[151] The problem of imported, unskilled, blackleg labour became less pressing than that of indigenous, skilled, and highly productive hewers being forced back to work through starvation.[152] So the debate shifted to inside the Association itself, and can been seen in the broadside, *A Dialogue Between Harry Heartless and Peter Pluck* (91). There is no hint here of any serious change of strategy or tactics, though religious faith is no longer invoked as a morale-booster. Instead, more materialist rhetoric is mobilised, including an exhortation to go out to 'beg' so as to experience solidarity at first hand. Yet the atomisation of the pit-village communities and of the activists within them is quietly attested to by the fact that this piece was 'Composed solely for the benefit of the Men of Framwellgate Moor Colliery By one of Themselves', and it may be that fear of victimisation led to its anonymity. However, towards the end of

---

149. *Advocate*, 29.6.1844, p.'123' – *ie* 132.
150. Compare *The First-DREST Man of Seghill* (17) from 1831.
151. Welbourne, *The Miners' Unions*, p. 78.
152. Owners were advertising for 'young, able-bodied and steady' men so far afield as Suffolk, though Dodds was quick to reprint the EC's response on June 22nd (NCL), which could have been spread via the trade union links with the Tyne seamen which dated back at least to 1825.

June, the tone and content of some broadside material printed in the Side began to shift. *Munkwaremouth Turn-out* (92) names names and uses a racy old tune and a 'phonetic' idiom to show full-hearted contempt for 'Viewers bums' and candymen, the lumpen petty criminals, brawlers and riff-raff. And yet, for all the strong-toothed good-humour and sarcasm, this piece too ends by lining up with Executive's policy. On the other hand, Henry Holliday of Greencroft Colliery's *A New Song* (93) illustrates the tension between the official, peaceful line and how rank-and-file strikers felt about those who oppressed them. Prayer, and perhaps reasoning, have given place to a recognition of the need to take and use power, not only by giving blacklegs 'the dreggs' after the strike but also by tackling the employers. Holliday's idea of how to get a 'fair price for our labour' depended not so much on the strikers' own efforts as on the alternative Chartist leadership of Roberts.

Strikers and their supporters continued to get fund-raising verse into print. Elizabeth Gair, described as a 'Collier's Wife', had her *The Colliery Union, A New Song* (94) printed by Robert Henderson at North Shields and then by Dodds. On the one hand, like Roberts in public, she accepted the quietist strategy for victory 'Without either sword or gun'. On the other hand, she represented herself as the Biblical widow whose 'Crouse of Meal...never did run out', and she seems to have believed that the Lord helped those who helped themselves. Above all, Gair thought that Roberts and Beesley were crucial for the strikers to 'gain your victory', and not the Executive, and she counselled the men accordingly. However, the supply of suitable newly-made material for broadsides seems to have slackened later in June, and so Dodds reissued *The Pitmen's Union* (29B&C) from the defeated strike of 1832 with Roberts' name substituted for Hepburn's, plus a few minor emendations to punctuation and spelling. This was highly ironic, given that Roberts was being represented as the potential saviour of a strike he thought premature and too local and of a strategy he felt was politically naive. The only other potential ally, in this perspective, remained God, the hero of G.A.'s maudlin *Song of the Oppressed* (95), yet its author marvels at the 'soulless courage' of blacklegs and the 'blackguards' who protect them, and offers no active strategy on how to do the opposing and the fighting which are rhetorically announced.

Class-based anger did sometimes get put into verse. William Roxby's *A Song to the Blacklegs and all thats not in the Union* (96A) drips with hate, but his text failed to appear in the *Advocate* or even on a Dodds broadside. Instead, it was used as the basis for the versified part of *A Dialogue between three Coal Viewers after being in search of men*, illustrating the employers' difficulties in recruiting skilled hewers as blacklegs. Roxby's text is highly mediated by Daniells (**96B&C**): verses are shortened from six lines to five; exclamation marks are sprinkled about liberally; idiom and syntax are altered towards a supposedly 'poetic' standard, and what the verse gains in smoothness it loses tenfold in rage. Above all, Roxby's chosen mode of individual address – as though to a particular blackleg, within arms' reach – is lost, as is his appeal to 'your Commerade brothers' who might change the traitor's perceptions. Whereas Roxby wanted the blackleg to feel, as he did, the physical pain of exploitation, the printed text misses out the 'thy' and impersonalises the address, diffuses the potent mixture of criticism and exhortation and so ruins the political effectiveness of the song.

The condition of the original manuscript of *A New Song* (**97A**) and what happened to what remains of it indicate the level of respect Daniells had for the work of his poetic correspondents. There is no evidence for Daniells' first verse – though the top of the sheet has been torn away – but every line of the remaining text is substantially altered (**97B**). The author evidently shared the common faith in God's fairness and Roberts' powers, but understood that such a perspective involved serious risks of martyrdom and defeat. Whereas the original text recognises the existence of 'class', Daniells alters that to 'poor men', and though certain forms of defensive violence were evidently becoming acceptable in the coalfields, Daniells' mediation assumes a divine intervention. Thus the tension between bleeding martyrdom and returning blow for blow was magically resolved in the Side, but not in the pit villages, where activists were now obliged to act independently of the Association officials.

The earliest two manuscripts of *Auld Lang Syne* (**98A&B**) are folded into the form of a letter, sealed and addressed to 'Mr Tho Dodds'. The packet contained two song texts, one of them signed by J.Matthews of Wingate Colliery, and the other (which may be in the same hand) left unsigned. There is also a brief note to 'Mr Doods' – 'ple[ase] prent 400 of this song, and we will pay for them when we start,' subscribed 'I am yours', signed by 'Adam Murray' and dated from Trimdon Colliery on June 20th 1844. This package is interesting on a number of counts. Firstly, its sender confidently assumes that Dodds extended credit to strikers. Secondly, activists from neighbouring pits knew each other well enough to swap ideas and material independently of the Association in Newcastle. Thirdly, there was not always a local printer who could or would produce four hundred broadside copies of a piece, and so people like Murray came to rely on the good offices of Thomas Dodds. Fourthly, a local colliery-based committee could organise fund-raising activities. However, J. Matthews' 'fair copy' is further mediated by Daniells (98C&D): spelling is rigorously standardised, 'poetic' expressions are substituted for matter-of-fact ones and idiom is banished. By themselves, such changes can seem trivial, or even preferable; yet the overall effect is to 'polish' the teeth-gritting fatalism of the song into bland inconsequentiality, while still ascribing authorship to 'J. Matthew'.

Such a process may not have been necessary with *Reason's Claim, or, The Miners' Plea to the Owners* (99A&B), which got into the *Advocate* at the end of June, and then (with only three tiny emendations) onto a broadside. It was probably by Joseph Philip Robson, and preaches cross-class unity under God at a period when those 'scattered interests' were getting wider by the day: Londonderry and the Coal Trade Committee refused even to meet the Association's officers. But what is interesting about this text is its concentration on the hearts and minds of the (male) liberal bourgeois people who had helped to free the slaves, on those 'Men of Britain' who might pity hungry and homeless women and children in the coalfields and who might influence the owners to reach a settlement with their own 'ill-used slaves', some of whom had reached then end of their tether.[153] In June an eighteen year old miner from Elswick Colliery died from hunger, and the capitalist press sometimes reported the level of suffering in the coalfields:

> Multitudes of them resort to the sea shore living & sleeping amongst the rocks, where they exist on refuse fish, and any other eatable matter they can collect; many of them are provided with Guns, and the small birds which they procure by this means have for some time contributed to afford them the means of subsistence; and begging is extensively resorted to.[154]

---

153. Fynes, *The Miners*, p. 73; Meech, *From Mine to Ministry*, p. 11.
154. Colls, *The Pitmen*, p. 300.

However, in some pit-villages like West Rainton, there was hope, as in William Walker Story and George Watson's *The Pitmen's Union* (100), which was set to the interestingly ambiguous tune of 'And a nutting we will go'. Like many of the other broadside and 'slip' songs, this was almost certainly put to work by the 'many who were travelling the country to collect subscriptions grouped together in musical bands'. The tone of this song suggests at least a public optimism about staying out on strike, and of being supported by other workers in doing so, whatever people like the 'Noble Marquis' might do in the way of evictions, though singers were sometimes harassed by magistrates.[155] Topped by the old symbol of unity, clasped hands, this piece eschews all idiom and all but the most tangential references to religious ideology.

For some Christian strikers the owners' attrition and the systematic use of blacklegs and candymen seem to have caused a severe spiritual crisis as June came to a close. Nicholas Cowey's *A Copy of Verses referring to the preasant state of things* (101A), sent from Shotton Colliery on June 28th, suggests that blacklegging had taken on the character of sin. His verse is full of hate, communicated directly and meant to be taken personally by the target, though with asides directed at any who doubted the Christianity of Cowey's tactics – 'They:l: Stand all the hissing that Nature Can give'. It has a pattern of punctuation which seems to articulate both outrage and the difficulty of expressing it smoothly. Most confusing to the author is that 'No Reason, Or Religion: Can make them to yield': immoral force seemed to be winning. On its transition to print, Daniells saw to it that Cowey's personal religion – Moses was 'mosses' to him, and he knew a strike-breaking 'judas' when he saw one – was blurred and not a line escapes emendation or even complete recasting. Given that owners like Londonderry were then meting out harsher treatment to strikers the more pious they were, it is not at all surprising that the ideological confusion felt by people like Cowey resulted in a chiliastic rhetoric; but Daniells simply chopped off Cowey's last three near-Revelationary verses, and so the painful transition to this-worldy activity effected there – the identification, isolation and shaming of blacklegs, and their continued pariah status after the strike – is completely lost.

---

155. Fynes, *The Miners*, p. 101.

July–August 1844

By July, 'Hundreds of the men on strike were...away in other parts of the country, some of them staying with their friends and relatives, some working at other places with their friends during the strike'. Others evidently continued to go out raising funds. *The Miner's Doom* (102A&B), 'Composed by Henderson Fawcett, Miner, South Wingate', has the air of a piece targetted at the hearts, minds and spare change of non-strikers. The text's politics are parliamentary and reformist and its tone descends from sentimentality into melodrama, after the manner of J.P.Robson. The same faith in the impartiality of the law is also exemplified in *Mr. Roberts the Pitmen's Friend* (103), issued at around the time the lawyer's responsibilities grew to cover all Association legal business. However, there is a sharper tone towards blacklegs – 'They will wish when we do get our rights they had been union men' – as well as an uncritical encomium for Roberts. In public, Roberts chimed in with the official Association stress on keeping the peace, and so, rather like Arthur Scargill in 1984–85, he failed to differentiate his politics from those of the most active amongst the striking rank and file.[156] Even so, rhetorical support came from sections of the London press, and more material aid came from other groups of workers. In Bury and Radcliffe, for example, a network of collectors accountable to the Bury District Committee operated in alehouses, but their example was apparently not generalised and much stress was placed by the Association on the legal consequences of direct action.[157] Even the printed appeal to blacklegs of July 20th was aimed at the consciences of those 'religious men who are working' for having 'sowed dissension in almost every religious body in the two counties'.[158] Londonderry had no such scruples and produced a peremptory, pompous and not wholly grammatical poster, 'Pitmen's Strike', in order to mobilise members of his class, above all the magistrates and clergymen, to put pressure on the shopkeepers who were giving credit to strikers' families, especially in 'his town of Seaham'.[159]

---

156. Fynes, *The Miners*, p. 101. Callinicos & Simons, *The Great Strike*.
157. A handbill for use amongst 'the Trades and public of Lancashire' and another detailing the sentences of those convicted after the early July 1844 'Sheffield Colliery Riots' were offered for sale by Mr John Turton in 1990. See below p. 75 note 194.
158. 'To the Deceived and Deluded Workmen now employed on the Collieries in Northumberland and Durham' (Editor's collection).
159. Fynes, *The Miners*, pp. 78–79, 85–91; Challinor, *A Radical Lawyer*, pp. 70, 121, 126, 130, 136; C & R, *The Miners' Association*, pp. 136, 246. Compare

On July 13th Daniells reprinted *Union!* (53D) in the *Advocate* rather than any of the 'poetic pieces' he had on hand, and in the next issue he explained why: 'Our poetical friends must have patience, we have not less than one hundred pieces by us, many of which are not of sufficient merit to warrant their insertion'.[160] What was of merit evidently, was *Wonderful!* (104), a bizarre piece by C. Ratcliffe of Seghill, written almost six weeks before, which claimed that 1844 was a year 'when masters fear a flogging'. Also acceptable was John Martin's *Song of the Oppressor* (105), which suggests that Daniells and the *Advocate* were all that was needed to secure liberty. The weakness of such a strategy was emphasised painfully by Daniells himself:

> FREEDOM OF THE PRESS. – We stop the press to announce to our readers that we have just been honoured with a GOVERNMENT PROSECUTION. If the Government or Coal Kings think by these harsh proceedings to frighten us from the advocacy of the Pitmen's rights they will be miserably disappointed. However (till the "Advocate" becomes stamped) to steer clear of law sharks and base informers the "Advocate" will, in future, be published once per month.[161]

Consequently, towards the end of July, with the threat of state prosecution hanging over their paper, the Executive had to rely even more on mass meetings, demonstrations and staged public events such as that in Newcastle's Music Hall on July 25th, where they 'Earnestly requested that all Miners will keep away in order to give the Tradesmen and Public an opportunity of attending', though a hand-picked set of respectable miners was specially invited.[162] In the coalfields, officials saw to it that 'committees formed to take goods away to pledge', but the distribution of the proceeds was not tied to the level of contribution.[163] Dodds, meanwhile, found himself printing extracts from a sympathetic Dublin newspaper, a notice of yet another attempt to organise sympathetic members of other trades

Continued from p 58

Londonderry, *Lady Anne*, p. 235.
160. *Advocate*, 27.7.1844, p. 148.
161. *Advocate*, 27.7.1844.
162. A poster, and a handbill, '*Means and Ways!!!*', were offered for sale by Mr John Turton in 1990.
163. Fynes, *The Miners*, p. 93.

and the order of march of one more 'Procession' to Newcastle Town Moor, which Fynes took to be 'a most convincing proof of their determination'.[164]

That determination could have been read quite differently, as could *The Pitmen Determined to be Free* broadside **(106A)**, which was in print by early August. The title-phrase had been much used by orators since the beginning of the strike – by Mark Dent, for example – and there is some evidence that printed verses found their way onto placards, or vice-versa, as the fourth stanza of this piece seems to have done on July 30th.[165] But what is particularly interesting about W.N.'s text is its silence about Roberts' supposedly pivotal importance, its apparent reference to the old radical tradition of Marat's *Chains of Slavery*, its notably unchristian lack of forgiveness for blacklegs and its determination to fight for freedom to the death.[166] The author insists that the enemy is on this earth and needs to be confronted there by strikers, not in some putative after-life by a God whose services, to all intents and purposes, were no longer required. Remarkably, only a little of that conviction is lost in the transition to print, suggesting that perhaps Daniells had nothing to do with the editing process; and what is probably William Hornsby's *A New Song* **(107A)** continues the secularist tendency. But for all its wish-fulfilling fantasy element – the owners' Committee had no intention of negotiating with anybody – it has a note of anger in the manuscript version which does not wholly survive the transition to print, and the regularisation of the woman's idiom detracts further from the attempted realism of the text. Given Londonderry's treatment of actual old women and children, it seems difficult to

---

164. The first two handbills were offered for sale by Mr John Turton in 1990. The third is reprinted in Fynes with Dodds and Daniells named as 'Conductors'. Thirty thousand strikers and supporters marched behind a banner proclaiming 'Peace, Law and Order', and only fifteen hundred men had then left the union (Fynes *The Miners*, pp. 94–100)

165. Fynes, *The Miners*, pp. 57, 94–100; C & R, *The Miners' Association*, p. 142.

166. The Methodist historian Robert Wearmouth did not believe that 'local preachers prayed for blacklegs to be injured', yet the Chartist-influenced Ranter leadership at Earsdon Colliery 'showed so strong a disposition to violence that a force of half a company of infantry, some cavalry, several mounted policemen, and from eighty to ninety special constables, was established at and near this colliery (from 18th of July to 24th of September)' (Wearmouth, *Methodism*, p. 189 note, 190. Compare Siegel, *The Meek and the Militant*, pp. xii, 29, 97, 197).

credit that the heroine of what Daniells called *The Old Woman and the Coal Owner* would be taken as having won an argument and changed a decision through moral superiority or threats of God's punishment in the after-life. Instead, such a piece might get a wry grin out of pit-villagers – people who had also been turned out of their houses back in May and who could also see only the long road ahead – and perhaps a penny out of sympathisers amongst other coal trade workers, shopkeepers or artisans.

As July came to a close, the need to address waverers within the strikers' ranks became crucial. *A Dialogue between Peter Fearless and Dick Freeman* (108) has the air of a last-ditch attempt to prevent strikers giving in, rather than that of a fund-raiser. All the arguments had been well-rehearsed before the strike and could hardly come as a revelation to 'Dick, though 'Peter' at least was drawing this-worldly, materialist and class-based conclusions, and professed cautious optimism about the Association's strategy and the owners' eventual defeat. However, 'Dick' no longer saw the point of a long trek to yet another Newcastle demonstration, so what begins as an account of the original grievances ends with a rhetorical (and perhaps not wholly ironic) denunciation of possible 'treason', as though the Executive had an authority equivalent to that of the state. This paternalism is reinforced by the combination of orthodox syntax and grammar with idiomatic/phonetic spelling, as though the author wanted to address those less formally literate. *Fish Bettys Account of herself* (109A) was evidently another last-ditch attempt to shame strikers from going back in a particular pit-community by ridiculing one person, and the text draws consciously on an older, urban satire, *Billy Oliver*. The identity of Fish Betty is not known, though it is interesting to see that women could be represented as taking contradictory positions on the strike and that the influence of some of them in getting strikers back to work was well understood. The song's strategy is basically a moral critique with a class component. It plays heavily on Betty's pride, her exploitation of her sexuality, her individualistic short-sightedness, her overdressing in chapel and her pretentious airs and graces. But the mediated manuscript seeks for some sort of 'standard Geordie', and takes away much of the pith, heavy irony and parody of the original.

At this point, if not before, other interested parties made interventions in printed verse. *The Miner's Prayer* (110A) may have been written by the Sunday School Union supporter, teetotaller and bookseller, James Rewcastle.[167] Roberts' talents and the strikers' solidarity are irrelevant in this perspective: salvation on earth is an individual matter. So, while the text acknowledges the strikers' oppression, it links that with their sinfulness – 'A slave to man, a slave to sin/A slave to satan too' – and suggests lugubriously that individual pitmen had only to 'trust and praise the Lord', bearing the 'land of glory' in distant view. If this wasn't simply a Rewcastle initiative, perhaps Dodds perceived a market amongst pious sympathisers: the psalm-like original appears all but totally unmediated in the imprintless broadside version. The same goes for *The Saviour's Death* (**111A**), though here the first three stanzas are part of a longer printed text. The remaining four stanzas are in manuscript and are treated with some liberty by whoever edited them for **111B**. Perhaps printed piety paid. Yet however successful the collections may have been, the tone of this piece suggests that defeat was now accepted in some religious quarters and that forgiveness was all that remained amongst strikers represented almost as Christ crucified. It is as though Dodds and Daniells were looking for material which would help to prepare the strikers for defeat. For example, *Job, the Patient Man* (**112**) makes a separation between sheep and goats on this earth, but the only hope it offers is equality after death, the grave and Revelation.[168]

A religiose tone now became more evident in the Association's official posters and handbills, though it is often uncomfortably combined with very materialist content. On August 3rd, for example, Thomas Forster signed an appeal for solidarity which noted the 'constant attacks which of late years the capitalists made upon labour' and stressed that a defeat for the miners would lead to the 'subjugation of every industrious section of the community', but he ends with the slogan, 'May God Defend the Right'.[169] Whether he spoke with contradictory voices, or whether he was attempting to

---

167. Rewcastle operated in Dean Street, Newcastle, from 1841 to 1847, specialising in Nonconformist and Temperance literature. He was the first President of Newcastle Temperance Society and also wrote verse (Hunt, *The Book Trade*, p. 77; Allan, *Tyneside Songs*, pp. 464, 491).

168. Daniells may at this point have reissued a piece from May 1831, *The Pitman's Complaint* (**20A**) as *Verses on the Cruelty of the Masters to the Pitmen* (**20B& C**), in preference to the hundred and more others he had spiked.

169. Editor's collection.

address two polarising audiences at the same time, is unclear. What is clear from an circular marked 'N.B. PRIVATE. FOR MEMBERS ONLY.', dated August 5th and referring to the 'present embarassed state of the general fund',[170] was that the Executive Committee's efforts at generalisation on a class basis were too little and too late.

The strike began to crumble unmistakably in the second week of August, and by the 10th up to six thousand hewers are said to have been back at work. Sometimes, patience snapped: the shooting of the Ravensworth Colliery brakesman Thomas Robson on August 11th may have had some connection with the state of the strike, though a link was never proven. On August 13th, only twelve hundred people supported a meeting called by the Executive on Newcastle Town Moor.[171] There was a meeting of ten thousand strikers in County Durham on the 14th, but the Northumberland strikers failed to support a planned mass meeting that same day. From August 15th, the strike began to go down in County Durham, too, leading to some outbreaks of blackleg-disciplining, though without much physical violence. Durham activists were victimised by the owners, and were forced to seek work in Northumberland, adding to the demoralisation and confusion. However, Thornley workers stayed out on strike until August 23rd, and one of Londonderry's pits remained defiant until August 31st.[172]

Aftermaths

By the time Mrs. Mainwaring of Sheffield's *The Collier's Complaint* (113) and the anonymous acrostic sent from Bolton on Matthew Pasquill (114) were published in the *Advocate* for August 24th, the strike was virtually over. Compared to the venom which went into *The Pitmen's 'Torney-General* (115) and the racist *A New Song* (116) – where the attempt at idiomatic writing seems to have something of a North

---

170. Wigan.
171. For that evening posters advertised a 'Musical Melange', for 'the benefit of the UNEMPLOYED MINERS of Northumberland and Durham' (Editor's collection). Tickets were printed and cultural connections mobilised: Mr. Joseph Fawcett rendered *The Battle of Minden* and *The Miner's Doom* (60 or 102), see above p. 35, note 105. Another such event was advertised for August 15th on a handbill offered for sale by Mr John Turton in 1990.
172. Fynes, *The Miners*, pp. 102–14, 140–41, 186; Meech, *From Mine to Ministry*, p. 14; Burt, *An Autobiography*, pp. 37–38, 41; Manders, *A History of Gateshead*, p. 93; Colls, *The Pitmen*, pp. 300–1; Galloway, *Annals*, Volume 2, p. 178.

Riding twang to it, and the piece seems to have been designed to finally demoralise the remaining Durham strikers – such pieces were bland indeed. The Association's national membership had reached one hundred thousand members,[173] but Daniells wanted no more verse from strikers. He asked only for prose accounts of the strike so he could write its history. However, there was no money to pay Thomas Dodds for Association work between August 13th and 30th. Between September 6th and October 12th he received over half the District's total expenditure for printing the *Advocate* and the notices and placards apparently designed to help stamp out local organisation, especially if it was being led by Chartists. Unofficial printing was generally out of the question, especially for destitute former strikers,[174] and only verse which supported the Executive's strategy was used in the paper.

---

173. Compare C & R, *The Miners' Association*, p. 145.
174. Thornley militants had a placard printed calling for a Shadon's Hill mass meeting on September 16th, but John Hall issued a counter-placard, declaring the meeting unconstitutional (Wigan). Dodds tried to keep his business going by turning back to the commercial trade, after the flow of work from the Colliery-based committees stopped abruptly and his work for the Association trickled away to almost nothing after January 1845. A proof of *The Boat Race. Clasper, v. Coombes* with a manuscript date of 'December 1844' survives (NUL Loose), though the type-face looks rather worn. An Association handbill with Dodds' name on it appeared in January 1845, advertising a meeting on the 10th at a Bishop Auckland inn, to be addressed by Roberts ('if health will permit') and a Mr Halliday, who may possibly have been the author of 93. If 68B relates to April 1845, the absence of Dodds' colophon and the address of the *Miners' Advocate* office at the Sun Inn suggest either the office had moved, or it had been turned over to another use. Publication of the *Advocate* was suspended in February 1845, to resume only in May, with a smaller format, still printed by Dodds, but published from the Executive Office at Martin Jude's Sun Inn, Side, Newcastle. (At around this time, Roberts closed his *Magazine*, though its circulation had varied between three and five thousand copies an issue, and Roberts' career had years to run.) In November 1845, Dodds was printing the *Advocate* from 61 Grey Street, where he seems to have remained at least until 1855 (Hunt, *The Book Trade*, p. 31). However, in February 1846 the Association moved its offices to Preston in Lancashire, and its paper-publication to the Isle of Man, in order to avoid stamp duty – though Dodds continued to print the paper until April 1846 (Challinor, *A Radical Lawyer*, pp. 138–139; Challinor, *The Lancashire and Cheshire Miners*, pp. 39, 287 note 38). Daniells presumably went too, though in January 1847 he chaired a meeting in Lancashire and he was still listed at his Castle Street address in the 1847 Newcastle directory. In 1848 the Association handed the paper over to Daniells completely, 'with all risk and responsibility'. It folded in 1849 (C & R, *The Miners' Association*, pp. 181, 191, 200).

C. Ratcliffe's *The Coal King and the Pitman* (**117**) was published in the *Advocate* on September 21st. Even in the militant centre of Seghill, the awareness of class difference in his verse, and the posing of appropriate, materialist questions of 'greedy wealth' do not allow the author to see beyond the 'bloodless fight' that had been defeated. In the issues for October and November 1844, Daniells saw fit to print anonymously G.P. Codden's fatalistic *The Pit Boy* (**118**), *The Collier's Worth* (**119**) – sent in anonymously from Normanton in Derbyshire – and Samuel Bamford's *God Help the Poor* (**120**). It is difficult to see what such verse was intended to achieve, including one of the last manuscript texts produced in relation to the 1844 strike, Robert Martin's *Poetry Composed on job the 14 Chapter* (**121A**). The strong Biblical element and the way conventional hand-signs are placed at points where a gesture might be appropriate from a pulpit, plus its hymn-like form and metre, suggest that Martin may well have been a preacher – one of those for whom the 'prise' was rest in the 'upper sky' and not the 'watery deep' of this sinful world. Apart from a few details of spelling, syntax, grammar and scansion, his text needed little mediation in the Side.

The defeat led to a huge crisis for the Ranter cadre.[175] According to a Wesleyan from Seaton Delaval[176], there had been dissension in both major sects from the outset:

> All our ministers discouraged the strike. This was the general case. The Ranters used their influence to disaffect our members towards the body. I know some of their local preachers who were obliged to leave their own body because they would not join and encourage the strike.[177]

And while each colliery committee tried to organise a dignified return to work, the Ranter leaders – first evicted and worst treated during the strike – were victimised most. They could accept this suffering piously: 'Kind heaven look down upon us, and guide us the way to get clear of this oppression, for the miner's cup is about full. No human being can bear the treatment which is daily inflicted upon

---

175. Fynes, *The Miners*, p. 108; Burt (1882), 394; Burt, *An Autobiography*, pp. 37–38. Compare Meech, *From Mine to Ministry*, p. 6.
176. Wesleyans were officially informed in 1842 that Chartism was incompatible with their continued membership of the body (Wearmouth, *Methodism*, p. 152).
177. Wearmouth, *Some Working-Class Movements*, p. 305 – see also p. 189.

us'.[178] Or, in a situation where the Monthly Bond gave Viewers the power to sack anyone they did not like very quickly indeed, they might draw more materialist conclusions.[179] Frederick Engels, a Manchester businessman writing for a German audience, believed that the 1844 strike 'had not been in vain':

> this nineteen weeks' strike had torn the miners of the North of England forever from the intellectual death in which they had hitherto lain; they have left their sleep, are alert to defend their interests, and have entered the movement of civilisation, and especially the movement of the workers. The strike, which first brought to light the whole cruelty of the owners, has established the opposition of the workers here, forever, and made at least two-thirds of them Chartists; and the acquisition of thirty thousand such determined, experienced men is certainly of great value to the Chartists. Then, too, the endurance and law-abiding which characterised the whole strike, coupled with the active agitation which accompanied it, has fixed public attention upon the miners.[180]

In April 1845, Roberts also believed that there had been a significant shift: 'A large experiment had been tried – and it has failed. It was an experiment, however, which colliers were perfectly justified in making'.[181] Writing in 1846, Tremenheere apparently agreed: during the strike most of the activists had been under thirty, and though they included several Ranters, he estimated that two-thirds had no religion at all.[182]

---

178. Wearmouth, *Methodism*, p. 188; Colls, *The Pitmen*, p. 192; Manders, *A History of Gateshead*, p. 93.
179. Edward Richardson and Martin Jude never worked in a pit again and died in poverty. Christopher Haswell was eventually re-employed, but the leaders of 1844 were all replaced by 1847. Ben Embleton was reduced to writing a begging letter to the *Advocate*. Beesley went back to his native Accrington, where he agitated and was victimised. North and South Shields Primitive Methodist Circuits' membership halved during the strike, and Darlington Circuit had a 'vast number' of untaken membership tickets (Fynes, *The Miners*, pp. 112–13, 140–41, 186; Challinor, *The Lancashire and Cheshire Miners*, pp. 39, 287 note 39; C & R, *The Miners' Association*, pp. 137, 195; Colls, *The Pitmen*, p. 151; Colls, *The Collier's Rant*, p. 204 note 19).
180. Marx & Engels, *Collected Works*, Volume 4, p. 545.
181. Challinor, *A Radical Lawyer*, p. 138.
182. Fynes, *The Miners*, p. 142.

In spite of Engels' optimism, a radical Chartist political perspective failed to displace a discredited religious hegemony before Chartism went into decline, though we find Roberts arguing for the Irish 'rebels' to join forces with mainland Chartists against the state in 1848 and getting a positive response from at least some North East colliers.[183] What did emerge from the defeat were ideas of class-based trade union solidarity, evident in the presence of Joseph Wilson, agent of the North Shields Sailors' Association, at a Horton miners' meeting in 1849, and when Martin Jude returned the compliment during the 1851 Tyne seamen's strike.[184] Also in 1851, Tremenheere complained bitterly about the 'infidel and Chartist' reading habits of NE pitmen,[185] and while serious political development went at a slow tempo, it had at least begun. Martin Jude, the arch pacifist of 1844, was one of three Tyneside radicals who presented the Italian bourgeois nationalist Garibaldi with a sword bought by the penny contributions of Tyneside workers in 1854,[186] though the presence of the Liberal capitalist Joseph Cowen on the same platform indicates the roundabout journey that North East working class political maturation was beginning.

183. Challinor, *A Radical Lawyer*, p. 95.
184. Fynes, *The Miners*, p. 139; Welbourne, *The Miners' Unions*, p. 108.
185. Wilson (1986), 91.
186. Colls, *The Collier's Rant*, p. 158.

CHIEF SOURCES OF THE MANUSCRIPT AND BROADSIDE TEXTS

Picton Library, Liverpool

The 'History of the Coal Trade' collection (call number Kf3) includes two volumes of unpaginated material entitled 'Workmen's Strikes'. The printed frontispiece pasted into both these volumes is an engraving celebrating 'The Pitmen's union, 1832', and the printed title-page reads as follows:

> Collections forming a General History of Coal, Collieries, Colliery-Engineering, & Mining, Together with the Local History of the Collieries and Coal Trade of the North of England...London: printed by John Gray Bell, 17, Bedford Street, Covent Garden.

These volumes contain all the manuscript songs and verse reproduced here: Volume I contains texts **47A**, **49B**, **72A**, **72B**, **80A**, **89A** and **90A**, and the remainder are in Volume II. The provenance of this material seems fairly clear. The volumes contain printed material relating to the Great Strike of 1844. Three of the manuscript items, **98A**, **77A** and **93**, are addressed to 'Mr Dodds', 'Mr. Thos. Dodds' and 'Mr Tho Dodds', respectively, and **98A** also contains a request from Adam Murray, dated June 20th 1844, for 400 copies of the enclosed 'Song'. Murray's text and note are not sealed and bear no stamp, so the document was almost certainly delivered by hand to Thomas Dodds' printshop in the Side, Newcastle. Nearly all the manuscript items in the Picton collection have a hole roughly punched through them, indicating that they had been 'spiked'. Many of the texts have been copied (and altered) in the same hand. The exception is **121A**, which has 'Miner Percy Main' added to it in the same hand as that of the 'fair copy'. This hand is different to that of all the other revised manuscript texts and appears to be the same as one of the hands in which print-run details are added to copies of several known Dodds' sheets: these numbers tally with those on the printed balance sheets in the Wigan collection. In addition, the printed version of this text is the only one apparently relating to the Picton manuscript collection which has Dodds' colophon attached, and it may have been printed so late as December 1844. It seems likely, then, that Thomas Dodds was the author of this one fair copy.

The other hand is almost certainly that of William Daniells, who edited the Miners' Association's newspaper, the *Miners' Advocate*, from December 1843, and for whom a balance-sheet records that a memorandum book and half a ream of notepaper were purchased in January 1844. Since all the manuscript copies appear on paper of a uniform size and quality – whereas what appear to be the originals are on paper of various kinds, with handwriting of various different characters – it seems reasonable to assume that all the edited versions of texts (including those for which no original survives) were Daniells' work. There is one apparent anomaly. A single piece, **53C**, was first published in the *Miners' Journal*, edited by William Beesley, and was later reprinted in the *Miners' Advocate* (**53D**). There is a surviving manuscript version of this piece, **53A**, which is closer to the first printed version than to that produced by Daniells (**53B**), but this does not mean that earlier edited manuscript could not have been taken to the paper's office in the Side before being tidied up for publication in the *Advocate*.

The authorship of some manuscript texts is indicated by signatures in the same hand on several items, by initials in a few cases, by attributions on some edited copies and by names printed on proofs or finished broadsides. In a few cases, otherwise anonymous texts appear to have similar handwriting to texts by known authors. None of the manuscript texts from Joseph Philip Robson or other petit-bourgeois authors appears in the collection. Similarly, the manuscripts of known full-time employees of the Miners' Association are absent, with the apparent exception of **72**, and none of the other texts used in the *Advocate*, with the exception of **53**, is to be found in the Picton collection. An apparent anomaly, the manuscript which forms **Appendix 1**, may have been the raw material for a non-political broadside which survived Dodds' change of orientation in 1843, or it may possibly be a satire which was too cryptic to be of use. For the rest, the unedited manuscript texts come from pit-village people, many of whom were proud to describe themselves as miners.

Sadly, neither of the texts attributed to women, **81** and **94**, survives in manuscript. All but seven of the Picton manuscript texts appear in printed form as broadsides, slip-songs or what look to be proofs. They are usually without Dodds' colophon, but use type-faces and layouts identical with those used by him elsewhere. It is possible that they were all published, but that their printed versions have not survived. Whatever was the case, we know that Daniells had received a hundred or more such manuscript items by the end of the strike and that he had jettisoned some which he had no intention of ever using. For these reasons it seems highly likely that the Picton manuscripts represent part of the contents of the office at 77 Side and were cleared out when the Association bureaucracy and the *Advocate* left Newcastle in 1846.

How and why these materials found their way to the Picton Library at Liverpool is less clear, since the Library was bombed in 1941 and many relevant records seem to have been destroyed. We know that John Gray Bell of the printed title-page was born in 1823, so he would have been 21 in 1844. He was the son of Thomas Bell and nephew of John Bell Junior, the 'Great Collector' – who had spent decades making up similar collections of manuscript and printed materials of this kind.[187] John Gray Bell was also directly connected to the North East and especially the Newcastle print-trade. In 1839 he and his brother William had taken over their father's bookshop in Union Street, Newcastle, and in 1841 they moved to larger premises at 5 & 6 Collingwood Street. In 1847 John Gray married Dorothy Taylor of North Shields, and in 1848 the couple moved to London, where he published a series of tracts on British topography, history and dialects, including several on North East matters. By 1854, they were living in Manchester, where they stayed until John Gray's death in 1866.[188] So the contents of the 'Workmen's Strikes' volumes probably came into his possession before 1854, and most likely they came with him from Newcastle in 1848. Perhaps he got hold of these materials in 1846, when the Association office – only a short distance from his own shop – was being cleared. It is also possible that the materials from 77 Side were shared by John Gray Bell and his uncle, since related material –

---

187. Harker (1971); Harker & Rutherford, *Songs from the Manuscript Collection of John Bell.*
188. Lockey, 'The Bell Family', pp. 15–16.

incuding printed songs and verse relating to miners and to the strikes of 1831, 1832 and 1844 – turns up in several other places.

Wigan Archives (formerly Wigan Record Office), Leigh Town Hall

The 'Pitmen's Strike Collection' (call number D/DZ A31) was described to me by Mr. N.E. Willis dated January 22nd, 1973 as 'bound together in a large scrapbook'. However, when I examined the collection in the mid-1980s there was no scrapbook to be found: the documents were kept in a large brown box, in loose-leaf form, and a printed version of 72 was missing, though several items not previously listed were present.[189] There are balance sheets of the Miners' Association and of its Northumberland and Durham District, which list payments of as little as one penny on minor items such as string, ink, paper and postage stamps, and were all printed by Thomas Dodds. Dodds also figures largely in the expenditure columns, but the documents in this collection appear to date from no earlier than February 1843, and while there are manuscript notes on some documents there are no wholly manuscript texts.

The provenance of this collection is suggested by the range of its contents. There are apeals to 'Tradesmen only' (encouraging them to form a 'Miners Friendly Protection Society'), bills with blanks for the insertion of dates, times and places of meetings, examples of receipts, Association Rules, Rules of the Miners' Benefit Society, requests to donate money in return for a notice in the *Miners' Advocate* and a large number of documents dating so late as November 1844. Several printed documents have print-run figures and date of publication written in what appears to be Thomas Dodd's handwriting.

The Wigan collection has over forty items of printed songs and verse, nine bearing Dodds' colophon and fourteen more using the same kinds of type-face and decorative borders as known Dodds texts. (Presumably, this was the result of the 'new assortment of type' mentioned in the *Advocate* of November 4th 1843.) In addition, there are five items by other known printers, two of which, **75A** and **94A**, seem to have been re-set by Dodds at least so far as proof stage. One

---

189. The scrapbook pagination had been supplemented by a new form of numbering, so I have adopted the new numbering and given any surviving previous numbering in round brackets. Where an item has no number of its own, I have given it as the verso of a text which has a number.

other text, **110A**, was re-set using decorative borders identical to
those used by Dodds, and another two texts, **102A/B**, appear with
another printer's colophon and without any form of identification,
but in remarkably similar type-faces and with virtually identical size
and layout. The fact that there are very few items with Dodds'
colophon dating from 1844 may be because what we have here are
proof copies, but it could also be the case that some colophon-less
texts were requested because they were to be used in ways which
were illegal.

So there are good direct and circumstantial reasons to suggest that
the Wigan collection derives from Dodds' printing-office at 77 Side,
Newcastle. How and when it came to Wigan is not clear, but its
relationship with the Picton collection is sure, and these two
collections may have remained together for a period even after they
left the Association office. This theory is reinforced by the facts that
one item, **53**, also appeared in the *Advocate* and that a second is by
William Hornsby, who sent another of his pieces to that journal.
Additionally, no fewer than twelve of these printed items correspond
closely to the edited manuscript texts in the Picton Library, while no
Picton manuscript corresponds to any Wigan printed item other than
those actually or probably printed by Dodds. None of the imprintless
texts in the Wigan collection use type-faces or decorative borders
different to those used on known Dodds texts. Moreover, three
Picton manuscripts are addressed to Dodds.

Northumberland Record Office, Gosforth, Newcastle

The Bell Mining Collection (NRO 3410/Bell) was formerly housed by
the North of England Institute of Mining and Mechanical Engineers.
In 1853, when the Institute was only one year old, one of its vice-
presidents, Thomas John Taylor, presented its library with 'twenty-
one folio volumes and one portfolio, containing memoranda relating
to coal and to the coal trade, and entitled "History of Coal
Mining"'.[190] The latest document appears to date from 1850.
However, while Liz Lockey thought it was the work of Thomas Bell[191]
and the Institute Librarian believed that the whole collection may
have been offered for sale by John Bell Junior, the 'Great Collector',
the printed title-pages are very similar indeed to that in the

---

190. Letter from Margaret Norwell, December 3rd 1985.
191. Lockey, 'The Bell Family', 33.

'Workmen's Strikes' volumes in the Picton Library, Liverpool, and name only J.G. Bell. So, the collection went through the hands of John Gray Bell before 1853, and, as we have noted, probably before 1848. It is posible that John Gray Bell's father or uncle may have kept the collection until 1850, but we know that John Bell Junior began what was probably his last such collection in 1851. There is no record of any collection on the 1844 strike in John Bell Junior's sale Catalogues of 1855 or 1865, so even if he did assemble a duplicate collection on this theme, as he is known to have done on other topics, it is still possible that John Gray Bell and his father could have assembled all the materials now held at Wigan, Picton and the NRO, perhaps drawing on John Bell Junior in the process.

No fewer than eleven items of song or verse in Volumes 11 and 12 of the Bell Mining Collection are also found at Wigan. These texts appear to be identical (or nearly so), and one pair – of 103 – have handwritten dates in what appears to be the same fist. Another pair, 85A/B, have differently-set headings but almost identical texts. Each bears a manuscript note, that from Wigan being in Dodds' hand and that from NRO in what is probably John Bell Junior's. However, the Wigan exemplar has been spiked, whereas that in the NRO is intact, probably because it was 'Bought 28 May 1844 price 1d'. There are several other signs of John Bell Junior's activity in relation to several of these collections. Dates and other notes on 85B in NRO appear to be in his hand, as do those on the duplicate of 85B at Wigan. The manuscript date on 102A at NRO is the same as that on 99B at Wigan, and may well have been written by John Bell Junior. Another note on 85B at the NRO is almost certainly by him, and tallies with notes on 7 and 20A in NUL B/W2, a collection he made. So, Bell could have built up one collection, taken out any duplicates and either sold them or given them away, before parting with the larger collection at a later date. Alternatively, he could have compiled all three overlapping collections and sold them off (or possibly given one away) at different times to different people. Finally, he could have made one huge collection and then broken it up gradually, a hypothesis supported by the separation of the proof, 29B, from its original, 29A, and from the finished broadside, 29C. We may never know, and sadly we may also never know what happened to the other broadside songs mentioned in a note on 85B, because when I first came to inspect this collection in the early 1970s these items were missing.

Newcastle Central Library

There are two main collections of relevant material at NCL. The first, the Thomas Allan Collection (Allan: SL 427.52), was donated to the library in the early 1970s. It contains eight relevant broadsides from before 1832, though none of the items in this uncared-for collection bear library reference marks. The second is a bound volume, 'Pitman's Strike 1844' (Pitman 1844: SL 331.89 Cr 31306). The 'ancient stock-book' of the Library records that this was presented on August 31st 1911, though the volume itself has a fly-leaf inscription to the effect that 'This book was given to the Reference Library of his native town, Newcastle on Tyne by William Malcolm Newton, born 7th Dec[embe]r 1845.'[192] In pencil above this is the name and address of George Clementson Greenwell, then of Poynton, Stockport, who worked as a colliery Viewer and compiled *A Glossary of Terms used in the Coal Trade*, first published in 1849. Greenwell returned from fourteen years at Poynton to settle in Tynemouth in 1877, and was President of the NEIMME between 1879 and 1881. Since he was four when Willie Carr, the Blyth 'Samson' died in 1825,[193] he would have been 23 in the year of the Great Strike of 1844. Moreover, he had been associated with the colliery Viewer, John Buddle, since at least 1840, so he was well-placed to collect the materials in this volume, which include some items of a distinctly anti-union nature. The absence of any materials which could not have been bought or clipped out of newspapers, and the fact that no item appears to have been spiked – or to be a proof copy, or to have come from a print-shop file – suggest that Greenwell was totally reliant on the commercial trade in printed matter. Several items derive from Dodds' press and some are similar to (or even identical with) items in other collections. The volume's prose materials appear to be arranged chronologically, but this is no reliable guide to the dating of verse materials, which are grouped together arbitrarily. Moreover it is not clear whether the rebinding of this material took account of whatever may have been the original order of its contents.

Newcastle University Library

NUL holds 'A Collection of Local Songs and Poems which have appeared in Print and circulated in Newcastle upon Tyne and its

---

192. Letter from Douglas Bond, October 28th 1985. The volume itself bears a
       presentation date of August 25th.
193. *Monthly Chronicle*, May 1887, p. 141.

Neighbourhood by John Bell, Landsurveyor, Gateshead' (B/W2: 821.04), which is not professionally or comprehensively paginated, and 'A Poetic Selection' (B/W13: W821.04-POE), which was 'Presented to Robert White Esqr. by Mrs. Setter[?] In remembrance of her dear Father the late Mr Thomas Wilson, May 7th 1862'. (Presumably, this was the poet who died in 1858.)

Cambridge University Library, Madden Collection

Volume M16 of the Madden Collection of broadside songs and verse, assembled by Sir Frederick Madden, contains 863 products of 'Country printers' working in Northumberland and Durham, though none relates directly to the 1844 strike. Perhaps the strike songs were not available commercially, though several items of a radical political character appear in the collection. Censorship or self-censorship may have played a role since the Madden Collection contains only fourteen of Dodds' numbered series (which runs at least as far as No 38), plus a few unnumbered and mainly imprintless texts which appear to be from Dodds' press. Unfortunately, the collection is less comprehensive for the later 1840s. Madden died in 1873, though his collecting may have petered out much earlier. In any case, it is unlikely that the trade in broadsides and slip-songs could have been sustained once songbooks took hold of the commercial market in the early 1850s.

The Goldstein Collection, Philadelphia

Professor Kenneth S. Goldstein, formerly of the Department of Folklore and Folklife, University of Pennsylvania, possesses a run of broadsides published by George Walker Junior of Durham, consisting of numbers 1–14, 16–21, 23–24, 27–28, 30–33, 36–40, 55–61, 64 and 67–69, all of which he was kind enough to photocopy for me.[194]

---

194. Materials dating from the 1844 strike are still circulating as commodities. In November 1990 I was offered several items (some of which may be unique) by Mr John Turton, the Willington bookseller, who had very properly offered them first to the Newcastle Central Reference Library. Mr Turton believes they came from the Barnard Castle library of the Watson family, via a Christie's sale in London in 1990, but I have been unable to trace any further information about their provenance. There were no song or verse items for sale. It remains my hope that items once held in collections at Wigan and the NEIMME will one day find their way back into public stewardship.

PRINCIPLES OF SELECTION AND ARRANGEMENT

The overall aim has been to reproduce all surviving printed and manuscript verse and song texts concerned with the representation of North East pit-village people and pitwork between c.1780 and the end of 1844, including the strikes of 1831 and 1832, the Chartist period, the Miners' Philanthropical Society, the Miners' Association, the Great Strike of 1844 and its immediate aftermath. This volume includes all relevant manuscript songs and verse from the Picton Library, Liverpool, 'History of the Coal Trade', 'Workmen's Strikes' volumes. It also contains all other relevant printed broadsides and proofs in the Picton Collection, the 'Pitmen's Strike Collection' at Wigan Record Office, the Northumberland Record Office Bell Mining Collection and the Newcastle Central Library 'Pitmen's Strike 1844' volume, together with all versified material from the Miners' Association newspaper, the *Miners' Advocate*, up to the end of 1844, plus some material from other periodicals. Some broadsides from the Bell/White Collections at both Newcastle University Library and Newcastle Central Library, from the NCL Allan Collection and from the Cambridge University Library Madden Collection are also reproduced here, together with one item from the British Museum Roxburghe Collection and another from Glasgow University Library. In addition, because of the song's association with the Great Strike, the various versions of *The Blackleg Miners* have been placed in **Appendix 2**.

The aim has been to present this material, so far as possible, in chronological order of publication (or of writing, in the case of unpublished items). When a text was reprinted it is included here along with the earliest publication.

EDITORIAL CONVENTIONS

Wherever possible, differing versions of the same piece have been taken to be variations on the **A** text, which is thought to be the earliest version, and their points of difference are given in the margin in chronological order as **B**, **C** and **D**. For the **A** text only, every effort has been made to reproduce spelling, capitalisation and punctuation exactly as in the original manuscript or printed text. Differences of these kinds in subsequent texts are not noted. In a few cases, where a mediated text is arguably a new composition, a single compound text has not been attempted. Original titles for the **A** text are reproduced verbatim, but with capital letters for the main title and lower case for the remaining material, ignoring the original typography. Where no title exists for the **A** text, one supplied in subsequent mediations (or by the editor) is given in square brackets.

The long 's' is replaced by its modern equivalent throughout, though the appearance of the former is noted in the margin on its first occurrence in each text. In addition,

* *next to a word or at the beginning of a line* refers to a gloss or notes in the margin. Where there are several marginal notes, they are divided by a semi-colon, except where there are differing readings in later texts, in which case they are divided only by a comma.

⌊⌋ *in the text* indicate the limits to a phrase which is different in subsequent versions, and any alternative readings are supplied in the margin.

† *in a gap between words or before the beginning or beyond the end of a line* refers to an addition in a subsequent version of the text, which is supplied in the marginal note.

+ refers to a footnote immediately beneath the text.

{} enclose interpolations. Where interpolations are retained in subsequent versions of a text, no note is made of them except when this might cause confusion.

<> enclose a legible deletion. Where appropriate, note is sometimes made of what happens to deletions in the A text in subsequent versions.

<?> indicate an illegible deletion.

[ ] enclose letters or punctuation supplied by the editor.

[?] enclose doubtful readings.

TEXTS

1. CALL THE HORSE, MARROW

Call the horse,* marrow,*
For I can call nane,
The heart of my belly
Is hard as a stane:
As hard as a stane,
And as round as a cup,
Call the horse, marrow,
Till my hewer* comes up.

long 's', here and elsewhere;
mate, especially pit work-
mate

pit face-worker

Me and my marrow,
And Christy Craw Hall,
Will play with any three in the pit
At the foot ball:
At the foot ball,
And at the coal tram,*
We'll play with any three in the pit
For twelve-pence a gam.

underground pit coal-wagon

Hewing and putting*
And keep in the sticks,*
I never so laboured
Since I took the picks;
I'm going to my hewer's
House on the Fell Side,
He hews his coals thick,
And drives his boards* wide.

job of pushing *trams*
? roof-supports, or a reference
to sword dancing

excavations between *pillars* of
coal

The rope and the roll*
And the long ower tree,*
The devil has flown over
The heap with them all three:
The roll it hangs cross the shaft,
De'il but it fall,
And stick in the thil;*
Twenty-four horn'd owls run away with the mill.

engine cylinder
? support for *roll*

coal-seam floor

I'm going to my hewer
Where ever he be,
He's hipt of a buddock,*   suffers from an over-strained
And blind of an eye;   buttock muscle
He's blind of an eye,
And lame of a leg;
My uncle Jack Fenwick,
He kiss'd my aunt Peg.

Print. B/W2.   Broadside. Woodcut. No colophon. See also Lloyd, *Folk Song*, pp. 336-37, and *Come all ye bold miners*, (1978), pp. 28-29.

Late 18th century. According to Lloyd, *Folk Song*, pp. 336–37, this 'oddity' was 'already falling into decrepitude before it was printed, but it conveys some of the curious flavour that early distinguished miners' songs from the folk songs of other labouring men, a compound of hardness and affection, peppered with craft jargon and salted with inconsequentiality'. With odd inconsequentiality, Lloyd, *Come all ye bold miners*, (1978), p. 341, drew attention to an apparent link between stanza four and a mining disaster of 1862. See Harker, *Fakesong*, for a critique of the term, 'folksong', and for an analysis of Lloyd's ideas and methods.

2. THE COLLIERS RANT.

As me and my Marrow was ganning to wark;
We met with the Devil it was in the dark;
I up with my pick, it being in the Neit,
I knock'd off his Horns likewise* his Club feet.   *long 's' here and elsewhere*

Follow the horses, Johnny my Lad Oh!
Follow them through my canny Lad Oh!
Follow the horses, Johnny my Lad Oh!
Oh Lad ly away, canny* Lad Oh!   kindly, good, gentle

As me and my Marrow was putting the tram,
The low* it went out and my marrow went wrang   light
You would have laugh'd had you seen the Gam'
The Deil gat my marrow but I gat the Tram.
Follow the Horses &c.

Oh Marrow, Oh Marrow what dost thou think,
I've broken my bottle and spilt a' my drink.
I' lost a' my shin splints* amang the great stanes.   leg armour
Draw me t' the shaft its time to gane* hame.   go, be going
   Follow the Horses &c.

   Oh! marrow Oh! marrow where hast thou
      been;
Driving the drift* from off the low seam,   exploratory or ventilation-
Driving the drift &c   shaft
Had up the low lad, Deil stop out thy een.
   Follow the Horses &c.

   Oh! marrow, Oh! marrow this is wor pay week,*   our fortnightly pay
We'll get penny loaves and drink to our beek;*   nose, ie fill
And we'll fill up our bumper and round it shall
     go.
Follow the horses Johnny lad Oh!
   Follow the horses &c.

There is my horse, and there is my tram;
Twee horns full of grease will make her to gang;
There is my hoggars,* likewise my half shoon,*   stockings without feet; toeless
And smash* my heart marrow, my putting's   shoes
    a' done.   God smash, ie an oath

   Follow the horses my Johnny Lad Oh!
   Follow them through my canny Lad Oh!
   Follow the horse[s] Johnny my Lad Oh!
   Oh! lad ly away; canny Lad Oh!

Print. British Museum Roxburghe Collection. No.352. Broadside. Woodcut. No colophon. Pasted within a decorative border of later date. First published in a songbook by Ritson, *The Northumberland Garland*, p. 67, then in a John Marshall chapbook (Thomson, *Newcastle Chapbooks*, p. 62), and subsequently in Bell, *Rhymes*, p. 35, Marshall. *A Collection of Songs*, p. 44, Sharp, *The Bishoprick Garland*, p. 52, Anon, *Tyneside Songster*, p. 56, Fordyce, *Newcastle Song Book*, p. 53, Robson. *Bards of the Tyne*, p. 41 and several later collections. Mediated by Lloyd, *Come all ye bold miners* (1952), p. 20 and (1978), p. 27. Recorded by the High Level Ranters on 'Along the Coally Tyne' (Topic Records: 12T189, 1962).

Late 18th century. For John Marshall, see Hunt, *The Book Trade*, p. 65. Lloyd, *Come all ye bold miners*, (1952), p. 17, noted that the song 'may have been in existence for generations before Joseph Ritson printed it' in 1793. Lloyd, *Folk Song*, p. 336, suggested that 'something of the same epic wind that inspired the legend-makers blows through' the piece, though by 1793 'it was already so old that its words had become corrupted and its story hardly coherent. But if part of the song is now lost or sunk into burlesque, some of its old epic force remains'. According to Lloyd, *Come all ye bold miners*, (1978), p. 341, the melody was first published in Robert Topliff's *Selection of the most popular melodies of the Tyne and the Wear* of c.1815. Questions about the text's alleged mythic qualities, superstition and incoherence relate more to the petit-bourgeoisie's perception of pit-workers than to its alleged 'folksong' status.

3. BOB CRANKY'S 'SIZE* SUNDAY,   Assize
SECOND EDITION.

Ho'way and aw'll* sing* thee a tune, mun,	I'll; *long 's' here and elsewhere*
'Bout hus seein my Lord at the town, mun,	
A's seer* a' was smart now	I am sure
Aw'll lay* thee a quart now,	bet
Nyen* o' them aw' cut a dash like Bob Cranky.	none
When a' pat* on my blue coat that shines se,	put
My jacket wi' posies* se fine see,	floral patterns
My sark* sic sma' threed, man,	shirt
My pig-tail se greet, man,	
Od smash! what a buck was Bob Cranky.	
Blue stockings, white clocks, and reed garters,	
Yellow breeks, and my shoon wi' lang quarters,	
A' myed wour* bairns cry,	our
Eh! sarties!* ni! ni!	certes, *ie* certainly
Sic verra* fine things had Bob Cranky.	very
A' went to awd* Toms and fand* Nancy	old; found
Kiv a',*+ Lass thou's myed to my fancy,	? Said I
A' like thou as weel	
As a stannin pye heel,*	crust
Ho'way to the town wi' Bob Cranky.	

As up Jenny's backside* we were bangin,*   house-back; rushing
Ki Geordy,* How,* where are ye gannin,   generic pitman's name; hello
   Wey't see my lord 'sizes,
   But ye shanna gan aside us,
For your not half se fine as Bob Cranky.

Ki Geordy, We leve i' yen raw,* weyet,*   row of pit-houses; yes
I' yen corf* we byeth gan belaw, weyet,   hazel basket
   At a' things ave* play'd   I have
   And to hew a'm not flay'd,*   frightened
Wi' sic in* a chep as Bob Cranky.   siccan, *ie* such

Bob has thee at lowpin* and flingin,   leaping
At the bool,* foot-ball, clubby,* and swingin,   bowls; clubby-shaw, a shinty-
   Can ye jump up and shuffle,   like game
   And cross ower the buckle,*   difficult dance steps
When ye dance? like the cliver Bob Cranky.

Thou naw's* i' my hoggars and drawers,*   knows; pit-trousers
A'm nyen o' your scarters* and clawers,   scratchers
   Fra the trap-door* bit laddy,   mine ventliation door
   T' the spletter,* his daddy,   splitter, *ie* pit ventilation-
Nyen handles the pick like Bob Cranky.   specialist

So Geordy, od smash my pit sarik,*   sark, *ie* shirt
Thou'd best had thy whisht* about warik,*   hold your tongue; work
   Or all sobble* thy body,   I'll thrash
   And myek thy nose bloody,
If thou sets up thy gob* to Bob Cranky.   mouth

Nan laugh'd, t' church we gat without 'im,
The greet crowd, becrike* how a' hew'd 'em   by Christ
   Smash'd – a keelbully* roar'd,   coal-barge-man
   Clear the road – whilk's* my lord?   which is
Owse* se high as the noble Bob Cranky.   anything

A' lup* up an' catch'd just a short gliff*   leaped; glimpse
O' Lord trials, the trumpets, and sheriff,
   Wi' the little bit mannies
   Se fine and se canny,
Ods heft!* what a seet for Bob Cranky.   God's command, *ie* an oath

Then away we set off to the yell-house,*   ale-house
Wiv a few hearty lasses and fellows,
    Aw' tell'd ower* the wig   talked about
    Se curl'd and se big,
For nyen saw'd se well as Bob Cranky.

Aw' gat drunk, fit,* and kick'd up a racket,   fought
Rove my breeks and spoil'd a' my fine jacket,
    Nan cry'd and she cuddled,
    My hinny* thou's fuddled,*   pet; drunk
Ho'way hyem* now, my bonny Bob Cranky.   home

So we staggcr'd alang fra the town mun,
Whiles gannin, whiles byeth fairly down mun,
    Smash'd a Banksman* or Hewer,   winding-engine man
    No not a fine Viewer,*   colliery manager
Durst jaw* to the noble Bob Cranky.   speak

What care aw' for my new suit a' taters,
Twe black een, od smash a' sic maters,
    When my lord comes agyen, mun,
    Aw'l strive every byen,* mun,   bone
To bang* a' wor Concern, ki Bob Cranky.   beat

O' the flesh and breed day when wor bund,* mun,   ie, annual contract day
A'll buy clase* far bonnyer than thon,* mun,   clothes; sic, ie thou
    For od smash my neavel,*   blow, ie fist?
    As lang as wor yebble,*   able
Let's keep up the day, ki Bob Cranky!

Newcastle, 1804.

+ *Kiver awa*, was a local military drill slogan; but whether this is in any way related to 'Kiv' is unclear.

Print. B/W2.   Broadside. Colophon: Newcastle, 1804. M. Angus and Son, Printers. The song appeared on another B/W2 broadside and in chapbooks by Margaret Angus and John Marshall (Thomson, *Newcastle Chapbooks*, pp. 32, 62). See also 'Songs, Sung at Mr Tayleure's Benefit, Friday, April 14th 1809', 'Printed for J. Bell, Quayside, Newcastle' (B/W2). The piece remained a firm

favourite in Tyneside songbooks up until Allan, *Tyneside Songs*, pp. 88–90, and
Stokoe and Reay, *Songs and Ballads*, pp. 88–89.

Dated 1804. For a fuller account of this song, its author, John Selkirk, its
mediators and its historical significance, see Harker, 'The Original Bob Cranky',
where the manuscript text is reproduced in facsimile. For the Angus family, see
Hunt, *The Book Trade*, pp. 3–4. For John Bell, see Harker, 'John Bell', and Harker
& Rutherford, *Songs from the Manuscript Collection of John Bell*, pp. xii-xxxiv.

4. A NEW SONG, ON XYZ; OR, PITMEN'S LUCK.

Smash, Jemmy, let us buss*, we'll off an see   kiss
    Newcastle races,
Set Dick the trapper for sum syep, we'll seun wash
    aw wor faces:
There's ne'er a lad o' Percy Main's be bet this day
    for five or ten;
Wor pockets lin'd wi' notes an' cash, amang the
    cheps we'll cut a dash;
  For XYZ, that bonny steed,
  He bangs them aw for pith an' speed,
    He's sure to win the Cup, man.

We reach'd the moor wi' sairish tews,* when they   a hard struggle
    war gaun te start, man,
We gav a fellow two-pence each te stand upon a
    cart, man,
The bets flew round fra' side te side, the field
    agyan XY they cried,
We'd hardly time te lay them aw, when in he
    cam, Hurray! hurray!
  Gad smash! says I, XY's the steed,
  He bangs them aw for pith an' speed,
    We never seed his like, man.

Next te the tents we hied, te get sum stuffin for
 the bags,* man,   stomach
Wi' flesh we gaily pang'd* wor hides, smoak'd stuffed
 nous but patten shag, man,
While rum an' brandy soak'd wor chop, we'd
 jackey* fine an' ginger pop,   gin
We gat what myad us winken blin', when
 drunkey* aw began te sing,   drunkenly
  Od smash, XY, thou is the steed,
  Thou bangs them aw for pith an' speed,
   We never seed thy like, man.

Next up amang the shows we gat, where folks aw
 stud i' flocks, man,
Te see a chep play *Bobbin Joan,* upon a wooden
 box, man,
While bairns an' music fill'd the stage, an' sum by
 gocks* turn'd grim wi' age,   by God
When next au'd grin* a poney browt, cou'd tell at *ie* the showman
 aince* what people thowt,   once
  Od smash, says I, if he's the breed,
  Of XYZ, that bonny steed,
   Thou never seed his like, man.

But haud when we cam te the toon, what thinks
 tou we saw there, man,
We seed a blackey puffin, sweaten, sucking in
 fresh air, man;
They said that he cou'd fell an ox, his name was
 fighting Molinox,*
But ere he fit anuther round, his marrow fell'd Molyneux
 him te the ground;
  Od smash, says I, if thou's sic breed,
  As XYZ, that bonny steed,
   Thou never seed his like, man.

Next 'board the Steamer boat we gat, a laddie
    rang a bell, man,
We hadn't sittin vera lang, till baith a sleep we
    fell, man;
But the noise seun myad poor Jemmy start, he
    thowt 'twas time te gan te wark,
For pick an hoggars he roard out, he myad sic a
    noise it waken'd me;
    Od smash, says I, XY's the steed,
    He bangs them aw for pith an' speed,
        Aw never seed his like, man.

When landed, straight off hame aw gans, an'
    thunners at the door, man,
The bairns lap owr the bed wi' fright, fell smack
    upon the floor, man;
But te gar the wifey haud her tongue, show'd her
    the kelter* I had won: cash
She'd with a cinder brunt her toes, an' little Jacob
    broke his nose,
    The brass I've gotten at the race,
    Will buy a patch* for Jacob's face;   ?plaster
        So now my sang is deun, man.

June, 1814.

Print. B/W2.   Broadside. No colophon. In B/W2 there is a broadside version
published by John Marshall in Newcastle and another, paired with *Cappy* (7),
'Printed for W. Smith, by J. Marshall, Newcastle'. Two more versions were
published by Marshall in Newcastle (CULM 16/457; Allan). Marshall also
printed this song in an 1816 chapbook, *The Budget; or Newcastle Songster*,
published specifically for the Union Lodge of Oddfellows in Newcastle (of
which the author was a member), and in Part III of his 'The Newcastle
songster' (Thomson, *Newcastle Chapbooks*, pp. 21, 62). Thereafter, it became a
regular in the local songbooks of the 1840s, and up to Allan, *Tyneside Songs*,
pp. 138–41, and Stokoe & Reay, *Songs and Ballads*, pp. 164–66.
    Dated June, 1814. The author was William Mitford (sometimes, 'Midford'),
who became a singing landlord in the 1820s – see Allan, *Tyneside Songs*,
pp. 132–36; *Newcastle Weekly Chronicle*, October 4th 1879 and October 4th
1884.

5. BOB CRANKY'S ACCOUNT OF THE ASCENT OF MR SADLER'S BALLOON, FROM NEWCASTLE, SEPTEMBER 1st, 1815.

Howay a' my marrows, big, little, and drest*,   *long 's' here and elsewhere*
    The furst of a' seets may be seen;
It's the balloon, man, se greet, aye faiks!* its ne jest, faith, *ie* by my faith
    Tho' it seems a' the warld like a dream.
Aw read iv the papers, by gocks! I remember,
    It's to flee* wivout wings iv the air,   fly
On this verra Friday, the furst of September,
    Be it cloudy, wet weather, or fair;

And a man, mun, there means in this verra
        balloon,
    Above, 'mang the stars for to fly,
And to haud a convarse wi' th' man i' the moon,
    And cobwebs to sweep fra the sky.
So we started fra heame by eight i' the morn,
    Byeth faither and mother and son,
But faund a' wor neibors had started before,
    To get in gude time for the fun.

The Lanes were a' crouded, some riding, some
        walking,
    I ne'er seed the like iv my life;
'Twas Bedlam broke out, I thought by their
        talking,
    Every bairn, lad, lass, and the wife.
The folks at the winders a' jeer'd as we past,
    And thout* a' wor numbers surprisin;   thought
They star'd an' they glowr'd, an' axed in jest,
    Are all of you pitmen a rising?

Aw fand* at the town* te, the shops a' shut up, found; *ie* Newcastle
    And the streets wi' folks were se flocken,
The walls wi' balloon papers se closely clag'd* up, stuck
    By cavers!* it luckt like a hoppen.*   an oath; country fair
A fellow was turnin it a' into joke,
    Another was a' the folks hummin*,   deceiving
While a third said it was a bag full of smoke,
    That ower wor heads was a cummin.

To the furst o' these chaps, says aw, nane o' yur fun,
   Or aw'll lay thee at length on the stanes;
Or thy teeth I'll beat out, as sure as a gun,
   And mevies* aw'll choke ye wi' banes.   maybe
Ti' the beak o' the second, aw held up ma fist,
   D—m aw'll bray* ye as black as a craw,   beat, hammer
Aw'll knock out yur ee, if aw don't, aw'll be kist,
   An mump* a' the slack* o' yur jaw.   slap; ?lower part

Aw put them to reets, an' onward aw steer'd,
   And wonder'd the folks aw had seed,
But a' was palaver that ever aw heard,
   So aw walk'd on as other folk did,
At last aw got up on the top o' some sheds,
   Biv* the help of an' ould crazy ladder;
And owr the tops of ten thousand folks heads,
   Aw sune gat a gliff o' the bladder.

D—m, a bladder aw call it! by gocks aw am reet,
   For o' silk dipt iv leaditter* melted   India rubber
Its made of, an Lord what a wonderful seet,
   When the gun tell'd it was *filated*.
'Twas just like the boiler at wor Bella Pit,*   ?Isabella Pit, Ellison Main
   O'er which were a great cabbage net,   Colliery
Which fasten'd by a parcel of strings se fit,
   A corf for the manny to sit.

As aw sat at ma ease aw cood here a' th' folk,
   Gee their notions about th' balloon;
Aw thout aw shud brust* when aw heurd their   burst
     strange talk,
   About the man's gawn to the Moon.
Says yen iv a whisper, aw think aw hev heard
   He is carryin a letter to Bonny,*   Napoleon Bonaparte
That's ower the sea, to flee like a burd:
   The thout, by jingars,* was funny.   an oath

A chep wiv a fayce like a poor country bumpkin,
   Sed he heurd, but may hap tis'nt true,
That th' thing whilk they saw was a great silken
     pumpkin,

Bim'y* eye, what a lilly-ba-loo!   By my
Another said Sadler, (for that is the nayme
    Of the man) ma pay dear for his frolic,
When he's up iv the clouds (a stree* for his fame!) straw
    His guts may hev twangs of the colic.

The man a' this while the greet bladder was
        filling,
    Wiv stuff that wad myake a dog sick,
It smelt just as tho' they were garvage* distilling,   garbage
    Till at length it was full as a tick.
They next strain'd the ropes to keep the thing
        steady,
    Put lilly white bags iv the boat;
Then crack went the cannon, t'say it was ready,
    An' aw seed the bladder afloat.

Not a word there was heurd, a' eyes were a staring
    For the off gawen moment was near;
To see sic a crowd se whish'd* was amazen,   quiet
    Aw thout aw fand palish and queer.
After waitin a wee, aw seed him come to,
    Wiv his friends round about, sic a croud;
Of his mountin the stage aw had a full view,
    But they crush'd him se vulgar and rude.

Aw hands then left go, and upwards he went,
    Shuggy-shuing* his corf iv the air: swinging
Aw heads were turn'd up, wiv looks se intent
    To see his flag awaving se fair.
It went its ways up like a lavrick* se hee,   sky-lark
    Till it luckt 'bout th' size of a skyate;*   skate, ie a fish
When like tiv a pear it was lost t' th' ee,
    Aw wisht the poor man better fate.

Print. B/W2.   Broadside. Colophon: Angus, Printer. This song also appeared
in a John Marshall chapbook (Thomson, *Newcastle Chapbooks*, p. 62), in
Marshall, *A Collection of Songs*, p. 75, Anon, *Tyneside Songster*, p. 45 and
Fordyce, *Newcastle Song Book*, p. 42.
    Dated 1815. Also written by Mitford. See Colls, *The Collier's Rant*,
pp. 24–56 and the critique in Harker, 'The Original Bob Cranky?'.

6. A CURIOUS DIALOGUE Which took place, a few
days ago, between A Pitman and his Wife, in
Newcastle, Respecting the present Hard Times.
Containing The whole Conversation that passed;
During which the Wife managed the Argument so*   *long 's' here and elsewhere*
well, that she shewed, and persuaded her Husband,
how they might still live happy, although he
considered himself on the Brink of Misery.

Sweet, dear and loving Wife,
My senses are at strife,
About this careful life,
    For we decline;
Times being grievous hard,
All trading spoil'd and marr'd,
I have a sweet regard
    For thee and thine.
I thank you for your care,
Yet, husband, don't despair,
Let us with patience bear
    These troubles here.
Dear love, 'tis all in vain
To weep, sigh, and complain:
Love, we may thrive again,
    Be of good cheer.
My dearest love, said he,
How can I cheerful be
While pinching poverty
    Knocks at the door,
And will not hence depart,
But wounds me to the heart?
I never felt such smart,*   *pain, hurt*
    Sweet Wife, before.
Dear husband, do not make
Such moan, for heaven's sake,
Of me this counsel take,
    Your bosom friend:
By patience put your trust,
In him that made you first,

When times are at the worst -
   Sure they will mend.
Dear love, it may be so,
But while the grass doth grow,
The steed may starve, you know,
    When 'tis too late,
So my dear family,
Which want a quick supply,
By long delays, may die,
    Oh! cruel fate!
Sweet husband, don't despair,
Avoid distracting care,
I will the burden bear
    Along with you.
Our sons and daughters they
Shall work, and if we may,
Get bread from day to day,
    Love, that will do.
Pine not for worldly pelf,*   money, goods
Bless God, we have our health,
And that is more than wealth,
    Be thankful then.
Job lost abundance more,
Besides his body sore,
Yet he with patience bore,
    While tidings came,
How all in ruins lay,
He patiently did say,
God gives and takes away,
    Blest be his name!
Job did not frown and fret,
When with these things he met.
Dear loving husband, let
    Us imitate
His patience when in pain;
Job found it not in vain,
God rais'd him up again,
    And made him great.
Love, I have often read,
How Job was comforted,

Yet I am full of dread
   And fear, for why?
Our family is very large,
Six children are some charge,
We fall within the verge
   Of poverty.
Dear husband, don't repine,
Nor grudge this charge of thine,
Blest be the powers divine,
   Sweet babes they are:
When we shall aged grow,
With locks like winter's snow,
They may. for ought I know,
   Lesson* our care.   *sic, ie* Lessen
It is a great offence,
To distrust Providence,
Whose blessed influence,
   Takes special care
Of all the sons of men;
Husband, be cheeerful then,
God will be gracious when
   Thankful we are.
My fingers do not itch
To be exceeding rich,
May we but go through stitch,*   ? the eye of a needle, *ie* a
   Keep from the door   Biblical reference
The greedy wolf of prey,
And all our dealers pay,
Believe now what I say,
   We need no more.
I and my children dear
Will work, than* never fear,   *sic, ie* then
But we shall something clear,
   Tommy shall weave,
The girls shall all begin
Forthwith to card and spin,
Which will bring something in,
   Then never grieve.
I value not to dine
On sumptuous dishes fine,

With rice and racy wine,
　　From foreign parts:
Good wholesome bread and beer,
Instead of better cheer,
Let us receive, my dear,
　　With thankful heart.
In all conditions still,
Let us not take it ill,
Since 'tis His blessed will
　　It should be so;
Whether we rise or fall,
Our substance great or small,
Content is all in all,
　　My dear, you know.
O most indulgent mate,
After this long debate,
My comforts they are great
　　In a kind wife.
Tho' some may think it strange,
My fancy seems to range,
But now a happy change
　　Doth bless my life.
For to my joy I find,
A sweet composed mind;
I wish that all mankind
　　Were full as well.
Despair's a dreadful thing,
And does poor mortals bring
Unto the bitter sting
　　Of death and hell.
Sweet wife, and heart's delight,
I had been ruin'd quite,
In death's eternal night,
　　Hast thou not been
The happy instrument,
That ruin to prevent,
Love, joy, and sweet content,
　　I now am in.
Tho' slender is my store,
Yet I'll despair no more,

that man is truly poor
    That wants content:
But where content's increas'd,
'Tis a continual feast,
Praise God, I am releas'd,
    Death to prevent.
As God does give me grace,
This counsel I'll embrace,
Despair shall not take place
    In me henceforth.
Farewell, litigious strife,
And come, my loving wife,
Thy words have sav'd my life,
    God bless us both!
And all mankind likewise,
From the calamities,
Which do, as fogs, arise
    From foul despair.
Let doubtful Christians fly,
In there* extremity,   *sic, ie their*
To God, who sits on high,
    By fervent prayer.
He is man's friend in chief,
The fountain of relief,
When I was lost in grief,
    And at the worst.
My dear indulgent bride,
Her counsel was my guide,
In God I'm satisfied,
    In him I trust.
My children, wife, and I,
We will ourselves apply
To true industry,
    And leave the rest
To providence divine:
Henceforth I'll not repine,
I hope that me and mine,
    Shall still be blest.
Thus, by the good wife's care,
The husband in despair,

Was brought at length to bear
   His sorrows rife.
The bitter cup of grief,
Her words did yield relief,
She was his friend in chief,
   And faithful wife.
Good men and women pray,
Who hear me now this day,
Labour, without delay,
   To live in love;
Assist each other still
In fortune, good or ill,
Then you'll have a blessing still
   Come from above!

Print. B/W2.   Broadside. Woodcut. Colophon: J. Marshall, Printer,
Newcastle.
      Probably c.1815. A virtually identical broadside – except that the 'pitman'
becomes a 'sailor', 'Newcastle' becomes 'North Shields', the type-face is more
modern (not using the long 's'), and there are fewer misprints – is also in
B/W2, with the imprint of 'Pollock, Printer, North Shields'. For James Kelly
Pollock, see Hunt, *The Book Trade*, pp. 73–74.

7. CAPPY; OR THE PITMAN'S DOG.
      Tune:- *Chapter of Donkies.*
   +*Wrote by William Mitford Shoemaker in the Back Row Newcastle*

In a Town near Newcassel a Pitman did dwell,
Wiv his wife nyemd Peg, a Tom Cat, and himsel,
A dog called Cappy, he doated upon,
Because he was left him by great uncle Tom;
   Weel bred Cappy, famous au'd Cappy, Cappy's
      the dog,
      Tallio, Tallio.

His tail pitcher-handled, his colour jet black,
Just a foot and a half was the length of his back,
His legs seven inches frev shoulders to paws,
And his lugs like twee dockins* hung ower his jaws: dock leaves
    Weel bred Cappy, &c.

For huntin of varmin reet cliver was he,
And the house frev a' robbers his bark wad keep
        free:
Cou'd byeth fetch and carry: cou'd sit on a stuil,
Or when frisky wad hunt water rats in a puil;
    Weel bred Cappy, &c.

As Ralphy to Market one morn did repair,
In his hat-band a pipe, and weel kyem'd was his
        hair,
Ower his airm hung a basket, thus onwards he
        speels,*   climbs briskly
And enter'd Newcassel wi' Cap at his heels;
    Weel bred Cappy, &c.

He hadent got farther than foot o' the Side,
Before he fell in with the dog-killin tribe:
When a Highwayman fellow slipt round in a crack,
And a thump o' the skull laid him flat on his back;
    Down went Cappy, &c.

Now Ralphy *extonish'd*, Cap's fate did repine,
While its eyes like twee little pyerl buttons did shine:
He then spat on his hands, in a fury he grew,
Cries, God smash, but I'se hev satisfaction o' thou;
    For knocking down Cappy, &c.

Then this grim luiking fellow his bludgeon he
        rais'd,
When Ralphy ey'd Cappy, and then stuid amaz'd:
But fearin beside him he might be laid down,
Threw him into the basket and bang'd out o' town;
    Away went Cappy, &c.

He breethless gat hyem, and when liftin the sneck,
His wife exclaim'd "Ralphy" thou's suin gettin back,
"Gettin back," replied Ralphy, "I wish I'd ne'er
    gyen,
In Newcassel they're fellin dogs, lasses, an men;
  They've knock'd down Cappy, &c.

If I gan to Newcassel when comes wor Pay Week,
I'll ken him agyen by the patch on his cheek,
Or if ever he enters wor Toon wiv his stick,
Weel thump him about till he's black as au'd Nick;"
  For killin au'd Cappy, &c.

Wiv tears in her e'e, Peggy heard his sad tale,
While Ralph wiv confusion an terror grew pale:
But while his transactions they were taukin ower,
He crap out o' the basket quite brisk o' the floor;
  Weel deun Cappy, &c.

+ Ernshaw, a Constable in Newcastle.

Print. B/W2.   Broadside. Colophon: K. Anderson, Printer, Newcastle.
Published on broadsides by Marshall and by Pollock (CULM 16/457; B/W2),
in Mitford's 1816 *Budget*, and in many later local chapbooks and songbooks
(Thompson, *Newcastle Chapbooks*, p. 7), including those of John Ross and
William Walker, up to Catcheside-Warrington, *Tyneside Songs*, Volume 2, p.
18. Recorded by Michael Hunt on 'Water of Tyne' (Decca: LK4902, 1967).
    Date c.1816. For Kenneth Anderson, who was mainly a book-printer, and
William Walker, see Hunt, *The Book Trade*, pp. 2-3,93. John Ross worked in
the Royal Arcade, Newcastle, from at least 1847 until 1852 or 1853, when the
business was taken over by John Gilbert (Hunt, *The Book Trade*, p. 80), and
around 1849 he issued a *Catalogue of Slip Songs, Histories, Song Books,..&c,
Offered to the Trade*, in which he advertised the first seven numbers of his '24-
page Song Books' of 'Newcastle Songs'.

8. THE PITMAN'S COURTSHIP.

One night as I came home from work,
Then who did I chance for to see,
Young Jemmy and Peggy a courting,
A canny young lassie was she.
I slid by the side of a hill,
There was nought but a valley between,
To hear what they said to each other,
I stood where I could not be seen.
   O my Peggy, my hinny,
    And O my jewel, said he,
     What with working and selling together,
     There will none be so happy as we.
Says Jemmy to Peggy, my lass,
We'll be married without more delay;
And I think it is the only plan,
To set up in the huixtery* way: street-trading
We will sell oranges, apples, and claggum,*   treacle toffee
Mint candy, spice horses, and all;
The pay we'll attend every fortnight,
Among the pit lads great and small.
We'll sell every thing you can mention,
I know very well we'll do fine;
You can catch the pay week upon Wear,
And next week come over to Tyne.
You can first give a call into Chirton,
To Dobson's, Northumberland Arms,
And if there be very few drinking,
Odsmash* you can sell to the bairns.   God smash, an oath
Then next you can go to the raws,*   pit-rows, houses
And from there to the sign of the Coach;
Odsmash our laddies will buy,
Whenever they see you approach.
They'll say, canny wife, what d'ye sell,
You will say, sweet meats of every kind;
Come buy away lads, and be handy,
I have the best stuff upon Tyne.
And when that you come from the Coach,
You can go up to Willington Square,

And there you will come to the pay house,
And see all the pit laddies there.
And there you will get your allowance,
Of full flowing glasses of ale;
What with eating and drinking together,
Odsmash you'll be as fat as a whale.
When you come from Willington Square,
You can go to the sign of the Swan,
You may just do among the pit laddies,
You may just do the best way you can.
Pray what do you sell, canny wife,
We will buy from you this very night,
I sell oranges, apples, and candy,
And spice cake to relish your kite.*   please your stomach
So when the Tyne pays they are o'er,
And you have sold all that you can,
I will buy you a canny new gown,
And for it I'll work like a man.
And then I will buy you a cuddy,*   ass
Next pay week to ride o'er to Wear,
And when you arrive at the pay house,
They'll think you some leddy come there.
Then first you will go in by Fatfield,
New Painshaw likewise Shiny Row,
Philadelphia, Newbottle, and Howton,
You may take them all in a row.
Then next you can go in by Rainton,
By Lumley you can come round,
Oddsmash my hinny with money,
And drink you'll be like to fall down.
The very last place you've to call at,
Is Wappen and Lambton by name,
And when you've sold all that you can,
You must just take away hame.
So I stood till their courtship was ended,
He call'd [h]er his joy and delight,
And when I come up from the pit,
I will meet you the very next night.

Print. B/W2.   Broadside. Colophon: Pollock, Printer. This piece has a
publishing longevity very similar to *Cappy*, from its appearance in Mitford's
1816 *Budget*, through various chapbooks and songbooks, up to Catcheside-
Warrington, *Tyneside Songs*, Volume 2, p. 16. It can be heard on Michael
Hunt's 'Water of Tyne' (Decca: LK4902, 1967).
   Probably c.1816. Another Mitford composition.

9. THE COAL TRADE. A NEW SONG.

Good people listen while I sing,
The truth from whence your comforts spring,
And may each wind that blows still bring,
   Success unto the coal trade.
Who but unusual pleasure feels,
To see our fleets of Ships and Keels,
Then Newcastle, Sunderland, and Shields,
   May for ever bless the coal trade.

May Vultures on the ciatiff* fly,   *sic*, caitiff, wretch
And knaw* his liver until he die,   gnaw
Who looks with evil and a jealous eye,
   Down upon the coal trade.
For if that should fail what would ensue,
What ruin and disaster too,
Alas! alas what could we do,
   If it were not for the coal trade.

What is it that gives us cakes of meal,
What is it that crams* our wame* se weel,   fills; stomach
With lumps of beef and draughts of ale,
   What is't but just the coal trade.
Not Davis' straits or Greenland oil,
Nor all the wealth that springs from that soil,
Could ever make our pots to boil,
   Like unto our coal trade.

Ye sailors' wives that love a drop,
    Of stingo* frae the Brandy Shop,   strong ale
How could you get one single drop,
    If it were not for the coal trade.
Ye pitmen lads so blythe and gay,
Who meet to tipple on pay-day,
Down on your marrow bones and pray,
    Success unto the coal trade.

May Wear and Tyne still draw and pour
Their jet black treasures to the shore,
And we with all our strength will roar,
    Success unto the coal trade.
Ye owners, masters, and sailors a',
Come shout till ye be like to fa',
And raise your voices, huzza, huzza,
    For we all live by the coal trade.

This country is in duty bound,
To pray for those who work under ground,
For 'tis well known this country round,
    Is kept up by the coal trade.
May Wear and Tyne and Thames ne'er freeze
Our ships and keels will pass with ease,
Then Newcastle, Sunderland, and Shields,
    Will still hold the coal trade.

I tell the truth you may depend,
In Durham or Northumberland,
No trade in them could ever stand,
    If it were not for the coal trade.
The owners know full well 'tis true,
Without pitmen, keelmen, and sailors too,
To this country they might bid adieu,
    If it were not for the coal trade.

So to conclude and make an end,
Of these few lines which I have pen'd,
We will drink a health to all those men,
    Who carry on the coal trade.

To owners, pitmen, and keelmen too,
And sailors who the seas do plough,
Without those men we could not do,
     Nor carry on the coal trade.

Print. B/W2.   Broadside. Colophon: W. Stephenson, Printer, Gateshead.
See also Marshall, *A Collection of Songs*, p. 135, Anon, *Tyneside Songs*, p. 18,
Fordyce, *Newcastle Song Book*, p. 146, Allan, *Tyneside Songs*, p. 277 and Stokoe
& Reay, *Songs and Ballads*, p. 140.
     Probably c.1818. The author was John Adley, 'A Pitman at Newbottle', who
also wrote *The Coal Trade, A Descriptive Poem*, 'printed by J.Marshall in the Old
Flesh Market, Newcastle, 1818, Price twopence' (Thomson, *Newcastle Chap-
books*, pp. 22, 30). For William Stephenson, see Hunt, *The Book Trade*, p. 85.

10. THE BOLD COLLIER

You gallants of England, come listen awhile,
And I'll sing you a song that will make you to smile,
It's of a rich lady that was gallant and gay,
And a French lord he wanted to steal her away.

With kisses and compliments he did begin,
Saying now noble lady if I can your heart win,
If I can you win, that is all my desire,
Or else my poor heart will be all of a fire.

It is your young collier I hold in disdain,
For he works all the day and its labour in vain,
But if you will marry me in a coach you shall ride,
And a jolly young coachman shall wait by your side.

Sir, its not your footman that I desire,
For it is my young collier I do admire,
He is a handsome young collier & works under ground,
And theres no such men in the world to be found.

In the middle of the courtship the collier came,
And saying now noble French Lord I have got you within
He stepped up to him and gave him such a fell,
Saying now noble French Lord you must pay for all,

O spare my life collier, and let me go free,
Dont let me be kill'd in a strange country,
For its fifty bright guineas I freely will give,
To the handsome young collier if he lets me live.

Come pay down your money, your money advance,
And go to your country that place called France,
And tell them you met with a collier by chance,
And he learned you a step call'd the new English dance.

Print. Allan.   Broadside. Woodcut. No colophon. (The woodcut was often
used by John Marshall c.1820–21.)
    Probably c.1821.

11. THE MINER'S BINDING.

It happen'd on March the twenty-third day,
When our binding came on, and we all went away,
And our miners of Backworth they all did agree,
And the number of them it was one hundred and
        three,
As I've told you before we agreed to a man,
To be true to each other and firmly to stand,
But we broke thro' our rules and began for to bind,
So we're all brought to nothing on both Wear and
        Tyne.

Our miners and keelmen, and sailors also,
Since our trade has come down are all very low,
The like of this binding we never did see,
Since the coal-trade commenc'd by land and by sea,

To take off our money I'm sure 'twas not right,
We lament our misfortune by day and by night,
When we push'd round the glasses but now must
      decline,
Since we're all brought to nothing on both Wear
      and Tyne.

We thought that the year nineteen it was bad,
It was all the whole cry there's no money to be had,
But it's nothing at all to this year twenty-two,
It's all the whole cry, alas! what shall we do,
The like of those times was ne'er seen I dare say,
Since the evening and morning became the first
      day,
The poor's been oppress'd this very long time,
Since we're all brought to nothing on both Wear
      and Tyne.

Tho' our binding money they've taken withal,
We may see better days yet in spite of them all,
To make themselves gentlemen I do protest,
They do not know which way the poor to oppress,
But since it is so we must do as we can,
We hope to see better days every man,
This year twenty-two now we always may mind,
That we're all brought to nothing on both Wear
      and Tyne.

We're all brought to hardships as plain you may
      see,
Which makes us lament now in every degree,
This binding we've had on our own native shore,
We ne'er will forget till our time is no more,
The way which now we are oppress'd every man,
It makes us down-hearted do all that we can.
Our wages is low and trade is on the decline,
And we're all brought to nothing on both Wear and
      Tyne.

So all you brave miners wherever you be,
I hope there is no one offended at me,
Altho' I did venture to pen out those lines,
I was urged to it now by the change of the times,
My song for to finish I will add little more,
But may the Great Ruler of both sea and shore,
Bring our island to flourish in a very short time,
And our trade it will rise then on both Wear and Tyne.

Print. B/W2.   Broadside. Colophon: Pollock, Printer, North Shields.
Reprinted, with a few minor alterations, as *The Miners' Binding* by Lloyd, *Come
all ye bold miners*, (1978), p. 217.
   Internal evidence points clearly to a date of 1822.

12. HETTON COALS. A NEW SONG.

Hetton-Main coal now is won,
We'll a' get drunk till we fall down:
The water is het we a' weel knaw,
But we'll tub* her back without a flaw.   wooden pit-shaft lining
   Hetton coal is very bonny,
   Hetton coal is best of ony;
   The water is het we a' weel knaw,
   But we'll tub her back without a flaw.

Hetton-Main coal is round and good,
It takes neither chips nor wood;
But makes a fire both brisk and braw,
Hetton coal it bangs* them a'.   beats
   Hetton coal is very bonny, &c.

Our master Cockrine he comes te,
'Lads you've won the colliery for me,
Good ale and beer you shall drink round,
And we'll a' get drunk in Hetton town.
   Hetton coal is very bonny, &c.

Our machines they're strong and good,
They're made of good metal and of wood;
And they're weel man'd so weel we knaw,
Hetton lads they bang them a'.
    Hetton coal is very bonny, &c.

Jowsey he comes swearing in,
'Smash her down lads to the seam;
The seam is good se weel we knaw,
Hetton coal it bangs them a'.
    Hetton coal is very bonny, &c.

Hopper and Stephenson did say
'Sharp your picks and hew away;
Carve them round and make ne sma;*   *ie* small coals
For Hetton coal it bangs them a'.
    Hetton coal is very bonny, &c.

Hetton colliery now is won,
The waggon way and a' is done;
The coals are shipping every day,
Amang them a' they bear the sway.*   take the lead
    Hetton coal is very bonny, &c.

Nesham's colliery and Lord Steward's te,
Our owners can win a' the three;
The coals they sell without delay,
Hetton owners carries the day.
    Hetton coal is very bonny, &c.

Now to conclude and make an end,
    Of these few lines which Jowsey pen'd;
Amang them a' in Wear or Tyne,
    Hetton owners takes the shine.*   come first
        Hetton coal is very bonny, &c.

Print. B/W2.   Broadside. Colophon: Stephenson, Print[er].
    Hetton Colliery was won in 1822.

13. ON THE SUFFERINGS OF THE PITMEN in the Dreadful
Explosion, In Staw Pit Townly Main Colliery, Stella, in the County of
Durham, by which upwards of 40 Men and Boy[s] were
instantaniously deprived of life.

O! how can a mortal or his pen describe,
The dangers of men who are buried alive;
The Sailors for dangers stand next in my sight,
Tho' never excluded from prec[i]ous day light.

The sun ne'er enlighten's the pitmen's dark damps,
They work by the light of their poor, glimmering lamps,
And the pitmen have dangers which none else endure,
Yet starved and oppressed, and wretchedly poor.

When they left their homes, this pit to descend,
How little they thought it would be their end.
Or little thought their wives or their children so dear,
The sound of their voices they'd never more hear.

Nor in these poor fathers a thought e'er arose,
That they'd ne'er more hear their prattling noise;
Nor could them dear mothers or else what dread moans,
That they'd ne'er behold more alive their poor sons.

Their homes they left cheerful with their bit of bread,
And along that dark cavern they went without dread,
Some hours they had laboured beneath the cold ground,
And very soon after they heard the dread sound.

A sound loud as thunder, a dreadful fire-damp,*   explosive methane gas
They say it proceeded from opening a lamp!
At a sound so distressing, I here drop my pen,
If affecting to write it. what was it to them.

But O! what distress next comes to our views,
When to the poor cottage did reach the sad news,
The pit it had blasted, and to them was made clear,
And they [k]new it contained all they held dear.

But for to describe it I know I'm not fit,
When with shrieks and lamenting they ran to the pit,
There in a dead silence I cannot relate,
When like a clock pendl'm their poor hearts would beat

When their poor remains were then brought to view,
Their hearts bled a-fresh and their sorrows renew,
With shrieks and sad wailings as of him we do read,
Would to God I had died my son in thy stead

But see them borne home to their own cottage door,
Them homes left in health but by them a few hours,
But now their pale corpse all lifeless and dead
No longer are needing their pittance of bread.

No, they had enough and perhaps bread to spare,
Why then ye vain mortals all this anxious care,
For death in a moment may extinguish your lamp,
Tho' you are not in danger of dreadful fire-damp.

Then to these poor widows who with trouble are tost
Remember poor Job when his children he lost,
Killed all in one moment this good man did say,
The Lord he has given and has but ta'en [a]way.

All worldly substance was ta'en from him, still
You read his afflictions when on the dung-hill,
And what was left him, it made him the worse
His own cruel wife bid him God for to curse.
*

He did in his anguish curse the day he was born, *no gaps between final three stanzas*
When those all around him he found did him scorn,
And no one to help him on this earthly ball,
He justly exclaimed you're tormentors all.

But I hope that Job's comfort will now be your lot,
Tho' they're dead and gone that you'll ne'er be forgot,
For thousands will assist you and will you befriend,
Like Job you may prosper in your latter end.

14. THE WIDOWS' LAMENTATION.

Good people all give ear we pray
   While we our sorrows vent,
Our loss is great you all must know,
   Which makes us thus lament.
We know that death's the common lot
   Of all poor Adam's race,
But he has ta'en our bosom friends,
   All in a moment's space.
In healths fair bloom that morning they
   Rose from their resting bed,
But erc another sun arose,
   They silent were and dead.
They left their homes that day in peace
   Their labour to renew,
But little did they think indeed,
   It was their last adieu.
That very night the damp* arose,   *ie*, fire-damp
   We bring it to your views;
How must our bosom throb with grief,
   At that appalling news.
O! had your bosoms dwelt in ours,
   But this we'll not desire,
When with shrieks & cries from house to house,
   The pit had taken fire.
While we their food contriving was,
   When their day's work was done,
But little did we think indeed
   That night they would want none.
And could we but lament indeed
   To see them dead and cold,
No, had we twice ten thousand tongues,
   Our grief could ne'er be told.
And can we but lament to see,
   Their dearest children then,
What must tha[t] mother's feelings be,
   That's left with children ten.
And can a mother but lament,
   Her only son when dead,

On which her constant hopes were hung,
　All for her daily bread.
Lament her son she may indeed,
　Tor* this of old was done,　　　　　　　　*sic, ie* For
For Jesus he did sure lament,
　And raised the widow's son.
We know our lamentations all,
　Can ne'er bring back to life,
But that cold heart which don't lament,
　Deserves not name of wife.
O may we not lament indeed
　As those that's got no hope,
For till grim death himself is slain,
　His rage will never stop.
Some in their bud, some in their bloom,
　And some in middle hours;
For when pale death puts in his scythe,
　Cuts down both grass and flowers.
Then hearken to the widow's cries,
　The fatherless regard;
And when in heaven we all do meet,
　Our God will you reward.

Print. NUL Loose.　　Double broadside. Colophon: Stephenson, Printer, Gateshead.
According to Fynes, *The Miners*, p. 149, Staw Pit, Townley Main Colliery, exploded on May 20th 1826, killing thirty-eight workers. Given the uncorrected errors (including the death-toll) and the way the colophon pushed the final three stanzas of **13** together, this may have been a proof copy.

15. COME, LAY DOWN YOR PICKS.
   Tune- *"The Campbells are coming."*

Come, lay down yor picks and awa', marrows,
   Come, lay down yor picks and awa';
The Drones are a hummin', the stewards are comin',
   And Liberty seconds the ca'.

      We'll drive a' Invaders awa', Willie;
      We'll drive the Invaders awa';
   The hand of Oppression we'll ever resist,
      As long as we've breath for to draw.

   Yor names they shall stand on record, Willie,
   Yor names they shall stand on record;
Posterity hence will applaud this event –
   That you did them Protection afford.
      Then we'll drive, &c.

   What got a' wor fine Silver Plate, Willie?
   What got a' wor fine Silver Plate?
That Asserter of Right* he has taken a flight,   *ie* pretended beneficiary ?
   And he's now linkin' in wi' the State.
      Then we'll drive, &c.

   Where mun the Kye* gang and graze, Willie?   cattle
   Where mun the Kye gang and graze?
When the daisies maun cow'r, on wor Leazes and
   Moor,
   To Engines and lang Waggon-ways.
      Then we'll drive, &c.

   It's lang may the buttercups grow, Willie,
   Lang, lang may the buttercups grow; –
May the widow be cherish'd, Newcastle be nourish'd
   Wi' good wholesome milk frae the cow.
      Then we'll drive, &c.

Then here's to the Numbers that's met, Willie,
Then here's to the Numbers that's met;
Although there's fifteen on that morning not seen,
    Yet the De'il catch'd them a' in his Net.

    Then we'll drive the Invaders awa', Willie,
    We'll drive the Invaders awa';
  Our duty's our Cause, to abide by the Laws, –
    Still we're determin'd to conquer or fa'.

16. THE PITMAN'S SURPRISE.
Tune - *"The Hills o' Glenochie"*.

Aw wrought in a Pit by the side o' the Moor,
    Wiv Arthur Mc.Clashin, Dick Wishit and Harry,
Ne loop* to gan doon – nowther damp or foul air,   *ie, pit-shaft rope-loop*
    But scamper'd reet in through a hole in the
        Quarry:
Ne danger we dreaded – the creep* never heeded,   *lifting of pit-floor*
    Wi' hackin' an' smashin', new graithin'* an'   *? dressing a coal-pillar*
        trappin',
When drivin' wor wedges reet through a coal-
        dresser,*   *? ie damaging a pillar*
    We a' gat laid off, an' aw knaw nowse what's
        happen'd.

Extonish'd was aw when they enter'd the hole,
    We shew'd them a leet for to keep them frae
        bruises,
They each tuik a pick, an' was hewin' the coal,
    And they tuik a bit hyem for to put i' their houses.
Kiv aw to Dick Wishit, "We've getten fresh hands,
    Wiv hackers and hewers, onsetters* and viewers,   *shaft-bottom coal-loaders*
They drove out the naig,* an' knocked ower the   *nag, horse*
        trams:"
    "Odswuns!"* cried Mc.Clashin, "it's surely the   *God's wounds, ie an oath*
        Stewards!"

A Tailor he cam, wiv his fine dandy sark,
  Alang wiv a Painter, that stuffs the Pall* Parrots,   Poll
They bad us *persist*, and give ower the wark,
    Or else in due time we wad swalley* the   swallow, *ie* undermine
    barracks:
We left them, and fand others rivin' and tearin',–
    The Butcher that bowt the Cur-dog o' the
    Mugger,*   hawker
Was lendin' a hand, wi' Fat Robin, a queer'on,
    That's often seen follow the Barrels o' Shuggar.

The big ones they stuid iv a heap on the hill,
    The little'ns wrought like the foumarts* and   polecats; moles
    moudies:*
We cairted wor graithin'* te gan hev a gill,   equipment, gear, clothing
    Or else to gan hyem te wor wives an' wor
    crowdies.*   oatmeal dish
Aw says tiv au'd Potter, "Your horse is a Trotter;
    Ye brag aboot Jackey, se kittle and bobbish;*   ticklish and skittish?
The coal we've been workin', it's myed the grund
    totter,
    So gan to the watch-house, and load her wi'
    rubbish."

Print. NUL Loose.   Double broadside. 'Price Twopence.' Decorative border. Colophon: Printed for the Author, and sold only by J. Marshall, Newcastle. See also an NCL copy of Mackenzie, *History of Newcastle*, Volume 1, facing p. 710.

  The sheet is headed: 'Songs, Written to Commemorate the Resolution of the Stewards of the Incorporated Companies of Newcastle, to lay off working Coal in a Quarry near the Barracks, on the Town Moor, Friday, Dec. 5, 1828, in order to prevent further Encroachments on their Property in future, and Dedicated, by Permisssion, to that highly Respectable Body, By a Free Burgess'. The author may have been Robert Emery, for whom see Allan, *Tyneside Songs*, pp. 284–90. See also 'A Pitman's Wonderful Account of a Public Dinner', NRO, Bull 11/602.

17. FIRST DREST MAN OF SEGHILL, Or the Pitman's Reward for
Betraying his Brethren. – A New Song.

Come, all ye Miners, far and near,
   And let us all unite, o,
In bands of love and unity,
   And stand* out for our right, o.   *long 's' here and elsewhere*
Like Israel, these many years,
   In bondage we have been, o;
And if we do not still stand out
   Our truth will not be seen, o.
      With my fal lal la, &c.
No doubt but there may be some men
   Not bad for to deceive;
But to their ruin it will be,
   Just like our mother Eve.
Our mother Eve was sore deceiv'd
   By one that's call'd the Devil;
And by persuasion she was brought
   To do the thing that's evil.
Man a weak frail being is,
   And easy to deceive;
And by a man call'd black J R.
   Was made for to believe –
It was on March the 19th. day,
   Eighteen hundred and thirty one,
A man from Earsdon Colliery
   His brethren did abscond.
And to the Seghill binding he
   Did come with all his might,
For to deceive his brethren dear,
   He thought he was but right.
But when he came to Seghill town
   The men were standing off;*   *ie* refusing to be bound
He thought that he would then be bound,
   And he would make a scoff.
As other men were standing off,
   He would not do the same;
That idle work would never do,
   He'd rather bear the shame.

Black J.R. made him believe
   That he was in no danger,
And to the office he might go,
   Because he was a stranger.
He to the Seghill office went,
   All with a bad intent;
But ere he got to Murton town
   He was made to lament.
He to the office went with speed,
   As hard as he could batter,
And other two young lads, with him –
   We did give him a tatter.*   ? a ragging
Black J.R. made him believe
   That men would not molest;
He being acquainted with the man
   He was with faith possest.
We kept the fugal-man* in view,   crowd cheer-leader
   Which made us all so keen;
For it's an oath, by brethren all,
   No one they are to screen.
We went in chace of this bad man,
   For to give him a scar –
By coming to our bond, you know,
   To serve the man J.R.
And at the hour of two o'clock,
   As I was sitting cobbling,
A rout there came unto our house,
   I heard the women gabbling.
Away I went with all my speed,
   As hard as I could hie,
To see if I could catch the hares –
   It was my will to try.
We gladly found him at the pit,
   With J.R. and G. Sern;
But our hearts were fully bent,
   Not to stand there bothering.
But there were some upon the chace
   Long ere I got there:
With running so I lost my breath,
   And I could run ne mair.

But I will tell his travels here,
    As he went from the binding;
They stript him there of part his clothes,
    And left his skin refining.
Black J.R. was all the blame,
    He lost all but his lining:*   *?underclothes*
 But when he came to Hallowell
    His skin so bright was shining.
They left him nothing on to hide
    The good old man the, priest.*   *ie* penis
But there they put him on his hat,*   *ie* put his hat on him
    He was so finely drest.*   *ie* had an erection through fear
They set him off from there with speed
    To an ale-house by the way;
And there the Earsdon men did sit,
    A drinking on that day.
But what their minds I cannot tell,
    When they did see him coming,
The priest he had within his hat,
    And hard he then was running.
And all the way as he went home,
    By many was heard say,
That persuaded he had been
    To his loss upon that day.
The Earsdon men they set him off
    From there to the Machine,
That stands upon the allotment hill;
    He there himself did screen.
Then to the left hand road he took,
    The road that leads to Murton,
And there under a good whin bush
    The priest and him sat lurking.
The priest was almost starved there –
    I'm afraid he has got harm,
If I was only into bed
    I quickly shall be warm.
But unto Paradise I'll go,
    Where I will get no ill,
But never more will I go back
    To that place call'd Seghill.

But remember you that come
  Unto Seghill to bind,
You may think upon the man
  That we have treat so kind.

Print. B/W2. Broadside. Woodcut. Colophon: J. Marshall, Printer, Newcastle. See also Allan, NRO 3410/For/1/18 and Picton. Lloyd, *Come all ye bold miners*, (1978), p. 355, referred to a copy in Sheffield University Library, but its location remains a mystery. Lloyd, *Come all ye bold miners*, (1952), pp. 91–93,137 – or his source, 'J.S.Bell of Whiston, Lancashire' – admitted to having 'edited' the text. In fact, one or both of them retitled it *The Best-dressed Man of Seghill*, put it in stanza form, missed out whole verses and cobbled bits of verses together, so that a fifteen stanza text was cut to twelve. Lloyd, *Folk Song*, pp. 339–40, kept the changed title, altered the verse-structure from eight-line to four-line stanzas, cut down what had been twelve stanzas to ten and made a range of other lesser alterations. Lloyd, *Come all ye bold miners*, (1978), pp. 218–20, used the broadside title, printed all fifteen verses and made some effort to present the text accurately, but kept the four-line stanzas. In a letter to the Editor dated July 25th 1972, Lloyd blamed 'Mr. Bell' for making 'some "adjustments" notably towards the end'. Apparently John Spalding Bell was a Cambridge student in 1935 and later was a leading member of the General and Municipal Workers' Union. (Ian Mackillop, *F.R. Leavis: A Life in Criticism* (London, 1997), p. 164).

Manuscript notes on the B/W2 exemplar read: '10 Quires March 31st, 1831. Crown – 3 on a Sheet.' and (in a different hand) '31 March 1831'. The sheet had been 'spiked' by the printer. The Picton exemplar has manuscript notes: '(10 quires) Wednesday April 6th 1831' and '31 March 1831'. Lloyd, *Come all ye bold miners*, (1978), p. 355, indicated that the exemplar he located at Sheffield University Library was dated '31 March 1831'.

18. THE OPPRESSIONS OF THE PITMEN.
A New Song. Composed by Joseph Hall, Collier, Sheriff Hill.

Eighteen hundred and thirty-one, as I have heard them say,
The Pitmen of the Tyne and Wear met on a certain day,
To consult about their wages, which makes me for to sing –
Expecting for to meet them upon Shadon's Hill.

CHORUS
The oppressions of our country
　　　　We cannot now endure;
　　　The viewers they get all the brass,
　　　　And we are kept so poor.

The owners and the viewers are all a wicked crew,
They have been long contriving to punish me and you;
To punish me and you, as I have heard them say,
The viewers of the collieries caused men to run away.
　　The oppressions, &c.

Some have gone to America and Ireland also
For to maintain their families to Scotland they go,
For money in our country is now so bad to get,
The viewers they must have it – and so we go to wreck.
　　The oppressions, &c.

We are meeting about our 'greements – mind what I do say,
And if we do not stand true, we'll have to rue the day:
Our viewers they'll be harder still, our prices to reduce,
And if we do not stand true our meetings are no use.
　　The oppressions, &c.

There was Hetton and Russell, and Renton also,
Some from Piddington and Lambton, and some from Shiney Row;
There were from Harrington & Fatfield, & Ouston that we ken,
They all came for to meet upon the Black Fell.
　　The oppressions, &c.

When they came unto the Fell to each other did say,
We must have a committee to settle all this fray;
The committee was agreed on, that you shall understand –
Down the Fell to the Mill-house the delegates did gan.
　　The oppressions, &c.

When we came to the Mill-house, H[ebbur]n* he did say,　　i.e. Hepburn
There's two or three things in our bond we must have done away
There's lying off the three days before we can demand,
And sixteen hours for bits of lads – I think its ower lang.
　　The oppressions, &c.

There's many a man binds himself, and does not know what about
And when he is out of employ, the house they turn him out;
The house they turn him out, as I have heard them say,
The best thing is now to strive to have them done away.
　　The oppressions, &c.

When we came unto the Hill, Tommy U–[nthan]–k for to hear,
He read some papers unto us, which was very queer;
He said the viewers had a club, and other things we ken;
It's all to keep the owners blind as well as the poor men.
　　The oppressions, &c.

There was Willie D[awso]n, a man that we did ken,
Said that he would bind himself – he would not mind the men;
He being a treacherous rogue, besides a wildish rake,
They stript the clothes all off his back, and sent him home naked.
　　The oppressions, &c.

Now our times are all out, and dutiful we have been,
Such union amongst the pitmen before was never seen,
Such union among the pitmen the world did never ken –
The oppression of the Viewers causes this amongst the men.
　　The oppressions, &c.

Come all you bold pitmen, since it has come so near,
If we do but stand true, we'll have no cause to fear,
The viewers they'll have to comply, for they will plainly see,
That there will be a stick,* if they do not agree.　　　　　　strike
　　The oppressions, &c.

Print. B/W13.　　Broadside. Colophon: Printed for the Author by Douglas and Kent, Newcastle. See also NRO 3410/For/1/18, which supplies the missing names in manuscript and Lloyd, *Come all ye bold miners*, (1978), pp. 228–29.
　　Knowing references to Willie Dawson – see **17** – and to a strike in the future tense, suggest that this piece dates from immediately before April 5th 1831. For William Douglas and William Kent, see Hunt, *The Book Trade*, pp. 32, 57.

19. GRIEVANCES OF THE PITMEN, by a putter boy, Newbottle
Colliery.

In eighteen hundred and thirty one as I have heard them say,
There did begin a mighty Stick upon a certain day;
Not less than 50 Collieries there were in it convened,
By which the Viewers and Masters were very much alarmed.

It first began at Hetton, and then it spread around,
But mind 'twas not for nothing, for in misery we were found,
We scarce had any thing to eat, and destitute of bread,
We were constrain'd to this effort, by reason we were led;

And we went to Shadon's Hill, our grievances to state,
And said unto the Public, we've been oppress'd of late;
But now we do intend men to stand out for our right,
And to maintain our union, and that with all our might.

There was but one opposed us, and we did make him flee,
And would you know that person's name, his
          name is W.D.*   *ie* Willie Dawson
We stripp'd the clothes from off his back, (no
          more than he deserv'd)
For he behaved badly, and he got his just reward.

Our hewers work like horses, 'twixt eight and
          eleven hours,
And breathing clouds of noxious dust, sweat down
          their body pours,
And all this hardship undergone to get a scanty living,
Their wages fortnightly for this, scarce more than
          twenty shilling.

The Corves* we have are far too large, the fines   *plural* of corf
          also imposing,
And Corves set out* from time to time,   *ie* confiscated
          unreasonably oppressing;
But 'tis eleven days* we want, each day we want   *ie* eleven days' work
          three shillings,   per fortnight
Perhaps by this we may begin to get an honest living.

But working sixteen hours a day, it really is too
    long,
For Putters or for Drivers, and all off-handed   *all pit workers except hewers*
    men;*   *and putters*
The Corves they often stick at the roof, sometimes
    the side,
And thus they toil for sixteen hours, until they   *ie* up the shaft, leave
    have to ride.*

The Putter Lads work very hard for sixteen hours a
    day,
With head and shoulders at the Corf, compell'd to
    thrust away,
With bodies nearly naked, along the way they go,
'Midst thick and pitchy darkness in the dreary
    vaults below.

The boys that drive the horses, have fourteen
    pence per day,
And working sixteen hours, as I before did say;
The little Trappers also, they seem to be unwilling,
To work so long for ten pence, when they ought
    to have a shilling.

Of all the trades in England there's none to be
    compar'd
To Colliers' for danger, besides their labouring
    hard;
By leaving the Sun and suspended by a rope,
Descend many fathoms toward the centre of the
    Globe.

What a numerous train of ills do Pitmen undergo!
Destructive damps and noxious dust, infect the air
    below;
An instance I beheld myself, of death in awful
    form,
For he was crush'd beneath the weight of an
    enormous stone.

But many say we're ignorant! confessing this is
    true,
Our children have not half an hour to read a
    lesson through,
By being detained at work so long and labour in
    the Mine,
The fault is really not in us, nor has been all this
    time.

At a meeting at Pittington soon after Lumley binding,
A poor silly wretched man these men he was
    defending,
The men they quickly at him, and off his clothes
    they rent,
They stripp'd him quite stark naked, and to his
    home he went;

The Viewer quickly to him went right glad to hear
    the news,
Saying now my man I counsel you to bind for
    such abuse;
No! says the man, I've got a fright. I'll not go to be
    bound,
They've shamed me so I dare not go, no not for
    fifty Pound.

The Viewers and the Masters confessing they are
    wrong,
Have sworn in many Constables, the father 'gainst
    the son;
The Soldiers also they have brought, and that to
    save them too,
But we will never mind that, so let us stick it
    throngh.*   *sic, ie* through

Print. Allan.   Broadside. Decorative border. Colophon: J. Beckwith, Printer,
Houghton.
    Probably from mid-April 1831. For James Beckwith see Hunt, *The Book
Trade*, p. 9.

20. THE PITMAN'S COMPLAINT.*

B&C: VERSES ON THE CRUELTY OF THE MASTERS TO THE PITMEN.

O Lord hear the poor pitmen's cry
Look down on us with pitying eye;
With heavy bondage are opprest,
And all our families are distrest.

Thou heard the Israelites of old,
And led them to a blessed fold;
Deliver us from slavery
And set the Sons of Britain free.

In the dark pit where we are bound,
The iron hand of oppression's found;
Our labour's hard, our wages small,
Some days we work for nought at all.

As lions greedy of their prey,
They take our rights from us away;
To starvation we are driven,
Pale and wan we are ill thriven.

Our masters pinch us very sore,
We never felt such smart* before,
They ⌊have us so completely bet,⌋
⌊Not one in fifty's out of debt.⌋

fining
B&C: They wish to have us completely ruin'd
B&C: And keep us tethered to the ground

The Indian slaves for freedom groan,
We have a greater cause to moan,
You often pity slaves abroad,
But we have now a greater load.

Come, O ye rulers of our land,
Pray take our cause into your hand,
Then let us have fair Britain's* law,
And save us from proud Pharoah's paw.

C: Briton's

Beneath the harrow we are crush'd,*   B&C: crushed
Our blood lies mangled* with the dust;   B&C: mingled
Regardless of our cries and groans,
They suck the marrow from our bones.

As cannibals they have* eat our flesh,   B&C: *omitted*
Their bellies swell to great excess,
To quench their thirst have drunk our blood,
And left us wallowing in the mud.

Does not the trumpet sound reform,*   *ie*, Parliamentary Reform
And are we not free Britons born;
We want to have a jubilee,
The slavish pitmen now set free.

Our flesh pots now are stained with rust,
Our cup-boards* now without a crust,   B&C: cupboards
The tears run from the mothers' eyes,
They cannot bear their children's cries.

Arise my brethren from the dust,
And in the Lord let's put our trust,
Then all our foes he will confound,
And in the sea proud Pharaoh dround.*   B&C: drown

Print. **A:** B/W2. **B:** Wigan 108 (302). **C:** NCL 1844.   **A:** Broadside.
Colophon: Printed for the Author, by W. Fordyce, 48, Dean Street, Newcastle.
See also Bell 11/278. **B:** Broadside proof? No colophon [Dodds]. See also Bell
12/256. **C:** Broadside. No colophon [Dodds]. Lloyd, *Come all ye bold miners*,
(1978), pp. 221–22, 355, published a slightly altered version of this piece and
a note referring to it as *The Pitmen's Complaint*, which is also the title of **21**.

A manuscript note on A reads: 'May 13th. 1831'. Bell 11/278 is inscribed
'May 13th) 500)1831'. C was probably published late in the strike of 1844: it
appears amongst material dating to August 1844 in NCL 1844. For Thomas
and Henry Dodds, and William and Thomas Fordyce, see Hunt, *The Book
Trade*, pp. 31, 36.

21. THE PITMEN'S COMPLAINT. A New Song. – By J. Knox.

Ye Collier Lads, I pray attend
  To what I'm going to say;*
For I am not the least afraid
  But that you'll win the day.
The way that you conduct yourselves
  You have no cause to fret;
And if the Lord is on your side
  You never will be beat.

long 's', here and elsewhere

Stand true to each other, and never give way:
This the method you must take if you'd wish to win the day.

The Pitmen they've been long opprest:
  To their sorrow well they know;
But they intend to be redrest
  Before to work they go.
They'll never from their colours fly,
  But boldly they'll stand fast;
For town and country's on their side –
  They'll bring them to at last.
    Stand true, &c.

'Tis a pity that those collier lads
  Should be so sore opprest;
For they're exposed, when down below,
  To many a dreadful blast.
The pitmen all should be well paid
  For all the work they do:
Consider the danger they are in,
  When working down below.
    Stand fast, &c.

The pitmen they are hearty lads,
  As any men I know;
Although they work hard for their brass,
  Freely they let it go.
So drink success to those brave lads,
  And let their health go round:

Think on the danger they are in,
   When working under ground.
      Stand fast, &c.

The pitmen they are well belov'd,
   Throughout this country wide;
For there's not many men I know
   But what are on their side.
For conducting themselves so well,
   Is greatly in their favour:
There was never a stick* in all those parts,   strike
   Where the men had better behaviour.
      Stand fast, &c.

Lord cause the pitmen's stick to end,
   And grant them their desire:
You may depend this neighbourhood
   Have found great want of fire.
For not a coal is to be got –
   I know this to be true:
And if they don't get started soon,
   I know not what we'll do.
      Stand fast, &c.

Concerning now the pitmen's stick,
   A little more I'll say;
But I wish freely from my heart
   That they may win the day.
I hope their masters will consent
   To grant them their desire;
That those brave lads may hew once more,
   And we may all get fire.
      Stand fast, &c.

Print. Allan.   Broadside. ?Woodcut. Colophon: J. Marshall, Printer, Newcastle.
   Probably from late May 1831. For Jeremiah Knox, see above, p. 11, note 38.

22. THE PITMEN'S AGREEMENT A New Song. Written in
Commemoration of a great Number of them gaining their Rights,
after a very long Contention with the Coal-Owners, in the Year
1831.

Come all you honest pitmen lads,
   And listen a short while;
It is concerning the agreement,
   Your time I will beguile.

A glorious victory you have gain'd
   Over your stubborn foes,
(Makes me sing these lines with glee)
   Which every body knows.

Some of you have been badly used,
   Most shamefully used indeed;
For out of doors you have been turn'd,
   And left you without bread.

Some of you have been turn'd out of doors,
   Which I do still maintain,
Complying not with the demands of those,
   Whose house you did retain.

During the whole of your manly strike,
   Your conduct have* been brave –   *sic*
Which deserves the country's thanks,
   And the nation's praise.

All those men that are not bound
   Cheeer up your daring hearts –
Patience and Perseverance, my lads,
   Be still your nobler parts.

Should you any act of violence commit,
   [A] stigma on you will be;
The military force will interfere,
   Which you will plainly see.

All those men that have got bound,
   For their aid you must call;
To give you part of their earnings,
   For fear that you should fall.

After you have all agreed, my lads,
   (I hope you'll excuse my rhyme)
In a sacred bond join heart and hand,
   To support you 'nother time.

Now success to all the pitmen,
   Both on the Tyne and Wear;
May they continue to have their rights
   In each succeeding year.

Success attend their canny wives,
   And all their children dear,
Forgetting not the Delegates,
   Who had the cause to steer.

Print. B/W2.   Broadside. Colophon: Douglas & Kent, Printers, Newcastle.
See also Lloyd, *Come all ye bold miners*, (1978), p. 230.
   Mid-June 1831.

23. THE PITMEN'S STICK. A New Song. By Jeremiah Knox.

Ye collier lads I pray attend,
   To what I'm going to say,
For I am very glad to hear,
   That you have won the day.
Great many people did believe,
   That you would get the worse,
Because they thought your masters
   Were too strong in the purse.

But let their purse be e'er so long,
   Or be they ever so wide,
I always said that you would win,
   For the Lord is on your side;
For those who're in a righteous cause,
   Have never cause to fret,
For when the Lord is on their side,
   They never can be beat.

For many years we know it well,
   You have been much oppress'd,
You may thank the blessed Lord
   That you have got redress'd.
I hope those lads will be thought on,
   More than they were before,
For we've a right for to be glad,
   They've started work once more.

For they are the main support,
   Of this whole country side.
I'll sing their praise where'er I go,
   Throughout this country wide.
The Merchants in Newcastle town,
   They were greatly distress'd,
For they thought the collier lads,
   Would never be redress'd.

The landladies long faces made,
   Good right they had I know,
For many a pound those lads did spend
   When they had work below.
If they'd been much longer off work
   Our fate would have been bad;
For you know this to be true,
   Coals were not to be had.

Full seven weeks their stick did last,
   You know this to be so,
Before that any man did ride,
   For to work down below.
Great praise the pitmen all have got,
   Throughout this country round.
May God protect the collier lads,
   When working underground.

Their masters would have more feeling
   For their men I know,
If they had but one month to work,
   With their brave men below,
And be expos'd when down at work,
   To a blast of foul air;
Their prices they would ne'er abate,
   But sooner give them more.

Now their strike is over,
   And they've got their desire.
I hope we'll never have more cause,
   To cry out for want of fire:
And I hope they will ne'er have cause
   For to stick any more,
But live in comfort all their lives,
   As their friends have done before.

There never was so many men,
   Which every tongue can tell,
During the time of their strike,
   That e'er behav'd so well.
So let us drink a health to those
   Brave lads who hew the coal,
For I think they should be well paid
   For working in the hole.

Print. B/W2.   Broadside. Colophon: Douglas and Kent. Printers, 50,
Quayside, Newcastle. See also Lloyd, *Come all ye bold miners,* (1978),
pp. 223–24, 355, where no author is given.
    A manuscript note dates this piece to 'July 1831'. Hunt, *The Book Trade,*
p. 32, gives no Quayside address for Douglas and Kent.

24. THE PITMEN'S UNION; or, the Lads of the Wear and Tyne.

Now let the colliers' hearts be glad,
   While plenty round them shines,
And blest contentment flows along
   The banks of Wear and Tyne.
          CHORUS
   Still round our banners we will stand,
     In love and truth combine,
   And children yet unborn shall sing,
     The lads of Wear and Tyne.
Brave Hepburn and our delegates,
   Like rays of virtue shine,
Their fame shall long be echoed round
   The banks of Wear and Tyne.
On Bolden Fell our flags shall wave,
   Like victory's wreaths entwine,
But peace shall be the motto still,
   With lads of Wear and Tyne.
We envy not the rich and great,
   Whose dazzling greatness shine;
While we the hardy sons of toil,
   Can labour in the mine.
Our happy wives and children now,
   All former cares resign,
And sing with joyful mirth and glee,
   The lads of Wear and Tyne.
May he, who rides upon the storm,
   Protect with care divine,
From all the dangers that surround
   The lads of Wear and Tyne.
Here's a health unto the King,
   Likewise the Queen sublime,
Who gave the pitmen their applause,
   That dwell on Wear and Tyne.
Now to conclude and make an end,
   May luck around them twine;
O, bless the happy collier lads,
   On both the Wear and Tyne.

Print. B/W2.   Double broadside. Woodcut. Colophon: Stephenson, Printer, Gateshead. Printed next to *The glorious victory of the Reformers in St. Stephen's Bay*. Another copy is in Allan. See also Lloyd, *Come all ye bold miners*, (1978), pp. 226–27, 355–56.

Late July 1831. A manuscript note on the B/W2 exemplar dates this to 'July 1831' and the first song mentions July 12th 1831 in the past tense.

25. THE TOTAL BANISHMENT OF SELF-TYRANNY & OPPRESSION.
By John Forrest, Pitman.

CHORUS.

Let truth and reason be your guide,
Whatever come to hand;
For unity it is the strength
Of this our native land.

Come all my friends and neighbours and listen unto me,
I will tell you of a monster that hang'd he must be,
Or chained in some dismal cell there for to lie and pine,
Before that peace and unity to love they can be joined.

Now as I have taken pen in hand I mean to tell you true,
Besides this terrible monster there is other two;
But this old one is the worst, so mind well what I say,
And constantly beware of him and watch both night and day.

So if you want to know him I tell you his name is Self,
He is the founder of all mischief, besides a wicked elf,
For he will both rob and plunder, and murder you also,
And how we must get rid of him is all that I want to know.

Now for to tie him in a sack and throw him into the sea,
You know the monster will not drown, so then what must we do?
For to put a rope around his neck and hang him on a tree,
And now the villain he will not hang so he will ruin our country.

Some other way then we must have, this fellow to destroy,
  But he is so familiar with us we cannot him decoy;
Therefore we must take him by force, I solemnly declare,
  And send him to his native place of blackness and despair.

Then the way we can take him by force, I mean to tell you true,
  Let justice, truth, and reason, be placed firm on every brow;
With love, peace, and union, sealed firm on every heart,
  And then I will be bound we will banish Self, and all who takes
    his part.

Now let every man stand firm to truth, and mind what I do say,
  Let reason be his constant rule and justice bear the sway;
Take love and peace close to your side, they will go hand in hand,
  And unity it is the strength of this our native land.

Now the armour that I have mentioned I pray you put it on,
  And brave the field of battle I would have you ev'ry man;
And be sure and keep this armour bright, it will glitter like the sun,
  Then the monster Self, he will be beat and all his schemes be done.

Now my friends there is other two, which you all know full well,
  But for fear that any should mistake, their names to you I'll tell;
Tyranny it is the one, well known in all our land,
  And Oppression he is the other, with his strong iron hand.

Now this villain Tyranny he is Self's oldest son I say,
  His mother's name is Greed, she nurst him up straightway
To be a monster with a whip for to rule over man;
  And that monstrous Oppression, says I, will crush all I can.

Now I've described this family of monsters so severe,
  Then every man be on his guard and keep all of them clear;
For where the old man can get in, the other will be there
  So my friends beware of them and keep them where they are.

So now good people all, the armour I've described
  I beg you bind it firmly on, whatever you betide,
To conquer all those hellish foes, and bid them to be gone,
  And send them back where they belong, to their eternal home.

Now for to make an end of what has here been said,
  Let justice, truth, and reason, be still your constant guide;
Take peace, love, and union, with the other three also,
  And you will conquer all those enemies, wherever they may go.

Print. Allan.   Broadside. Colophon: E. Mackenzie, Printer, Newcastle.
  This piece probably dates from late 1831 or very early 1832. For Eneas
Mackenzie Senior, see Hunt, *The Book Trade*, p. 63, and Welford, *Men of Mark*,
Volume 3, pp. 117–18.

26. THE PITMANS UNION.

It's on the 5th of April, the days were long and clear,
So bright did shine the sun, and how cool did blow the air
I overheard a pretty maid how sweetly she did sing,
As she was sitting under her cow a milking.

I stepped up to her and bended my knee,
And asked her pardon for making so free;
Your pardon is granted, young collier. she replies.
But do you belong to the brave union boys?

Don,t* you see that I'm a collier as black as any   *sic*
      sloe?
And all this night Iv'e* been working down   *sic*
      bolow:*   *sic*
O, I do love a collier as I do love my life
For my father was a pitman all the days of his life.

Come all you noble gentlemen, wherever that you be,
O, never pull their wages down to break their
      unity;
You see they hold like brothers, like sailors on the
      sea,
To do their best endeavonrs* for their wives and   *sic, ie* endeavours
      family.

We've steam upon the ocean, we've steam upon the land,
And what can we do now at all without our colliermen?
They send their coal above the ground the country all round,
We know they work both night and day with danger under Ground.

She put her arms around him like violets round the vine,
You are the bonny collier lad that,s won this heart of mine
And since that you have won the day, and since you,ve won my
    heart
I' [l]l crown you in glory, and for ever take your part.

Come, all you pretty fair maids, wherever that you be,
Never despise a collier lad in any one degree;
For if that you do use them well, they'll do the same to thee;
There's no one in this world but a bonny pit lad for me.

Print. Glasgow University Library MU23 – y.1. No.15.   Broadside.
Woodcut. No colophon. See also Lloyd, *Come all ye bold miners*, (1978), p. 99.
    Lloyd, *Come all ye bold miners*, (1978), p. 345, dates this piece from the
1840s, but it may well have been published early in April 1832, since it refers
to a previous victorious strike, a threat to lower wages and the very day on
which the annual binding normally took place.

27. A NEW SONG.

In eighteen hundred and thirty two,
    Our leaders a meeting fix'd,
On the Black Fell where they spoke well,
    Aud* place and order for us fix'd,   *sic, ie* And
With love and peace they spoke like men,
    Saying to your cause stand true,
And trust to God 'tis only he,
    Your enemies can subdue,

Beware of black legs*, brethren all,
   They're a deceiving, treacherous crew,
Stand to your Union one and all,
   You'll ne'er have cause to rue,

*strike-breakers, recognisable by
coal-dust on their legs*

They strove to break our union,
   But that they cannot do,
With all the treachery they have used,
   They cannot us subdue,
We support the aged, sick and lame,
   And those out of employ,
So men be staunch, from your cause ne'er flinch,
   Our union they can't destroy,
     Beware, &c,

Ye pitmen all from Wear and Tyne,
   Mind well what ye do,
And walk in peace, let your love increase,
   Providence will bring you through,
Altho' you have been shamefully used,
   Deceivers will get their due,
So with patience wait, you'll see the fall,
   Of that backsliding crew,
     Beware, &c,

Pitmen in peace your trials stand,
   Think on that great command,
You know black-legs, blacksliders too,
   Are despised by God and man,
All honest men does their company shun,
   They're despised where'er their* known
If our owners they should find them out,
   Their time here will not be long,
     Beware &c,

sic, ie they're

Why should our union be despised,
   When in heaven there is one,
To support the aged, siek* and lame,   *sic, ie sick*
   I'm sure it injures none,
If our owners they were told all right,
   How things were carried on,
They would not despise our union,
   But send all black-legs home,
      Beware, &c,

Admiral Dee, and his black crew,
   On board the ship, Bad Fame,
Was sent to sink that gallant ship,
   The Union was her name,
But the admirall nor his black crew,
   The ship could not bring too,
The good ship union she is manned,
   With a gallant upright crew,
      Beware, &c,

Now brethren all we will conclude,
   As we mean harm to none,
But may our wrongs be brought to light,
   And clearly to all men shown,
Its our last agreement that we want,
   Why pull us down so soon,
'Tis the black-legs that's done all this,
   'Tis not our union,
      Beware, &c,

Print. Allan.   Broadside. Woodcut. Colophon: Stephenson, Printer, Gatesh[ead].
   Fynes, *The Miners*, p. 27, notes there was a mass meeting of union members at the Black Fell on April 14th 1832, so this broadside may have been prepared for that event.

28. A COPY OF VERSES. Written on the Pitmen being turned out from their Houses and Homes, by Special Constables & Soldiers, according to the Order of the Coal Owners.

Each feeling heart I pray attend,
    While I with pain unfold.
These verses which I hear* have penn'd,   *sic, ie* here
    As true as e'er were told.

'Tis of the pitmen, brave and kind –
    How they have been abused –
To bear the owners' tyranny
    They manfully refused.

The owners they've lead miners got,
    And put them in their place;
Depriving pitmen of their bread –
    Oh! horrible disgrace!

But their* is still a power above   *sic, ie* there
    Who knows each pitman's wrong,
And will restore them to their rights,
    And that e'er it be long.

May heav'n protect them and their wives
    Th[e]ir friends and children too;
And may they ne'er come to distress,
    But soon receive their due.

The lead miners they've proved false,
    All villains void of grace;
But hope that e'er it be long
    They all must quit this place.

At Coxlodge and Kenton too,
    They turn'd them to the door;
The soldiery they brought likewise,
    To assist the civil power.

A piteous sight it was to see
　　Their goods toss'd to and fro;
To those, that stood looking on,
　　It fill'd their hearts with woe.

Among them they'll no Judas find,
　　And each hath play'd his card;
For none will expose his comrade
　　For any bright reward.

When times are with the pitmen hard,
　　Mechanics feel the pain,
For on the coal depends the die
　　Where all do lose or gain.

The ship that ploughs the raging main,
　　Depends on their supply;
Both rich and poor without their help,
　　Would make a mournful cry.

To Thee, O God! they all submit
　　Their wives and children dear,
And hope thou will, e'er it's too late,
　　Protract* their foes' career.　　　　　　　*sic, ie* Protect [them from]?

Success attend the pitmen all,
　　Whose hearts and hands combine;
And may they long enjoy their rights,
　　Both on the Wear and Tyne.

The collier lads may God defend,
　　Long life and peace be given,
And when their life on earth doth end,
　　Receive a crown in Heaven.

Print. Allan.　　Broadside. Colophon: Printed for the Author by Douglas and Kent, Drury Lane, Newcastle. See also Bell 11/414.

June 1832. The lead miners referred to were used to satirise Thomas Beaumont in *The Lord of the Allendale Miners* (B/W13), published about this time by Hernaman & Perring at the Journal Office, Newcastle. For John

Hernaman, his short-term partnership with Perring between 1832 and 1833 and his publication of a 'Constitutional and Conservative' newspaper from March 1832, see Hunt, *The Book Trade*, pp. 48–49, 72.

29. THE PITMEN'S UNION.

To our camplaints* give ear,   **B&C:** complaints
   While we our case relate;
To you it must appear,
   That our distress is great.
To our petitions now attend,
And shew* that you're the Pitmen's friend.   **B&C:** show

In Union we* are join'd,   **B&C:** we're, *sic*
   Up fo[r]* our rights to stand;   **B&C:** for
Our masters are combin'd,
   To use the Tyrant's hand;
They long to see our Union end,
Which shews* they're not the Pitmen's friend.   **B&C:** shows

Our Union gives offence,
   If they it's* end could see,   **B&C:** its
All men of common sense,
   Know what our state would be.
Help us our Union to defend,
And shew* yourselves the Pitmen's friend.   **B&C:** show

You all must understand,
   That we indeed are poor;
Many, by wicked hands,
   Are turned to the door.
Who, who, the helpless will defend,
And shew* themselves the Pitmen's friend?   **B&C:** show

Long, long, may Hepburn* live;

Long may our Union last;

May God our souls receive,

When all our toils are past.

O, may we all to Heaven ascend,

And reign with Christ, the Pitmen's friend!

A: *deleted: manuscript addition:*
Mr Roberts ; **B&C:** Mr. Roberts

Print. **A** : Wigan 118 (verso). **B:** Bell 12/258. **C:** Wigan 118.   **A:** Broadside. Decorative border. No colophon. **B:** Broadside proof? No colophon [Dodds]. **C:** Broadside. Decorative border. No colophon [Dodds]. Lloyd, *Come all ye bold miners*, (1978), pp. 260, 358, gave his source as a broadside in 'Newcastle-upon-Tyne Public Reference Library', which cannot now be traced. C & R, *The Miners' Association*, pp. 109–10, and Challinor, *A Radical Lawyer*, p. 107, imply that there were two copies of this text at Wigan, but only one copy can now be traced.

Probably from early June 1832. Lloyd, *Come all ye bold miners*, (1978), p. 358, remarked that 'The pious tone of the final verse need not surprise; more surprising is that such a tone is not commoner in the strike songs' of 1844, though his own selections from the 1844 songs and verse ignored many militantly pious texts.

30. LAMENTATION OF WILLIAM JOBLING Who was executed at Durham, August 3rd, 1832 for the Murder of Mr. Fairless at Jarrow.

Good people all I pray draw near and listen unto me,

Of Jobling's lamentation and sad calamity:

He was charged with murder as I do understand,

His trial o'er and sentence pas'd and Jobling he is hang'd.

Oh hark it is the passing bell that breaks the gloom profound

It seams to toll my funeral knell, how awful is the sound

A few short hours he had to stand, expos'd to shame and scorn,

How sad and luckless was the day when Jobling he was born.

He was brought up at Jarrow near unto South Shields Town,

His parents rear'd him tenderly till he was a man grown,

A pitman then they made him to work an honest way,

Until one sad disasterous and unlucky day.

'Twas on a Monday Afternoon as I for truth was told,
When this murder was committed but not for sake of gold,
It was upon the eleventh of June, the truth it is well known,
When this deed was done my misery for to crown.

When his trial it had come on, he at the bar did stand,
Like Moses he stood waiting for the holy lord's command.
The Judge when passing sentence then made him this reply
You assisted in the murder so prepare yourself to die.

You must prepare yourself to die upon a gallows tree,
When hung the usual time then taken down must be,
Then hung up in chains near to the Jarrow slake,
And your sinful soul may our Lord and Saviour take.

A pain now rends my heart, such as no tongue can tell,
Prest with grief, prest with woe, all in this dreary cell,
And oh my wife and bairns how they will soon deplore
To see me hung in chains before my own house door.

So all young men take warning by my sad destiny,
For oh it is an awful thing to die upon a tree,
Avoid the drunkards path and shun bad company,
And happiness to all to all eternity.

Print.   NCL Bell Tyne Collection (L942.8 T987B) 3/180. Broadside.
Woodcut. No colophon. (Its woodcut is similar to that used by Stephenson on
24).
    Probably published on or before August 3rd 1832.

31. A NEW SONG.

Come all you canny pitmen here come listen to my song,
Of these few verses I have pen'd you will not think them long,
Stick fast to your integrity be sure and do not fail,
And we will make the coal trade flourish, my lads it shall go bail.

CHORUS.

Come let us all be cautious, and mind well what we do,
And not forget the rights we got in the year thirty two.

We in the year of thirty two all for our rights did stand,
To be true to each other we agreed to a man,
We did agree like Britons bold our rights to maintain,
We were true unto each other until the victory we did gain.

When we think of the days of old about twenty years ago,
When plenty flowed among us, how it fills our hear[t] with woe,
Eleven days a fortnight we did all get good employ,
But now we're glad of eight its little we can enjoy.

Our masters in the days of old upon both Wear and Tyne,
They gave us good encouragement both money and drink to bind
Let men and masters all agree as they have done before,
And then our trade shall rise again upon our native shore.

So all you canny pitmen lads be all of one mind,
And then our trade will quickly rise upon both Wear and Tyne
And we will get our rights again and all be in full glee,
And then we'll make the houses ring and spend our money free.

Consider all the hardships now our pitmen have come thro',
How sadly we have been pulled down in the year of thirty two,
But cheer up your hearts my pitmen lads, I hope you now will smile,
And we'll forget the weary time we've all had this long while.

We hope this year of thirty-six will put it to an end,
And free us of our hardships, and our trade will quickly mend,
Let men and masters all agree with harmony to combine,
And then we shall rejoice and sing upon both Wear & Tyne.

Now to conclude these lines we will say little more,
And wish our trade would rise again as it has done before,
And men and masters would agree before that it be long,
For the lord above now he does know that we're not in the wrong.

Print. CULM 16/777.   Double broadside. Woodcut. Colophon: George
Walker, Jun., Printer, Durham. [148]. Printed next to *The Wind Blew the Bonny
Lassie's Plaidy awa*. Re-titled by Lloyd, *Come all ye bold miners*, (1978),
pp. 238–39, 356, as *Come All You Canny Pitmen*, and published with other
minor alterations.
       1836. George Walker Junior took over his father's Sadler Street shop before
1835. He advertised 'a choice collection of Songs, Ballads, &c, &c,' until 1846,
but later concentrated on periodical publication (Hunt, *The Book Trade*,
pp. 92–93).

32. A NEW SONG, CALLED, THE HASSWELL BINDING. By a Coal-Hewer.

My hearty cocks come join with me,
And fill your glass with mirth and glee,
I hope we all content will be,
Masters and men at Haswell O.
Eighteen hundred and thirty six,
It took four men to sharp our picks,
And now two men can do our tricks
In the smith's shop at Haswell O.

The bottom seam you may suppose,
Was taken out by sturdy blows,
Caus'd many a man to blow his nose,
And cough and sneeze at Haswell O.
We beg'd the master to let it stay,
He knew that it was very gray,
And hurt the trade when sent away
With the good coals at Haswell O.

Before the Furnace we got lit,
We had many a sorry set,
And many a poor man's nose was wet,
Both night and day at Haswell O.
But since the Furnace we got on,
The atmospheric air is blown
Around the mine, would starve a stone
In the Hutton seam at Haswell O.

Then Mr Foster was so kind,
He said that if we were inclin'd
To take great pains then we should find,
He would ease our fines at Haswell O.
And from that time as he did say,
The shilling corves were done away,
And sixpence is the fine we pay,
For laid-out corves at Haswell O.

There was one rogue among the rest,
That sore upon the poor men prest,
The separation I protest
Disturbance made at Haswell O.
We wish'd he might be sent away,
Then Mr Forster he did say:
My lads he shall no longer stay
To make mischief at Haswell O.

So now transported he's to be,
But where to I care not a flea,
Some say he is going to Thornley,
But no more work at Haswell O.
He should be sent out of this land,
Along with many a better man
To Botany or Van Dieman's Land,
And come no more to Haswell O.

I hope amendment we have made,
And likewise better for our trade,
The putters they will be well paid
The price is raised at Haswell O.
The drivers they are not behind,
Their wage is rais'd, and that they'll find,
And shift work its come in my mind,
Was not forgot at Haswell O.

Now to Mr Forster and Mr Wails,
And John and Robert without fail,
May sorrow never them assail,
Man, wife, or child at Haswell O.
And Mr Hunter he is the Clerk
That pays the cash both light and dark,
And I dare say oft hits the mark,
To keep things right at Haswell O.

Now to conclude and make an end,
I hope these lines will none offend,
Still trusting that the times will mend
Both elsewhere and at Haswell O.
God speed them well that go away,
Success to those that are to stay,
May Mr Foster many a day
Our leader be at Haswell O.

Print. CULM 16/721.   Broadside. Colophon: Walker, Printer, Durham.
[159].
    The text mentions 1836 in the past tense, and is one of the last items on
Walker's *List of Songs* of c.1837. Mr Foster could be the person at Shotton
Moor Colliery mentioned in **49**.

33. THE PITMEN'S UNION

Ye pitmen who dwell near the Wear and the Tyne,
With heart and with hand together combine,
For our masters' oppression* doth grieve us full sore   *long 's' here and elsewhere*
So now we will all join in Union once more.

                    CHORUS.
    Huzza for the Union! stand to your Union –
    You pitmen all round the Wear and the Tyne.

The masters have join'd hand in hand, as we hear,
To pull down the Union, they vow and declare;
They say that our Unions will very soon
Rob them of their rights, so they'll have them down.

The masters are plotting their roguery to hide,
They want king and parliament both on their side;
But our tight little Union will smile at the fun,
For what they're intending will never be done.

Now let us stand firm as the king to his crown,
No underhand dealings will e'er pull us down;
For we are all join'd by the Powers above,
With true reformation and brotherly love.

Our hands are all join'd, and our hearts are the same,
And our tongues shall repeat the brave Union's fame;
For the sake of our country we ne'er would rebel.
We have suffer'd like martyrs, you all know it well

Now the Union for ever, my boys! – do not fret,
Be true to each other – we ne'er will be beat;
The Union's our laurel, and take it who may,
Before we resign, we will show them some play.

Tho' our masters the Union did pull down before,
When Grovers* they brought from the country all o'er;   lead miners, *ie* in 1832
But numbers of them did not long here remain,
So be not afraid, boys, they'll ne'er come again.

So now to conclude and finish my song,
Join like wedlock together, to keep yourselves strong;
Altho' in oppression our masters delight,
The Union, my lads, will soon put us all right.

Print. CULM 16/287.   Double broadside. Woodcut. Fordyce, Printer, 48,
Dean Street, Newcastle. [No.132]. Printed alongside *Remember the Poor*.
    Possibly c.1837, the latest date at which Hunt, *The Book Trade*, p. 36, can
trace Fordyce at this address.

34. A NEW SONG IN PRAISE OF WILLINGTON COLLIERY.

It was on the seventeenth day of March,
   Eighteen hundred and thirty-eight,
When the Willington lads to bind came in,
   With friendship and delight;
And when their masters met them there –
   Now, my brave lads, they cried,
We trust we'll bind you on such terms
   As will make you satisfied.

           CHORUS.
  We've got more than we did expect –
    This was the general cry;
  When they heard the name of Johnson,
    Their hearts were fill'd with joy.

You owners of each colliery
   Upon the Wear and Tyne,
A pattern take by Willington,
   And peace you'll constant find;
And when you meet your men to bind –
   Mind what I say to you –
Like our masters here, do what is fair –
   You'll have no cause to rue.
     Like the Willington lads they will stand true,
       If fair proffers you them give;
     Try that for once – you'll never rue
       As long as you do live.

Brave Johnson has a pattern shewn
   To all on Wear and Tyne,
We hope all owners hearing this,
   Will to the same incline;
So you merry lads of Willington,
   In chorus let us sing

In praise of all your masters,
   And Johnson, your good friend.
      May such coal-owners ever thrive.
        Seven-fold may they receive,
        And may their offspring happy be
        As long as they do live.

Now to conclude and make an end,
   There's none can think it wrong
To sing the praise of Johnson,
   The main subject of my song:
Ye colliers brave, with glass in hand,
   I'll tell you what I mean –
Drink a good health to Johnson,
   Also our gracious Queen.
      Huzza! for Willington Colliery –
        For Willington Colliery, huzza!
      And let the praise of Johnson,
        Be sounded every way.

Print. CULM 16/178.   Broadside. No colophon [W. & T. Fordyce]. [No.51.].
See also CULM 16/179, and, with *Dandy Wife*, No.51 in the Fordyce *Catalogue
of 4to. Slip Songs* of c.1841.
   March 17th 1838 is mentioned in the past tense. Since most pit-workers
were bound on or before April 5th this piece must have been produced before
that date to make any sense as propaganda.

35. THE COLLIER SWELL.*   B: THE PITMAN TURNED SWELL.

I used to be a vulgar clown, with cash and money
     short in,
Till my old uncle died in town, and left me all his
     fortune;
A collier* I was by* trade, I have* chang'd as you   B: pitman; to my; but; see
     may tell* sir,
And since a richer purse I've made, I'd* be a   B: ⟨?I'll⟩
     regular swell sir.

CHORUS.*   B: *two lines not four*
  But I'm so plagued with vulgar folks,
  Since ⌊I have cash for sporting,⌋   B: I've got cash to sport, sir
  Why ca'nt* a Collier* cut a swell,   B: can't; pitman
  ⌊When he has got⌋ a fortune.   B: since he's been left

I used to go with low-bred* chaps, &* talk to every   B: low bred; *omitted; ie* oddball
    gew-gaw,*
Get drunk in Tom & Jerry* shops and went a   B: tom-and-jerry; *ie* kicking; B:
    purring* foot ball;*   football
But now with all † fops in town, I sport my boot*   B: the; boots
    and tanners,
And I'm going up to London town to learn some
    genteel manners.
       †   B: But I'm so plagued, etc.,
                                            after every verse

And when I've been to London town I mean to go
    to France sir
To practice two or three times a week to learn to
    hop &* dance sir;   B: and
Besides I've got a quizzing-glass* to see* things far B: qui⟨ss⟩ing-glass; view
    and near O,
But the other day it caused me to fall over a
    wheel-barrow.

O* my family is a vulgar set, ⌊tho' they have⌋   B: *omitted*; though they've got
    clothes in fashion,
They put them on the ⌊wrong side⌋ out, which   B: inside
    puts me in a passion;
The lads when e'er* they go to church, ⌊tho'   B: whene'er; though they've
    we've⌋ got lots of riches,
They all go in their clogs, smock frock* and   B: frocks; working
    leather* breeches.

My wife she is the worst of all when we give
   genteel dinners,
She uses neither knife nor fork but pops in all her
   fingers;
And when they hand the wine about, she tells the
   gents it stinks †   B: ,sir,
Gets full her mouth, &* squirts it out, &* calls for   B: and; and; drink, sir
   treacle ⌊drinks.⌋
If I give a dinner to my Lord, and bid her make a
   good un,*   B: one
Perhaps she'll make some pea soup, or else a great
   black pudding;
And when the tea it is brought in, the tray she
   always flings sir,
Stirs up the sugar with her fist, &* then she licks   B: and
   her fingers.

My lord once ask'd us out to dine &* there we had   B: and
   a rum start,
Instead of her new carriage fine, she would ride in
   the dung cart;
And when he sent his horse to her, and wanted
   her to ride sir,
And* what do you think of the ignorant* jade, she   B: Pray; impudent; astride
   would get on a-stride* sir.

Print. **A**: NUL Loose. **B**: Wigan 112.   **A**: Double broadside. Two woodcuts.
Decorative border. Colophon: Walker, Printer, Durham. [28]. Published with
Anne Laurie. See also Goldstein. **B**: Broadside proof. No colophon [Dodds].
   Walker's *List of Songs* of c.1837 has a different pair of titles at this number,
so this piece may date from 1838 or 1839. Series numbers were regularly re-
used for fresh material once older texts had become unsaleable. The Wigan
proof is very rough. See also Colls, *The Collier's Rant*, pp. 102–3.

36. HASWELL CAGES.

Tune. – *The Wedding of Ballyporeen.*

Come all you good people and listen a while,
I will sing you a song that will cause you to smile,
It is about Haswell I mean for to sing,
Concerning the new plan we started last spring.
    And the very first thing I will mention,
    Without any evil intention,
    It is concerning this new invention,
        Of winding up coals in a cage.

It was in eighteen hundred and thirty eight,
We began to prepare to make the shaft right,
We put in the conductors from bottom to top,
The materials were ready prepar'd at the shop,
    From the top of the pit to the bottom,
    One hundred and fifty six fathom,
    And the distance you do think it nothing,
        You ride so quickly in the cage.

Now considering the depth its surprising to say,
The quantity of work we can draw in a day,
Five hundred and thirty tons of the best coal,
In the space of twelve hours we can win up this hole,
    About forty five tons in an hour,
    And viewers, overmen, and hewers,
    Our engines must have a great power,
        To run at such speed with the cage.

Then as soon as the tubs do come to the day,
To the weighing machine they are taken away
Where two men are appointed there to attend,
To see justice done between master and men.
    And when they leave the weighing machine, sir,
    Straightway they do go to the screen, sir,
    And the keeker* does see that they're clean, sir,   overlooker
        All the coals that come up in the cage.

I have wrought with the corves, I have wrought with the tubs,
I have wrought where the baskets came up by the lugs,
I have wrought by the dozen, I have wrought by the score,
But this curious contrivance, I never saw before.
   When we get in, they then pull the rapper,*   signal lever
   At the top it does make a great clatter,
   And the brakesman* they* know what's the   winding-engine man; *sic*
      matter,
     And bring us away in a cage.

And when the bell rings and the top we approach,
It oft puts me in mind of a new railway coach,
The number of passengers I cannot tell,
But she brings a great many I know very well.
   But I wish they may not overload her,
   And do some mischief on the road, sir,
   Too much charge makes a cannon explode, sir,
     And so will too much in the cage.

Now the young men and maids do sometimes take a trip
Out to sea in fine weather, on board a steam ship,
But if any be curious enough to engage,
For a trip down below, and a ride in our cage,
   It would be a fine recreation,
   For to go down and view the low station,
   I wish they may meet no temptation,
     When they take a trip in our cage.

---

36. Print. NUL Loose.   Double broadside. Woodcut. Decorative border.
Colophon: Walker, Printer, Durham. [31]. Published alongside *The Exiles Return*. See also Goldstein. Mediated by Lloyd in *Folk Song*, pp. 350–52, and *Come all ye bold miners*, (1978), pp. 45–47.
    The text refers to 1838 as 'last spring', so 1839 seems most likely, though 1838 remains a possibility. 'Tub guides and cages were introduced by T.Y. Hall in 1838 to replace haulage of men and coal in baskets' (Moyes, *The Banner Book*, pp. 17–18). Dated c.1839 and c.1840 by Lloyd in *Folk Song*, p. 352, and *Come all ye bold miners*, (1978), p. 342. Lloyd's assertion that this piece is redolent of 'mechanics' halls' seems misplaced: the tone, language and content of the piece seem both urban and petit-bourgeois. According to John Powell of Twizell, in the summer of 1849, 'as I passed over the old Tyne Bridge

I heard a man singing with all his might and selling copies of the *Haswell Cages'*, but who his audience may have been is unclear. Lloyd also believed that George Walker set up shop in 1839, but Hunt, *The Book Trade*, pp. 92–93, dates his activity from 1834 or 1835 at the latest. In his *List of Songs* of c.1837, Walker has a different title at this number.

The Tyne Exile's Return was written in 1824 by Joseph Philip Robson, when he was 19. This was published in the first number of John Ross' series of chapbooks, *The Songs of the Tyne*, as *The Exile's Return* (Robson, *Autobiography*, p. 4; Robson, *Bards of the Tyne*, pp. 381–82; Allan, *Tyneside Songs*, pp. 348–49) and on a broadside (B/W13). Robson was an orphan, but his father had been educated for the Catholic priesthood at Stoneyhurst College, before his failing health forced him to run a paint shop. Joseph was apprenticed to a plane-maker, but an accident unfitted him for manual labour and in 1830 he began working as a teacher in a Catholic School and publishing his poetry, including a volume printed by William Douglas in 1839 (Robson, *Autobiography*, pp. 3, 4, 6; Allan, *Tyneside Songs*, pp. 345–48; Harker (1972), xiv–xvi). Robson also wrote **60, 64, 66, 68** and **84**, and, probably, **65** and **99**.

37. O'CONNER'S VISIT TO NEWCASTLE.

You Chartists all both far and near
    That dwell around the Tyne and Wear,
Straight to Newcastle all repair,
    To welcome brave O'Conner,
For O'Conner is our country's pride,
    And by the poor man will abide,
The Charter he will gain besides,
    If you but prove true to him.
            CHORUS.
    So join the brave O'Conner,
        Your rights for to maintain,
    If you stand true unto him,
        The Charter he will gain.

Chartists, prepare to meet him,
    To Newcastle he is bound,
And give to him that hearty welcome
    That will make the air resound.
Then show both Whigs and Tories,
    That Chartism is not dead,
But through the brave O'Conner,
    Still will raise its mighty head.
        So join the brave, &c.

This God-like cause in England,
    He has spread far and wide,
The poor man's rights he has maintained,
    That long had been denied.
And may he go on conquering,
    This good cause to proclaim,
Till one and all do shout aloud,
    The victory we have gained.
        So join the brave, &c.

To London, Birmingham, and Leeds,
    This cause he has pursued,
And not forgetting Newcastle,
    The tyrants to subdue.
The poor men they will meet him,
    It will be a glorious sight,
Playing welcome conquering patriot
    Thy deeds are shining bright.
        So join the brave, &c.

There is Foreman's Row and Cramlington,
    Seghill, North Shields, and South,
And all the poor men of the North
    Who wish to hear the truth,
Unto Newcastle will repair,
    With flags of green and white,
Playing long life unto O'Conner brave,
    The defender of our rights.
        So join the brave, &c.

Britannia's sons what would you give
   To set your country free,
On the eighth day of November,
   Let both Whigs and Tories see
That by supporting bold O'Conner,
   The friend of the oppress'd,
That Britains will their Charter gain
   And with peace will soon be blest.
     So join the brave, &c.

Print. NUL Loose.   Broadside. Decorative border. No imprint [Dodds?].
   Probably from 1841. See also *Huzza for the Charter*, by 'A Chartist',
published in South Shields on June 24th 1841 (B/W2). For Thomas and Henry
Dodds, see Hunt, *The Book Trade*, p. 31, and above, p. 18ff.

38. STATE OF THE TIMES.

Come all you working people what shall we do now;
The world is fill'd with poverty with hunger it is bound;
The Farmers all declare the rents they must come down.

CHORUS.
Let you all say what you will and do the best you can,
Poor man and horse must work for all, to keep the
       like of them.

The German beggars are come o'er to travel the
       country round,
With tambarines* and organs go roaring up and   *sic*
       down,
They carry the brooms all in their hands, their
       clothes above their knees,
They tie their napkin round their heads the
       country to deceive.

We see the jolly farmers go whistling to the plough,
They plough and sow, they reap and mow, they   *sic, ie* cultivate
     cnltivate* the ground,
They plough and sow, they reap and mow, no one
     can on them frown
For nothing we can do at all without the useful plough.

We have steam upon the ocean, we have steam
     upon the land,
But what should we do now at all without the
     collier men;
They send the coals above the ground the country
     all round.
We know they work both night and day with
     danger underground.

You soldiers and you sailors who plough the
     raging main,
You fight for Queen and country your rights for to
     maintain;
But when that you have done your best, poor man
     can do no more,
They'll quickly turn you on the shore to beg from
     door to door.

Come all young men and maidens a warning take
     by me,
And never to the ale-house go, but shun such
     company;
The landlord will fiddle and sing, and he['ll] chalk
     down a score,
And when your money it is all gone, they'll turn
     you to the door.

Print. CULM 16/24.   Triple broadside. Decorative spacers. Colophon:
T. Dodds, Printer, 43, Head of the Side, Newcastle. No.9. Published above *Man
Little Thinks* and *Toasts*.
     Probably from 1841 or perhaps 1842.

39. NEWCASTLE & LONDON BOAT MATCH, FOR £100 ASIDE. On Saturday, July 16. Tune – 'The Campbell's are Comin'.'

Let canny Newcastle once more raise her head,
From the sod where she's long moan'd as tho' she were dead;
Let the sons of the Tyne once again bear the sway,
And though poverty reigns, gain the boat race to day.
For the pride of our navy, Northumberland's sons
Have long mann'd our yards and directed our guns,
May the Keel row and Boatie-row still grace the river,
And canny Newcastle yet flourish for ever.

For ages long past have our seamen been famed,
And Newcastle's blue jackets aye foremost are named;
On the topmast of fame long has Collingwood stood,
The dread of our foes and the pride of the flood[.]
Then to day let the skill of the past be display'd,
Nor of England's first boat crew be ever afraid,
Invincible long, may St.Agnes' crew reign,
The boast of Newcastle, the pride of the main!
    For the pride of our navy, &c

Combes, Newell, and Parish, the pride of the Thames,
Have in many boat races exalted their names;
But the pride of the Tyne they contend with to day,
And Newcastle's bright flag may direct them the way[.]
May the oars of the Glaspers* be pull'd well together,   *sic, ie Claspers
May their strength never fail as they bend to the weather,
May the Agnes fly over the waves like a swallow.
And the Cockneys brave crew be completely beat hollow.
    For the pride of our navy, &c.

How proud seems each head as it bends o'er the waves,
Though our pitmen and seamen work harder than slaves;
How bright is each eye, and how light is each heart,
As the boats are preparing and manned for the start.
The signal is given, they glide o'er the stream.
Like the arrow's swift glance, or the lightning's gleam;
Tho' we wish them all well, may the Agnes display,
For the pride of Newcastle, a conquest to day.
    For the pride of Newcastle, &c

May our canny blue jackets, our pitmen and lasses,
Dance lightly to night and replenish their glasses;
May misfortune's foul wind leave Newcastle to day,
And prosperity's sun shed a happier ray.
May friendship and harmony reign in each heart,
And the Cockneys confess when for London they start,
That the sons of Newcastle, tho' homely and plain,
Are the pride of the lasses, the stars of the main.
    For the pride of Newcastle, &c

Print. NUL Loose.   Broadside. Colophon: T. Dodds, Printer, Head of the Side No.25.
    A manuscript note gives '1842', and the text refers to a race on 'Saturday, July 16th'.

40. THE BONNIE PIT LADS.

As I walked forth one summer's* morn, all in the   B: summers
    month of June
The flowers they were springing and the birds
    were in full tune:
I overheard a lovely maid and this was all her
    theme,
Success attend the Pit Lads, for they are lads of
    fame.

I stepped up to her and bending on my knee,
I asked her pardon for making with her so free;
Your pardon is granted young Pit Lad, she replies,
Pray do you belong to the brave Union boys?

You may see I'm a pitman all* black as a sloe,   B: as
And all the night long I am working down below;
O, I do love a pitman as I do love my life,
My father was a pitman all the days of his life.

Come now my young pitman and rest here awhile,
And when I have* done milking I'll give you a smile,   B: am
He kissed her sweet lips while milking her cow,
And the lambs they were sporting all in the
          morning dew.

Come all you noble gentlemen wherever that you be,
Do not pull down their wages nor break their unity;
You see they hold like brothers, like sailors on the sea,
They do their best endeavours for their wives* and   C:wifes
          family.

Then she clapt her arms around him like Venus
          round the vine –
You are a* jolly pit lad, you've won this heart of   B&C: my
          mine;
And if that you do win the day as you have won
          my heart,
I'll crown you with honour and for ever take your
          part.

The Pit Lads are the best of boys, their work lies
          under ground.
And when they to the alehouse* go they value not   B&C: Ale-house
          a crown;
They spend their money freely, and pay before
          they go,
They work under ground while the stormy winds
          do blow.

So come all you pretty maidens wherever you may
          be,
A pit lad do not despise in any degree;
For* if that you do use them well they'll do the   B: Fer, *sic*
          same to thee
There is none in this world like a pit boy* for me.   B&C: pit-boy

Print. **A**: NUL Loose. **B**: Wigan 113 verso. See aso Bell 12/426. **C**: Wigan 112 (298). **A**: Broadside. Woodcut. Colophon: Hollis and Hodge, Printers, 136 High-street, Sunderland. **B**: Broadside. Illustration. Decorative border. Decorative emblems. Colophon: T. Dodds, Printer, Side, Newcastle. No.25. **C**: Broadside. Decorative border. Decorative emblems. Colophon: T. Dodds, Printer, No.77, Side, Newcastle. Lloyd, *Come all ye bold miners*, (1978), pp. 100–1, 345, gives a similar text – except that the 'Pit Lads' are 'colliers' and he uses the title, *Brave Collier Lads* – as 'From a broadside, n.d. published by W. and T. Fordyce, Newcastle-upon-Tyne'. No such broadside has been traced, though the Fordyce *Catalogue* does mention a piece with the title *Collier Lads* at No 144 – see CULM 16/306. Raven, *Folk-lore and Songs*, Volume 3, p. 16, gives as 'traditional' a remarkably similar set of words, entitled *The Brave Collier Lads*. See also C & R, *The Miners' Association*, p. 52.

A was probably first published in 1842 or early 1843. William Hollis worked at 136 High Street Sunderland at least between 1844 and 1850. Thomas Hodge operated at 37 and later 206 High Street from 1819 to 1850, but John Barlow Hodge also worked as a printer in Sunderland between 1841 and 1850, and he seems to have been active in Silver Street between 1841 and 1842 (Hunt, *The Book Trade*, pp. 49, 51). Dodds' No.25 text, **B**, was probably published soon after **A**, but **C** may not have been appeared until 1843 or even 1844.

41. THE WEAVER'S LAMENTATION.

O listen to our mournful tale.
   Of poverty and grief;
Let charity stretch forth her hand,
   And yield us from relief.

Our case is such as do request,
   Some favour from your hands,
Till we again with trade are blest,
   In once our happy land.

Our trade is now so very bad.
   That we have nought to do,
Our hearts would now be very glad,
   If you would help us through.

Our families in distress do live,
   Which pains our hearts to see,
We fain would now your mite receive
   Whilst in our poverty.

A mite from you though e're so small,
   Would greatly us befriend,
We hope you will no poorer be,
   But richer at the end.

We thank the Lord who reigns above
   For friends so good and kind,
Protect them with thy heavenly love
   Both us and all mankind

And when we reach that heavenly place,
   We sound thy praises high,
And live before thy gracious face,
   With saints above the sky.

Then shall we bathe our weary soul,
   In ease of heavenly rest,
And not a wave of trouble rowl.
   Across my peaceful breast.

Print. CULM 16/35.   Broadside. Woodcut. Decorative border. Colophon:
T. Dodds, Printer, 43, Head of the Side, Newcastle. No.37.
   Probably from 1842 or 1843.

42. THE POOR TRADESMEN'S LAMENTATION.

Neighbours, countrymen, and friends,
   Attend unto our cry,
For still our trade is very bad,
   Our wants do multiply.

Our case is such, we do request
  Some favour from your hand,
Till we again with trade are blest
  In our once happy land.

Sure Britons ne'er refuse to work,
  And yet how hard we fare
No Heathen, Savage, Jew, nor Turk
  Such hardships hath to bear.

A mite from you, though e'er so small,
  Will greatly us befriend;
We hope you will no poorer be,
  But richer in the end.

The man that doth the poor assist,
  And always them relieve,
On earth shall spend his days in peace,
  In glory after life.

The vineyard of our precious Lord
  Before his labourers lies;
And lo! we see a vast reward
  Await them in the skies.

May God the widow's ways protect,
  Ane* help the fatherless,   *sic, ie And*
With those who share the world's neglect,
  And languish in distress.

Give to our country commerce,
  Again our trade renew,
Let those rejoice who have got work,
  For we've got none to do.

Print. Wigan 110 (300).   Broadside. Decorative border. No colophon [Dodds].
    Probably also from 1842 or 1843, given its apparent borrowings from **41**.

43. THE CRIES OF THE POOR.

All you distress'd tradesmen in country and town,
Give ear to these few lines that I have penn'd down;
The state of the nation to you I will show,
And the hardships that thousands they do undergo.

My nerves they grow weak and my mind is confus'd,
When I think on the way British subjects are used;
Our Rulers and Statesmen lie snug and secure,
But they shut their ears to the cries of the poor.

They eat and they drink and they wear of the best,
The cares of this life don't disturb them of rest;
They are not afraid when they're sporting up by,
Their children at home they with hunger will cry.

They bind heavy burdens each year on the poor,
And oftentimes more than we're fit to endure;
They keep Rural Police to guard the highways,
To protect their properties and vagrants to seize,

If you are cruel to your beast you'll be fined
But the worst of cruelties they shew to mankind;
For seeking their rights, some the billows has cross'd.
At least it was so with Jones, Williams, and Frost.

There's some have not seen it, but then you have heard
What did befall Wilson, brave Hardie and Baird;
And forty-five more that were banished away,
As exiles for life unto Botany Bay.

Now trade every day it is on the decline.
Some mills they are idle and some on half time;
Two large mills in Glasgow by fire were destroy'd,
Which does cause some hundreds to go unemployed.

The bonny mill lasses to their work they do go,
In the winter season thro' cold, frost, and snow,
From six in the morning till half-past eight at night,
Some do work for fivepence a day, it surely is not right.

In Camlachie, Parknead,* Calton and Bridgton,   *sic, ie* Parkhead
The weavers and their families are greatly kept down;
Their wages are low and their porridge but thin,
They're working life out here to keep the life in.

In Paisley the people for bread they do cry
There eleven thousands are out of employ,
It is by subscriptions they daily are fed,
Their whole cry is now – give us trade and cheap bread.

The Irish have got no employment at home.
And in search of work they are foreed* to roam;   *sic, ie* forced
It's forty years since they lost their parliament.
The wealth of their natton* abroad it is spent.   *sic, ie* nation

Their poor are distressed in every town,
It's by oppression they are greatly kept down;
You've heard of what tyrants at Rathcormack has done,
They've robb[e]d widow Ryan and murdered her son.

It's some alterations they'll soon have to make,
Or hunger I fear through stone walls it will break;
You feed your dogs well Oh ye great men up by,
While millions in Britain for bread they do cry.

We did live in hopes, but our hopes now are fled,
Begging's not allowed and charity is dead
Bread to the hungry and freedom to the slave,
It's all that we want, and it's all that we must have.

Print. CULM 16/37.   Broadside. Colophon: T. Dodds, Printer, No.43, Head
of the Side, Newcastle.
    Probably from 1842 or 1843.

44. THE STATE OF THE TIMES AND THEIR CAUSES.

Ye have eaten up the Vineyard; the spoil of the poor is in your
houses, what mean ye that ye beat my people to pieces and grind
the faces of the poor, saith the Lord God of Hosts. – IS[I]AH*, III –
14, and 15.

Come all you philanthropists attend a while to
    me,
The cause of those distressing times I will explain
    to thee;
Providence provides us bonutifully,* that you   *sic,ie* bountifully
    must all allow,
Then why is times so bad with us the reason tell
    me now.

The Farmers, Tradesmen, and the Labourers search
    all the nations through,
Are deeply complaining that such times they
    never knew;
But there's a certain class of men whose
    complaints we never hear,
Who wring from other classes 50 million pounds a
    year.

If the people were all starving no complaints from
    them we hear,
Excepting when they want another million
    pounds a year.
If it pleases the Lord to eause* a drought and   *sic, ie* cause
    famine for to come
We then might say these are bad times, but let thy
    will be done.

The want of true religion upon our native land
Is the cause of all bad times if you will but
    understand.
We all complain of bad times, with plenty in the
    land,
But very few of any class do act by God's command.

To do as you'd be done by is God's command to
    you,
But to find the one that acts that part, you'll find
    but very few.
The reason why dissenters dissented from the
    church
Is because for their religion they had to pay so
    much.

Some clerg[y]men went fox hunting and horse
    racing ever[y] day,
The people's money for religion they squandered
    away.
The Wesleyans, and Baptists, and Calvinists began
To preach amongst the people, they had a fairish
    run.

But some rose so much in riches it filled them up
    with pride,
Like those who they dissented from they on the
    poor wou'd ride.
The Wesleyans divided in all sectarian tribes,
Called themselves by different names, built
    chapels every side.

There was new connexion, ranters, & sleepy
    waranites,*   ?Warrenites
Aftersaints,* anti-baptists, and poor Jerusalamites,   ?Latter-Day Saints
There's many I've not mentioned yet, about
    another score
Who every day are preaching for a living from the
    poor.

The more chapels there is built, and the more they
    preach I'm sure,
With all their great exertions still sin increase[s]
    more.
The all say they are striving to go to Zion's hill,
But yet there's some seem more inclined their
    coffers for ro* fill.   [sic, ie to

And though they are providing in Heaven to appear,
They rather seem inclined to stop a little longer here.
Each one does think there's nothing done but what he
        does himself,
They are every day contriving to accumulate the pelf.

Competition, monopoly, spouting preaching all the go,
If a poor man's got no money he to lucifer may go.
A rich man's soul will be valued very little more
Than the meanest wretch upon the earth let him be e'er so poor.

Then why do rich men treat the poor with scorn, simple noddies,
And make so much distinction about their thinking bodies,
The Jews will not turn christians while in this country,
And the reason why they will not few christians they can see.

Of sectarian divisions there are so many now,
Which is the christian church of God the Jews can never know.
If christians we profess to be let's go to church alike,
Without distinction, one and all serve God with pure delight.

Let all mankind do unto man as they wish to be done to,
And whatever religion they profess they'll find this is most true.

Print. CULM 16/39.   Broadside. Three woodcuts. Colophon: T. Dodds,
Printer, 43, Head of the Side, Newcastle.
    Probably from 1842 or 1843, but not in Dodds' numbered series.

45. COPY OF VERSES ON THE CASTLE EDEN TRAGEDY On Friday,
February 3rd, 1843.

Ye Working men of Briton's Isle,
   Tradesmen and labourers all
Attend to this sad tale I tell,
   Concerning my downfall.
Within the cell of Durham goal,
   I now lamenting lie
For the murder of my wife,
   Expecting for to die.

It was in the town of Sunderland,
   I formerly did dwell,
Where I married Margaret Yarrow,
   The truth to you I'll tell:
But Margaret I did ill use,
   And from her went astray;
My marriage vow I soon did break,
   But now I rue the day.

I am a Pitman by my trade,
   Robert Pearson is my name;
At Castle Eden I did live,
   And led a life of shame.
My loving wife I did forsake,
   And in adultry
With Kate Wearmouth I did reside,
   Which proves my destiny.

Aloud for mercy she did cry,
   And on her knees did fall;
Requesting me to let her pray,
   And on her God to call.
I struck and wounded her full sore,
   Regardless of her cries
Upon the floor she lifeless fell,
   And never more to rise.

It was on the 3rd of February,
    Eighteen hundred and forty-three,
My wife to Castle Eden came
    Her husband for to see.
But wishing to remove her
    Entirely from my sight,
I form'd the resolution,
    To take away her life.

Then I was taken prisoner,
    To Durham sent with speed –
To appear at the assizes,
    For the dreadful bloody deed.
May God have mercy on my soul,
    O Lord look down on me,
When at the bar I do appear.
    To hear my destiny.

'Twas Satan who tempted me
    To do the wicked deed;
And when I think upon the same,
    It makes my heart to bleed.
For when my trial does come on,
    I at the bar must stand,
Like Job waiting with patience,
    To hear the laws command.

In dungeon dark and Irons bound,
    I bitterly do weep;
The midnight bell, and thought of death
    Deprive me of my sleep.
My murdered wife to me appears,
    Her wounds she does display;
No rest at all then can I get,
    She's with me night and day.

Young men with speed your lives amend,
  And shun all wicked ways,
Lest like me your lot should be
  In shame to end your days.
My old companions all I pray,
  Take warning by my fate,
Beware of passion's fatal sway
  Before it is too late.

Print. Wigan 9.   Broadside. Colophon: Hollis and Hodge, Printers, Sunderland.
    1843. Probably published to coincide with the execution of Robert Pearson. Verses 4 and 5 seem to have been transposed. A printed prose account (Wigan D/DZ A31/8) is dated February 3rd 1843.

46A. A NEW SONG COMPOSED AND WRITEN FOR THE MINERS PHILANTHROPIC SOCIETY OF ENGLAND SCOTLAND AND WALES.

Vrs 1.. Come Hither all Miners Kind, Honoust Social and free
        for Sacred this day is to You and to me
        Should Care Venture {hither} all wrinkled and Pale
    We'd Shew him a trick and Put him up for Sale
    Chorous.. Unanimous then let.s drink and let,s Sing
        To our Friendship our Freedom our Commerce and king

2..   United Philanthropy is the Science we boast
        of all other the unions our toast
        all love of mankind may from this be infered
        His Kindness* extended to fish beasts and birds   *long 's', here and
            Unanimous let.s, &c   elsewhere

3..   Whats welth or ambition, or titles or Power
        What are they but toys that may Please for an hour
        A Single good act. to a friend if distresst
        Will {make} them Seem Nothings, or trifles at best
           Unanimous let.s &c..

4..   All Party di[s]putes Shall be banished from hence
           As bane of good Humour as foes to good Sense
           True Sons of Philanthropy Never disagree
           Be allways true Honoust Sociel and Free
                Unanimous lets &c..

5..   Our Union is founded on Princeples of truth
           our Motto is Justice to age and to Youth
           let us love one and other in ivery degree
           and treat them with {silence} thats our Enemy
                Unanimous lets &c..

6..   Of all enemies injustice is the worst
           Falshood and Hypochrecy is Sure to be Curst
           But let us do Justice to all brothers liveing
           and that is the Road or the first step to heaven
Chorous.. Unanimous let,s drink and let's Sing
           To our Friendship our freedom our Commerce and our King

           By William Roxby

46B. A NEW SONG COMPOSED FOR THE MINERS' PHILANTHROPIC
SOCIETY OF ENGLAND, SCOTLAND & WALES.

Come hither all Miners kind honest & free,
For Sacred this day is to you & to me;
Should care venture here with thin vizage & pale,
We'ill shew him a trick and send him for Sale.
    Chorus. Then together let's <drink> {sing as we dance} on the green
             And drink Friendship & freedom our Commerce & Queen.

United Philanthropy ever we boast,
Our Science is Union, Union our toast,
And love to Mankind from this rule be inferred;
That we wish to extend our regard to a bird.
    Chorus &c –

What is wealth or ambition? what tittles* or power?   *sic*
The toys of the vain that delight for an hour:
A single good act, to a friend when distressed,*   *long 's', here and elsewhere*
Will make them seem nothings, or trifles at best.
    Then together &c.

All party disputes shall be banished from hence,
The bane of good feelings, the foe to Good Sense;
Then Sons of philanthropy ne'er disagree,
Be ever true hearted, consistent & free!
    Then together &c.

Our Union {we} <? is> found<ed> on the basis of Truth,
Our Motto is "Justice to Age & to Youth";
Let us love one another in every degree,
That our foes may confess we are honest & free!
    Then together &c –

Of all our stern foemen injustice is worst
Tis the bane of all pleasure, by all it is cursed
But let us do justice in every regard
And the bliss of high Heaven will be our reward!
    Then together lets sing as we dance on the green,
    And drink Friendship & freedom our Commerce & queen.

Wm.Roxby

Manuscript. Picton.   **A:** Hand: William Roxby (with interpolations by William Daniells). **B:** Hand: William Daniells.
    The Roxby manuscript may have been written as early as spring or summer 1843 so as to help spread propaganda about the Philanthropic Society and the unofficial trade union. Roxby also wrote **96** and may well have written **74**. He was probably beyond middle-age, given that he still used the long 's' frequently and he failed to take note of Victoria's coronation in 1837.

47A. A NEW SONG COMPOSED FOR THE MINERS'
PHILANTHROPIC SOCIETY.
Tune Free Mason Song.

Ye true Sons of union, like ⟨Brittains⟩ {Britons}, be bold,
And shrink not for tyrants nor bow down to gold;
But ⟨High⟩ {wide} let the banner of liberty fly,
Our freedom wee,'ll gain, or for freedom wee'il die

How languid's* the feeling, and cold is the breast,   *altered from* languid
That never Hath warm'd for his brother oppress,'d.*   long 's', here and
Still baser ⟨still⟩ ⟨than that is⟩* the father whose child   *elsewhere*
Wears the yoke of a tyrant by bribry beguiled   *reinstated?*

But foreign to Miners be feelings like these,
Want follows division, as death does disease,*   *altered from:* desease
⟨But⟩ wee,'l blend in ⟨?⟩ UNION our UNION,'S our all
By the Strength of our Union we Stand or we fall

Tis Ours to produce the Wealth of the Mines
Deep down the dark caverns where light never Shines
Be it ours tis all that we ask in Return
to partake of the bread that in dangers we earn

Shall we bow down in bondage nor Seek to be free
Sell to tyrants our Son's with our own liberty
No never no Never shall Brittons be Slaves
While the Son guilds our Shores as they washd by the Waves

We Want not A Sword we want not to fight
But peace and contentment possessing our right
But Should we be Branded and forced to the field
We'll glory in death that Scorns Ere to Yield

Our rule Shall be reason, by Union We,'re bound
While Blood warms our breast, wee,'l Echo the Sound
High High let the banner of Liberty fly
Our freedom weel gain, or fo[r] freedom wee'l die

47B, C & D.   A NEW SONG
COMPOSED FOR THE MINERS' PHILANTHROPIC
SOCIETY*

       Tune – Free Masons' Song.*

D: UNION AND LIBERTY,
D: omitted

Ye* true Sons of union, like Britons, be bold,
   D: Yea

And shrink not for Tyrants, nor* bow down to
      gold;
   C: now

⌊Let the gay flaunting flag⌋ of ⟨y⟩our* liberty fly
   D: But high let the banners;

⌊{For} ⟨Y⟩our⌋* Freedom to gain, or for Freedom to
      die!
   C&D: omitted [C: For our, D: Our; D: we'll; D: we'll

How languid the feeling ⌊&⌋ cold is* the breast,
   C: and how, D: and; D: as

That never hath* warm'd for his brother*
      oppressed;*
   D: has; C: brothers; B: long 's', D: oppress'd

⌊But baser than all is⌋ the father, whose child,
   [D: More base still this

Wears the yoke of a tyrant by brib'ry beguiled!*
   D: beguil'd

Oh!* ⌊far from the⌋ Miners be feelings like these,
   B: altered from ?; D: But; D: foreign to

Want follows division, as death doth* disease,
   [D: does

⌊To Union st[ill?]* blending, for⌋ Union's our all,
   D: But we'll blend into union, our; B: manuscript spiked, C: stil

By the strength of our Union we stand, or we fall!

Tis ours to produce the bright* Wealth of the
      Mines,
   D: omitted

Deep <u>in</u>* the dark Caves* where the* light never
      Shines;
   C: in, D: down; C: courses, D: caverns; D: omitted

⌊And all, that for toiling, we ask in return,⌋
   D: Be it ours (tis all that we ask in return,), [D: To partake;

⌊Is to eat⌋ of the bread that in danger* we earn!
   [d]angers

Shall we bow ⌊low to⌋ Bondage, nor Seek to be
      free,
   D: down in

Sell to tyrants* our Sons ⌊and our dear liberty?⌋
   B: altered from ?; D: with our own liderty

Oh,* never † shall Britons ⌊be forced to⌋ be slaves,
   [D: No; no never; omitted

While the Sun* gilds our shores* ⌊that are⌋
      washed* by the {waves!}
   C: suns, D: snn; D: nation; D: or its; C: wash'd, D: wnsh'd

We crave* not a Sword, ⌊nor are eager for⌋ fight,
   D: want; we want not to

⟨But⟩* {In} Peace &* Contentment ⌊we ever
      delight;⌋
   C: omitted; D: and; D: possessing our right

But Should we be branded &* forced* to the field,   C & D: and; D: forded
We will* glory in death, ⌊ever Scorning⌋ to yield!   D: We'll; but scorn e'er

* Our Rule shall be Reason, by Union we're bound,   B: *verse written vertically in margin*
While* blood warms our bosoms,* we'ill * echo   [D: Whilst; breast; C & D: we'll
    the Sound;
⌊Far, far⌋ let the Banner of Liberty fly,   D: High, high
Our freedom we'ill* gain, or for freedom we'ill*   C & D: we'll; we'll
    die.

A & B: Manuscript. **C & D:** Print.   **A & B:** Picton. **C:** Wigan 108 (302). **D:**
Wigan 115 (293). **A:** Hand: J. Matthews of Wingate[?], with changes by
William Daniells. **B:** Hand: William Daniells. **C:** Broadside. Decorative border.
No colophon [Dodds]. **D:** Double broadside. Two illustrations. Decorative
dividing lines. Colophon: No.52. T.Dodds, Printer, 77, Side, Newcastle, 'Who
has always on hand a large assortment of Songs'. Published as *Union and
Liberty* with *The Madman of Wingate* (51). See Bell 12/476 for an identical copy
of *Union and Liberty*, but without *The Madman of Wingate*.
    Probably written in the second half of 1843 though it may not have been
published until December that year or early in 1844. The author had very
similar handwriting to that of J. Matthews on **98**.

48. THE MINERS' PHILANTHROPICAL SOCIETY.
BY JAMES WARDHAUGH.

Come all you jolly fellows and listen unto me,
I will tell you of a Union that's in the country:–
In eighteen hundred and forty-two, November the seventh,
It was in Yorkshire it was formed and there its name was given.

CHORUS.

So you brothers all join heart and hand, – stand firm unto a man,
Never let it be said that we are afraid to join the Union.

There is Yorkshire, Durham, Northumberland, and other places
    round;
There is Ireland and Scotland, where men work under ground;
They're all in union combin'd, and swear they'll "stand test,"
Aud* shake off all oppression that the Masters on them press.   *sic*

There is oppression in our trade, and that we know full sore!
Masters together do combine to lay it on the more;
These Coal-pit Kings they're the devil's own, their bonds they are so
    false,
This Society they've forced us in, so they must stand their chance.

So unite my lads and firmly stand, your liberty's at hand,
The tyrants will tremble at our philanthropic band;
The colours of liberty we have hoisted them so high,
Tyrants may look at them, but oppression it shall die!

This Society, when rightly form'd, I am sure it will redress,
And give to each and all of us that right that is suppressed,
Then to conclude, and make an end, I wish not to offend;
It's just to let the Tyrants know their tricks are at an end.

Print. Wigan 108 (302).   Broadside. Decorative border. No colophon
[Dodds].
    Probably from late 1843, given the knowing reference to a Society 'when
rightly form'd' – that is, to a full-blown trade union. James Wardhaugh's
manuscript has not survived.

49 [VENTILATION]

Much has Been Said upon the them of {and much
more Remains Still to be Said} Ventelation Fire:
Called in questtion By a impulce a duty inculcated
upon me to Say a little Upon the Subject of
Venterlation upon Shotton moor Colleiry

B: Much has been said on the Theme of Ventilation, and much remains to be said. I feel myself called upon to Say Something on the Subject of the Ventilation of Shotton Moor Colliery

1 ⌊Come all yea miners*⌋ of wear and* tyne,

B: no numbers and three-line stanzas; Come ⟨All⟩ all ye men; &

That labours:* in: the Sunless* mine,
With ⌊Spark:'s: of Dissputetation⌋
⌊I hear doo*⌋ undertake: to Prove,
that Shotton will: ⌊Bid your doubts:⌋ Remo[ve]
⌊You have on Venterlation.⌋

B: labour; long's', here and elsewhere
B: sparks of disputation,
B: I hereby
B: all doubts
B: On Coal Mine Ventilation.

2 The Shotton Vewier: ⌊Who:'s: Name is C
Brow[n]⌋
A wothy* man: of hight* Renown
⌊Esteem:d: for Elaboration⌋
⌊Presidency doth Promp his⌋ Soul
True as ⌊a Needl to:o⌋ the pole.
⌊He's <?> Praise:d: for Venterlation,⌋

B: whose name is [Brown]

B: worthy; high
B: With great elaboration
B: With conscious honesty of
B: the needle to
B: Pursues his Ventilation.

3 Some talk of ⌊damp's that:s: caus:d: {the
do[om]}⌋
And huried* thousand:s: too* the toomb.*
By dullness* of: discretion,
No ⌊greaf invade:d and⌋ wounds his heart
For want of genius or of art,
He has it* in possession,

B: damp that caused the doom

B: hurried; to; tomb
B: dulness
B: grief invades, or

B: all

4 His work:s: to us his genius Show
⌊Perpettual Breess: on us⌋ Blow,
⌊Wich Envey has dissputed⌋
⌊By a flow of wit <?>⌋ we find
⌊He:s <?>{air goes}Whissling through the mine⌋
Leave:s: ⌊No Place: unsalluted⌋

B: He makes the Breeze thro' Mines to
B: Tho' Envy this disputed
B: But by his ready wit
B: That th[r]o' the Pit he Sends the wind –
B: nothing unsaluted.

5* Then W Whittle:s: most Noble fame,
    Doth Still Perpettuate his Name,
       Likewise his indagation
    No Blast on his:s Chrater:s: found,
    His Plans doth Show too all <?> around,
       His knolage of Venterlation.

B: whole page missing, presumably including stanzas 5 to 8

6*   Then Vallient thompson Blithe gand* grave
Income undaunted undissmayd.
    With a token of Contemplation
Hydrogin that:s: Cause thousand:s: woe,
    He drives to deep disspair the foe
      By art of Venterlation.

B: whole verse missing; A: sic

7* Then Erington Some will Sing his Praise
    As Bold as fancy:s: thougt Can Raise
      In Strains of Elevation
    He fill the wondering with Surprise,
    And hundred:s: on him Still Relies,
      And trust:s: his Venterlation,

B: whole verse missing

8*   Then Newerwrick that judicious dan
    Who Cut:s Contrives to keep he Can
      the air in agitation
    If Carbonic there for him to face,
      He drives her from her from her* Native, Place
      By Skill for Venterlation,

B: whole verse missing

A: sic

9   Then ⌊income:s: Noble Crock:s⌋ So free,
    A: man Renown:d:* for Repartee,
    ⌊No Limit:s in⌋ penetration.
    Where* he Susspect:s:* that danger lies,
    ⌊Destructtive Slaughters: he⌋ defies,
      By a* dextrous Venterlation.*

B: in walks noble Crooks
B: renowned
B: He lacks no
B: When; suspects
B: Then Slaughter he at once
B: omitted; Ventilation.

10 * Of doubts I:ve: drunk this* Bitter Cup,
    The Way the Subject:s:* taken up,
    ⌊It:s: Silence:d all dissputers:⌋
    You:v* Name:d to us the Noble Clan,
    Likewise the Clever Copious plan,
      But Where* the Executors:,*

B: ' – ie, a quotation; the
B: theme is
B: 'Twill silence the disputers
B: You've

B: show,; ' – ie, end of quotation

11 There* Hornby and there* Bolam too   B: There's; there's
 ⌊There Jaxon find:s: Something to doo⌋   B: There's Jackson show⟨s⟩
                                                      you what to do,
 All wothy* of their Station   B: worthy
 ⟨Of Care they {all} delight to take⟩*   B: line omitted
 With care they Strive {against the fall} ⟨?⟩*   B: omitted
 To* prolong the fate that waite's* us +   B: omitted; waits; all
    By ⌊Readeness, in Venterlation,⌋   B: art in Ventilation

12 ⌊There Stevenson and their Bates to⌋ find   B: Then Stevenson and Bates we
 Who Neither passionate or* Blind,   B: nor
    Or* Short of immitation,*   B: Nor; imitation,
 ⌊They act upon⌋ a prudent Plan,   B: Act always on
 Attentive hearing all they Can,
    Concerning Venterlation*   B: Ventilation.

13 There:s Wardle Next Who ⌊feel:s dissposed,⌋   B: felt disposed
 ⌊With Nicholas to have: his mind⌋ disclosed,   B: To have with Nich'⟨o⟩las all
    ⌊With friendship:s: fineniest*⌋ feelings   A: sic. B: By friendship's finest
 Resolved they are yet* more and* more,   B: still; &
 ⌊Too have⌋ the fluid to kiss the floor*   B: To make; Shore
 ⟨And⟩* Likwise {to} Seep* the Sealing*   B: omitted; sweep; ceiling

[14] ⌊There Jeverson One that:s in⌋ the Clan,   B: There's Jefferson belongs
 And ⌊Burdiss proved a Noble⌋ man,   B: Burdis too, a worthy
    With a* Virtuous inclineation*   B: omitted; inclination:
 ⌊While they With: Caution heard Complaint:s:⌋   B: They heard with caution
                                                      each complaint ·

 Resolve'd: No New: distrest* to Paint   B: distress
 For Want of Venterlation,*   B: Ventilation.

[15] There:s fletcher too: Who Strives with Care
 ⌊With Coall to Safe: Conduct⌋ his air,   B: ⟨With⟩ {Oer} Coal to safely
                                                      send
    ⌊Strong in disjudication⌋   B: Preventing desolation
 While* Envey* Seem:s: ⌊⟨t[o]⟩ Smile on fault:s:⌋ B: omitted; Envy; on faults to
                                                      sneer,

 ⌊There Sence improves: their Better thoughts:⌋   B: Their Sense improves and
                                                      makes it clear
 They ⌊have on Venterlation,⌋   B: Knaw good Ventilation.

[16] ⌊There patten to⌋ we doo* Admire: B: Theer patent too; do
And Richardson will Not Retire,
      Without deliberation
   ⌊There:s Hertherington and⌋ Hogg we know,   B: There Hetherington &
      Resign:d:* to Share the Joys:* or woe,*   B: Resigned; joy; wo
      Of Shotton Venterlation *   B: Ventilation

[17] ⌊The * Elastic fluid She:s Now Return:d,⌋   B: Th' ⟨fluid⟩ elastic {fluid}
To Serch* the Secrets* Places Round: now is found
Sent ⌊⟨of⟩ {in,} Exagitation⌋ +   B: search; secret
To Joseph that Atentive man,   B: in by agitation
   ⌊Not a⌋ Whit Behind the Noble Clan,
      For Schem:s in VenterLation *   B: No
                                                  B: For Schemes on Ventilation.

[18] No ⌊mistes: are are⌋ Left Behind   A: sic. B: mists are ever
No damp Stagnating air to* find +   B: we
   ⌊No Buxom hid in Corners:⌋   B: In holes no (Buxom?)
                                                  Keeps, –
The* Elastic fluid So* quickly flies, +   B: Th'; omitted
And fills all Part's:* with fresh Suplies*   B: parts; supplies
   And ⌊comfort's those that {murmers}⌋ +   B: dries the damp that sleeps

[19] The foe ⌊that:s cause⌋ Lamenting Strains   B: that caused
   ⌊Behold Behold the gloomey Scenes ⌋+   B: Is banished from the
      The* direful Devastation   mining plains B: And
   ⌊Carbonic that mangling warrior⌋ falls +   B: With ruthless chief
                                                  Carbonic
She's:* driven from her* Native wall:s   B: ⟨She's⟩ {He's}; his
      By power of Venterlation* +   B: Ventilation.–

[20] ⌊There {M} T: Foster:s: illustrious⌋ Name   B: But let illustrious Forster's
   ⌊Must Shine Enroll:d: {in Lists of fame}⌋ +   B: Shine on the glorious roll of
      ⌊Through. Successive generrations:⌋   Fame, B: Tho' coming
                                                  generations
With air his mines* he w{e}ll Suplies*   B: mine; supplies
the mangling Bolt:s. of death⟨:s⟩* defies +   B: Death
      By Best of venterlation.*   B: Ventilation.–

          Nicholas Cowey Shotton Moor Colleiry*   B: Colliery

+ *written on same line as one above*

Manuscript. **A & B:** Picton.   **A:** Hand: Nicholas Cowey. **B:** Hand: William Daniells.
    Probably from late 1843.

50. THE PITMAN'S UNION.

You Britons all, where'er you be,
I pray you listen unto me,
And then you will with me agree,
    That union is now wanted.
The Queen is good I mean to say,
Because she cannot have her way,
Her brave men would not go astray,
    If we were all united.

CHORUS
Oh dear! oh dear, what times are these,
The rich will just do as they please,
The poor are starving by degrees
    All for the want of union.

The rates and taxes are so high,
All trades are ruined now or nigh,
Which makes the working man to sigh
    All for the want of union
This is the truth I mean to say,
That England once look'd fresh and gay
But now is mouldering to decay,
    All for the want of union.

The poor man he holds down his head
The children they are wanting bread,
There's thousands starving still with dread
    All for the want of union
By tyrants some the seas are cross'd
Twas so with Jones Williams and Frost;
By tyranny we'll all be lost
    If we dont join the union.

They said Reform would do us good
It has not yet I wish it would.
For thousands they are wanting food,
   All for the want of union.
It is no use to talk at all,
The weakest must go to the wall,
And every day still lower fall,
   If we do'nt join the union

The Farmer cannot sell his wheat,
The poor cannot get bread to eat,
The world is ruined now complete
   All for the want of union
The work is all a standing still,
The next that stands will be the mill.
All trades are fast going down the hill,
   All hands must join the union

When unions through the nations made,
Which then for work we shall be paid;
And tyrants too they will be laid
   All by the poor men's union.
To put oppression to an end,
And make the tyrants with us bend:
Like britons all join heart and hand
   Within the bonds of union.

Print. Wigan 114 (300).   Double broadside. Colophon: No.47. T. Dodds, Printer, No.77, Side, Newcastle. Published alongside *The Female Auctioneer*. For another copy, without either a colophon or *The Female Auctioneer*, see Bell 12/427.
   Probably from late 1843.

51. THE MADMAN OF WINGATE.
Tune – Betsy Baker

The man who's got so strong an arm,
  Has grown weakish in the brain sir,
Too doubtful he's got so alarm'd,
  He'll ne['e]r be right again sir.

They say that he's outgane his wits,
  About this combination,
The union's flaid him into fits,
  Without exaggeration.

He's fare frea* fit to hae his scope,*   from; be let loose
  He's grown se outrageous,
We'll bind him round with wire rope
  And put him in the cages,

They say for lang he's had nea sleep.
  And oft they do him haud man.
Yall* neets* he dances round the heaps,   All; nights
  Just like another mad man,

Although he crack'd his dormant brains,
  By suffering oppression out,
His mind unshaken still remains,
  He never had possession out.

For they that made him first to scrawl
  Had judged one power was plenty,
For surely he had wanted all,
  Supposing h[e] head twenty.

Now since that he['s] gane past hiss sell,
  I hope delirium will last him,
And all his frantic notions swell,
  Until we all get past him.

To fight and bawl a'* hea nea skill,   1
  Indeed a' niver intend it,
But I'll skrudge* yea wi my hamely quill.   *crowd, *ie* bother, trouble
  Be pleas'd or be offended.

Print. Wigan 115 (293). Double broadside. Two illustrations. Decorative dividing lines. Colophon: No.52. T. Dodds, Printer, 77, Side, Newcastle, 'Who has always on hand a large assortment of Songs'. Printed alongside *Union and Liberty* (47D).
  Probably from late 1843.

52. THE WINGATE GRANGE ⟨FOX⟩* BLUE   B: *omitted*
HOUNDS IN PURSUIT OF A FOX.
          † Cappy,s the dog   B: TUNE

1st* Tis* of a fox hunting which latley* took Place B: *no numbering;* 'Tis; lately
    The dogs were unmuzzeled* and fitted for   A: *altered from ?*, B: unmuzzled
      Chase
    The fox got a peep at the dogs coming nigh
    He Stopt not to parley but of* he did fly   [B: off
      † ⌊Hadaway Herry haddoway &c⌋   B: CHORUS.; Hadaway
                                        Harry;Tally-ho, Harry,/Harry's
                                        the dog, Tally-ho, Tally-ho!

2nd there was Butcher an* Davy an* one {or} two B: and; and
      mair
    they look:ed* not behind them but cut   B: look'd
      th{r}ough the air
    They cracked* and they creacked* like a Ship A: *altered from ?*; *aletered from*
      in full Sail   *?*, B: creaked
    But big Slashing Harry left all at his tail
      ⌊Hadaway Herry ⟨to⟩ haddaway &c⌋   B: Hadaway, Harry, &c. *after*
                                        this and remaining verses

3rd the fox he Kept jigging* and quicking* his
     pace   B: jogging; quick'ning

He distanc:d* the dogs as he led on the   B: distanced; chase
   chace*

He cross:d* and he winded they cud:ent* tell A: *long 's'.* B: cross'd; could not
  how

But Herry *Still ran as he puff:ed and he Blue* B: Harry; blew
  Hadaway Herry ⟨Tol⟩

4th Then away to the cover wor foxey* He   A: *altered from ?,* B: foxy
   bounds

an puzzel:d* baith* Hunter and Hunting   A: *altered from* pussel:d?, B:
   blood Hounds   puzzled; B: both

But on they Still ran through* the taties they A: *altered from ?*
  went

An* there they gave in for ⌊they:d farley lost A: *altered from?,* B: And; B:
  Sent⌋   they fairly lost scent
  Hadaway Herry Tol

5th then not Half contented with what they had
   done

they Branded* each others* "why dident*   B:'braided; B: other; didn't A:
  you run"   *altered from ?;*

They Huffled* and Scuffled and covered* A: *altered from* Scuffld; A:
  their* face*   *altered from* coverd; A: *altered*
                                 from there; B: faces

Wi' their ⌊tail 'twen⌋ their legs they came B: tails 'tween; places
  Back to the Place*
   Hadaway Herry Tallio Harry
   Harrys the dog tallio tallio

A: Manuscript. B: Print. A: Picton. B: Wigan 109. See also NCL 1844. A: Hand: unknown (with changes by William Daniells). B: Broadside. Decorative borders. No colophon [Dodds].

    Possibly from late 1843. The tune derives from that for 7, above, though it was originally called *The Chapter of Kings.* Catcheside-Warrington, *Tyneside Songs,* Volume 2, pp. 18–19, gives an arrangement.

53A & B. *UNION

A: To the editor of the Coal Miners Journal Sir the insertion of the following will much oblige yours in the Bond of union I.N.

[1st]* Sweat* union let the echo fly
    the spacious earth around
    O* may the tear and mournful sigh
    ⌊no more 'mang us be⌋ found

B: *eight-line stanzas, no numbering;* A: *ie,* Sweet,
B: Hail
B: Oh
B: Again, be never

2nd   ⌊<of ?> sweating Balm spreads all around⌋
    And* our oppresses* see
    ⌊Once more in union we abound⌋
    To strive for our* liberty.

B: Thy healing balsam spreads afar
B: Let; Oppressors, A&B: *long 's', here and elsewhere* [B: That fixed in Union firm we are [B: *omitted*

3rd   The foe too Long has had the* sway
    Death is his Legal due
    O hasten ⌊sweat &⌋ happy day
    with liberty* on thy Brow.

B: his

B: blest and
B: Freedom

4th   Sweat* liberty we hail ⌊the sweat⌋
    When miners shall ⌊be free⌋
    When the † monster we shall meet
    ⌊Old Acursed⌋ tyranny.

B: Hail; thee sweet
B: agree
B: dread
B: And dare his

5th   Let wisdom ⌊peace power &⌋ grace
    in all our hearts <be found> {a bound}*
    Let us as miners Keep our plac[e]
    Firm* to our post* be found.

B: and let Peace and
B: abound

B: True; posts

6th+   O* Let our* flag of freedom fly
    in front of our communion
    ⌊And shout with one unaminous⌋ cry
    Success unto* the union.

B: Oh; the

B: With loud unnumbered Voices
B: attend

7th ++ Ye miners all both far &* near
    Attend unto the call
    ⌊your standard rally give⌋ the chee[r]
    ⌊To see appression⌋ fall –

B: and

B: Sorround your Standard – raise
B: <Behold>{And see} Oppression

†

I.N.

B: *final quatrain added:*
Hail Union! let the echo fly,
   The spacious earth around,
And may the tear and
   mournful sigh
Again be never found!

+ **B:** *this stanza was moved to become the first quatrain of
   the fourth and final eight-line stanza*

++ **B:** *this stanza was moved to become the second
   quatrain of the third eight-line verse*

53C & D. † UNION!

Hail, Union! let the echo fly,
   The spacious earth around,
Oh! may the tear and mournful sigh,
   Again, be never found!
Thy healing balsam spreads afar,
   Let our oppressors see,
That fixed in union firm we are,
   To strive for liberty!
The foe too long has had his sway,
   Death is his legal due;
Oh! hasten blest and happy day,
   With freedom on thy brow!
Hail liberty! we hail thee, sweet,
   When miners shall agree;
When the dread monster we shall meet,
   And dare his tyranny.

C: TO THE EDITOR OF THE
MINERS' JOURNAL. Sir, the
insertion of the following will
much oblige, in the bond of
union. I.N.

Let wisdom and let peace and grace,
　　In all our hearts abound;
Let us as miners keep our place,
　　Firm to our posts be found!
Ye miners all, both far and near,
　　Attend unto the call;
Sorround* the standard, raise the cheer,　　　　　D: Surround
　　And see oppression fall!
Oh! let the flag of freedom fly,
　　In front of our communion;
While loud unnumber'd voices cry,
　　"Success attend the union!"
Hail union! let the echo fly,
　　The spacious earth around;
Oh! may the tear and mournful sigh,
　　Again, be never found!

　　　　　　　　　†　　　　　　　　　D: J.N.

A & B: Manuscript. C & D: Print.　　A & B: Picton. C: *Miners' Journal*, No.2.,
November 4th 1843, p. 16. D: *Miners' Advocate*, July 13th 1844, p. 140. A:
Hand: I.N. B: Hand: William Daniells.

I.N.'s manuscript was probably written in October 1843. The manuscript
has been folded and 'spiked', but there is no sign of a fair copy of the version
that appeared in the *Journal*, over the initials, 'I.N.', or in the *Advocate* as by
'J.N.'.

54. AN ADDRESS TO THE MINERS OF SCOTLAND.

Ye Scottish sons who daily toil
Beneath the rich luxuriant soil,
     And dig from thence the ore;
When you your limbs and lives expose
To gain your porridge and your brose,
     What men can venture more.
And will you then contented toil
Like other moles beneath the soil,
     Who seldom see the sun?
In misery will you waste your time,
Destroy your health in youthful prime,
     Till life itself be done?
Hark to the trumpet's pealing sound,
From east to west – nay, Scotland round,
     Re-echoes unity!
Your English brothers now declare
They willing are with you to bear,
     If you united be.
And will you still content remain,
And daily drag the servile chain,
     And bear a tyrant's frown!
Then if you will with us unite
You shall obtain a Briton's right,
     And break oppression down.
Arouse then from your apathy,
And be determined to be free,
     Give to the winds your fears.
Tho' in the strife you may contend
Success will crown the happy end
     And bless declining years.

WILLIAM HAMMOND.

Print.   *Miners' Advocate*, December 2nd 1843, p. 8.
     Probably written in late November 1843. For William Hammond, who also
wrote 55 and 72, see above, p. 33 and note 98.

55. UNION!

Sons of slavery come with me,
Join the bond of unity!
Let us now join heart and hand,
Bring oppression to a stand!
Long have we been servile slaves;
Long been duped by heartless knaves;
But we soon can wander free
If we join blest unity!

Now no longer drag the chain;
Willing slaves no more remain!
Bondage chains will broken be
By this giant unity!
Union is the tyrant's dread;
Union strikes oppression dead;
Tyrants cannot bear to see
Men who walk in unity!

Union, great in matchless power,
Renders even slaves secure,
Makes the blind his right to see;
Hail unconquered unity!
Hasten friends, make no delay,
This the year, and this the day –
This will prove a jubilee
If you now united be.

Send your might to break the chain,
And like men your rights maintain;
Give your tyrants proof to see
You are strong in unity!
Then in friendship's heavenly light
You will bask as freemen bright;
Justice then obtained must be,
For right's the soul of liberty.

WILLIAM HAMMOND.

Print.   *Miners' Advocate*, December 2nd 1843, p. 8.
    Hammond also wrote **54** and **72**.

56. THE MINER'S COMPLAINT.

"Alas! what will become of me,
What help for wife and family,
    When work I cannot get!
Our bread is now become so small,
Our children crying, one and all,
    'Oh, give a little bit!'

"How mournful such a tale to state,
Starvation seems to be my fate –
    No food can we procure.
My tender wife exclaims 'My dear,
I'll die for want of bread I fear;
    Three days! – can I endure?'

"Ah! this I cannot bear, dear wife,
Upon the road I'll venture life,
    And there in ambush lie:
And should a traveller appear,
I'll cry, tho' trembling in my fear,
    Your money or you die!"

"Speak not, my husband, thus," she said,
Then sighing faint, she droop'd her head,
   And died – OF HUNGER DIED!
"My helpless babes, your mother's gone,
The spirit from starvation's flown,
   From grief and sorrow's tide,"

His children to his heart he pressed,
With bitter anguish sore distressed;
   His thoughts what tongue can tell.
His wasted visage semed to say,
"Ah! short will be my earthly stay
   In this cold world to dwell."

He thus addressed his children dear,
While on his cheeks a rolling tear
   A piteous story told –
"Sweet innocents! draw near my bed,
Ere I consign my weary head
   In death to slumber cold.

"There was a time, some years ago,
When poverty we did not know,
   And strangers to a sigh!
Employment good, and payment sure,
No hunger we had to endure,
   Or yet a weeping eye.

"From school you came, with toys you played,
Till your dear mother kindly said.
   ' 'Tis time my babes to rest.'
You clasp'd your hands, you bent the knee,
And pray'd to God most fervently
   To be your constant guest.

"Alas! I feel my strength is done,
I die – my breath is nearly gone;
   May Heaven supply my place."
He kissed them all, and sighed "Farewell!"
Blest with his Saviour he doth dwell;
   He sees him face to face.

Husband and wife have joined the throng
Of angels where they sing the song
   Of Jesus, ever new!
And, oh, it was these parents' prayer
That God would shield with tender care
   Their children – orphans too!

These orphans in a Bastile* dwell,   workhouse
Their treatment there I may not tell,
   To know would make you sigh.
No mother hears their sad complaint,
Placed under prison-like restraint,
   And yet they dare not cry.

And shall the oppressors of our land
Escape, tho' they go hand-in-hand.
   Tho' they be rich and great?
Tho' '*Honourable*' they are called,
With horror they shall stand appalled,
   And curse their pride to[o] late.

Yes! then these tyrants shall appear,
Who now nor God nor mortal fear,
   And tremble at His bar.
For Heavenly justice heedeth not
The grandeur of their mortal lot –
   Satan once a shining star!

But can we thus in hunger waste,
Our wives and children pine to taste
   The joys of daily bread.
Rise, Britons, rise! let despots know
That Heaven will deal the avenging blow!
   Our hearts too long have bled!

South Wingate, Nov. 6, 1843.   R.H. FAWCETT

Print.   *Miners' Advocate*, December 16th 1843, p. 16.
   For R. Henderson Fawcett, who also wrote **102**, see above, p. 33.

57. AN ADDRESS TO THE MINERS OF BRITAIN.

Come all ye brave Miners and listen,
 Attend for a moment to me,
While tears in my eye sadly glisten
 Such monstrous oppression to see.
The masters against us united,
 But longer we'll be not supine;
At their threats we will not be affrighted,
 Ye brave lads of Tees, Wear, and Tyne!

We have laboured in servile debasement,
 For ten years we've carried the yoke;
And the thought fills my head with amazement,
 That we've patiently suffered the stroke.
But the voice of fair freedom inviting,
 Bids the day-star of Union shine.
Then around her gay standard, uniting
 We'll crowd, lads of Tees, Wear, and Tyne!

Remorseless, our rights they have taken,
 Every shadow of justice denied;
Like tyrants their hearts are unshaken –
 Oppression is brother to pride!
But our fetters, that too long have bound us,
 We'll scatter like billowy brine,
For our Union with courage hath crowned us,
 Brave lads of the Tees, Wear, and Tyne!

Let friendship and peace ever guide us,
 Our hearts will be free of all fear;
To our leaders, whatever betide us,
 Let us cheerfully – firmly adhere!
To our brethren in want let us render
 Assistance, and never repine,
Then Heaven will be our defender,
 Brave lads of the Tees, Wear, and Tyne!

Let us patiently move – persevering,
　For soon will the struggle be o'er;
Our masters will see it appearing,
　And conscience will trouble them sore.
Be firm – ever watchful – united,
　And never your efforts resign,
Then freedom shall meet you delighted,
　Brave Lads of the Tees, Wear, and Tyne!

Ye Miners of England combining,
　With Ireland, with Scotland and Wales,
Success to the bond of your joining,
　Success fill the breadth of your sails!
Let us stand for our rights like the heroes
　That battled in days o' lang syne,
And the Goddess of Conquest will cheer us,
　Brave lads of the Tees, Wear, and Tyne!

Shotton Moor Colliery.   WM. HORNSBY.

Print.　*Miners' Advocate*, December 30th 1843, p. 24.
　　Probably written in November 1843, since the *Advocate* of December 2nd 1843 noted that this piece was 'under consideration'. See also C & R, *The Miners' Association*, p. 109. For William Hornsby, who also wrote **89** and (probably) **107**, see above, p. 34 and note 100.

58. ACROSTIC.

J ust is the cause which in union we are combined,
A nd each Miner everywhere should heart-and-hand be joined.
M idst troubles and oppression, firm to our post be found,
E ach Miner's liberty to gain through all the nation round;
S tern tyranny may frown and rage, yet all will prove in vain,

S till all their efforts we'll counteract each Miner's right to gain.
M ay every honest, feeling heart look to the Miner's wrongs,
I n justice and in legal right which unto them belongs.
T o all my brethren in the land, before I do conclude,
H ail to the Miner's gallant band, let none on them intrude.

Print.   *Miners' Advocate*, January 13th 1844, p. 31.
    James Smith is noted in the *Miners' Journal*, October 21st 1843, p. 2, as being the temporary secretary of a union committee. He later became a member of the Association Executive.

59. THE WORKHOUSE BOY.

The light of day had scarcely dawn'd
    Upon my humble birth,
When death deprived me of my last
    And only hope on earth.
My father ere a month had pass'd
    Lay in a grassy mound,
And I, a helpless orphan boy,
    Was in a workhouse found.

As reason dawn'd I saw that I
   Was scarcely welcome there,
And grudgingly to me they gave
   The scanty workhouse fare!
And when upon my strawy bed
   I laid my orphan head
A wish arose that I could work –
   For strength of limbs I pray'd.

And strength was mine when years had flown –
   A farmer's boy was I,
Who laboured hard and joy'd to see
   A smile from friendship's eye.
How hard so'eer my labour was
   It still afforded joy,
And glad was I when now no more
   A helpless workhouse boy!

Each Sabbath morn saw me array'd
   In clothes by labour won,
And after, with a cottage maid
   I ey'd the setting sun.
But now her fate with mine is joined,
   To share my woe or joy,
And health and peace are inmates with
   The once poor workhouse boy!

WILLIAM THOMASON.

Print.   *Miners' Advocate,* January 13th 1844, p. 32.
   Daniells informed Thomason in the *Advocate*, December 30th 1843, p. 21, that his poem would appear 'in our next'. For Thomason, see above, p 35, note 102.

60. THE MINER'S* DOOM.

Written expressly for the Miner's* Advocate.*
+ By the author of "The Tyne Exile's Return."*

* 'Twas evening, and a sweeter balm on earth was
    never shed,
The sun lay in his gorgeous pomp on ocean's
    heaving bed;
The sky was clad in bright array, too beautiful to
    last,
For night, like envy, scowling came, and all the
    scene o'ercast.
'Tis thus with hope – 'tis thus with life, when
    sunny dreams appear,
The infant leaves the cradle-couch to slumber on a
    bier,
The rainbow of our cherish'd* love, we see in
    beauty's eye,
That glows with all its mingled hues, alas! to fade
    and die!
'Tis dark, still night, the sultry air scarce moves a
    leaf or flower;
The aspen, trembling, fears to stir in such a silent
    hour;
The footsteps of the timid hare distinctly may be
    heard
Between the pauses of the song of night's
    portentious* bird.
And in so drear a moment plods the Miner to his
    toil,
Compelled refreshing sleep to leave for labour's
    hardest moil;
By fate's rude hand the dream of peace is broken
    and destroyed,
*The savage beast his rest can take, but man must be
    denied.**
And why this sacrifice of rest – did not the Maker
    plan
The darksome hours for gentle sleep, the day for
    work by man?

C: Miners'

B:Miners', C: *line omitted*
[B&C: *line omitted*

C: *lines split, and second half indented*

C: cherished

C: portenteous

B: *no italics,* C: *no italics except for* man

Yes! but the mighty gods of earth are wiser in their
    laws,

*They** hold themselves with pride to be *their*   **B:** *no italics*
    *creatures'** first great cause.

The Miner hath his work begun, and busy strokes
    resound,

Warm drops of sweat are falling fast – the coal lies
    piled around.

And what a sight of slavery! in narrow seams
    compressed

Are seen the prostrate forms of men to hew on
    back and breast.

Fainting with heat, with dust begrimed,* their   C:begrimmed; **B:** meager
    meagre* faces see

By glimmering lamps that serve to show their
    looks of misery.

And oft the hard, swollen hand is raised to wipe
    the forehead dews,*   C: forehead's dew

⌊He breathes a sigh⌋ for labour's close, ⌊and then   [C: And sighs are heaved; But
    his toil renews.⌋   toil they must renew

And manly hearts are throbbing there – and
    visions in that mine

Float o'er the young and sanguine soul like stars
    that rain and shine.

Amid the dreariness that dwells within the
    cavern's gloom

Age looks for youth to solace him – waits for his
    fruits to bloom.

Behold! there is a careless face bent from yon
    cabined nook,

Hope you may read in his bright eye – there's
    future in his look;

Oh, blight not then the fairy flower, 'tis heartless
    to destroy

The only pleasure mortals know – anticipated joy!

Oh, God! what flickering flame is this? see, see
    again its glare!

Dancing around the wiry lamp like meteors in the
    air.

Away, away! – the shaft, the shaft! – the blazing
    fire* flies;   C: ruin
Confusion! – speed! – the lava-stream* the   C: lava stream
    lightning's wing defies!
The shaft! – the shaft! – down on the ground and
    let the demon ride
Like the sirocco on the blast, volcanoes in their
    pride!
The *choke-damp** angel slaughters all – he spares   B: *no italics*
    no living soul!
He smites them with sulphureous brand – he
    blackens them like coal!
The young – the hopeful, happy young fall with
    the old and gray,*   C: grey
And oh, great God! a dreadful doom, thus buried
    to decay
Beneath the green and flowery soil whereon their
    friends remain,
Disfigured, and, perchance, alive, their cries
    unheard and vain!
Oh, desolation! thou art now a tyrant on thy
    throne,
Thou smilest with sardonic lip to hear the shriek
    and groan!
To see each ⌊mangled, writhing⌋ corse to raining   C: scorched and mangled
    eyes displayed,
For hopeless widows now lament, and orphans
    wail dismayed.
Behold thy work! The maid is there her lover to
    deplore,
The mother wails her only child that she shall see
    no more!
An idiot sister laughs and sings – oh, melancholy
    joy!
While bending o'er her brother dead, she opes the
    sightless eye.
Apart, an aged man appears, like some sage Druid-
    oak
Shedding his tears like leaves that fall beneath the
    woodman's stroke;

His poor old heart is* reut* in twain – he stands   C: was; A: *sic*, B & C: rent
    and weeps alone,
The sole supporter of his house, the last, the best
    is gone!
This is thy work, fell tyrant! this the Miner's
    common lot!
In danger's darkling den he toils, and dies
    lamented not.
The army hath its pensioners – the sons of ocean
    rest,
When battle's crimson flag is furled on bounty's
    downy breast.
But who regards the mining slave, that for his
    country's wealth
Resigns his sleep, his pleasures, home, his
    freedom, and his health?
From the glad skies and fragrant fields he
    cheerfully descends,
And eats his bread in stenchy caves where his
    existence ends.
Aye! this is he that masters grind and level with
    the dust,
The slave that barters life to gain the pittance of a
    crust.
Go read yon pillared calendar, the record that will
    tell
How many victims of the mine in yonder
    churchyard* dwell.   C: church-yard
Hath honour's laurels ever wreathed the despot's
    haughty brow?
Hath pity's hallowed gems appeared when he in
    death lay low?
Unhonoured is his memory, despised his
    worthless name,
Who wields in life the iron rod in death no tear
    can claim.

Newcastle-upon Tyne, Dec. 18th, 1843.*   B & C: *line omitted*

+ **B:** Written expressly for the "Miner's Advocate," and recited by Mr. Jos. Fawcett, a practical Miner, at a Concert held in the Lecture Room, Nelson Street, Newcastle-upon-Tyne, on Tuesday, August 13, 1844, for the Benefit of the Unemployed Miners of Northumberland and Durham.

Print.   **A:** *Miners' Advocate*, January 27th 1844, p. 40. **B:** Wigan 90. **C:** Robson, *The Monomaniac*, p. 220. **B:** Broadside. Decorative border. Colophon: Newcastle-upon-Tyne: Printed at the Miners' Advocate Office, 77, Side, by T. Dodds. Reprinted in the *Advocate* (New Series, No.8, December 1845, p. 128) over Joseph Philip Robson's name.

A is dated from Newcastle-upon-Tyne on December 18th, 1843, and the subsequent *Advocate*, December 30th 1843, p. 24, noted that 'The "Collier's Doom", by the author of "The Tyne Exile's Return", shall most certainly appear. The writer has our warm acknowledgements'. In the following *Advocate*, January 13th 1844, p. 32, readers were told to expect 'The poem entitled "The Miner's Doom" in our next', but whether the title was changed by Daniells or by Robson is not clear.

61. THE MINERS'* COMPLAINT.   **B:** Miner's

On the twenty fifth of November last,
    We Thornley* men did strike;   **B:** Thornly
Our masters they did rob us, –
    We knew it was not right.

        CHORUS.

Cheer up, my lads, ⌊for Roberts is⌋ bold,   **B:** Roberts's
    And well defends our cause;
For such a drubbing he's gi'en them
    With their* own class-made laws.   **B:** there

We went unto the Magistrates,
    Of our masters to complain,
The Magistrates made this reply –
    The* entreaties are in vain.   **B:** Your

Then we sent unto our Advocate,
    Whose counsel we do prize,
He bade us turn to work again, –
    Thus did he us advise.

The boxes on the bank were placed,
    Each man his rights to get;
But when the men returned from work,
    Great numbers were in debt.

Then the men they all resolved,
    That this they would not stand;
Before this tyranny they'd bear,
    They would leave their native land.

This oppression they have borne,
    Of it they did complain,
And oft unto* our masters went,   **B:** into
    But it was all in vain.

The police then came to town,
    To drag our men away;
They pounced upon poor Lumsdon,
    And seized him for their prey.

Our men proved Britons bold,
    And set our brother free;
A glorious victory we achieved,
    As you may clearly see.

Now to conclude and finish,
    It's here we make an end;
Here's a health to Mr. Roberts,
    For he's proved the Miner's friend.

Print.   **A:** Bell 12/258. **B:** Wigan 58.   **A:** Broadside proof? No colophon
[Dodds]. Another copy (Wigan 106) has a decorative border. **B:** Double
broadside. No colophon [Dodds]. Published below *A New Song, Called the
Wonderful Shaver, Or Tom R—d—n's Life,* for which see **62.**
    Probably from January 1844. The text recalls November 25th 1843 as
'November last', when a dispute at Thornley Colliery involved, amongst other
grievances, a wire-rope. See also Challinor, *A Radical Lawyer,* p. 107.

62. A NEW SONG, CALLED THE WONDERFUL SHAVER, OR TOM R—D—N'S LIFE.

Come all you good people and listen to my song,
While I sketch a story concerning shaving Tom,
He is a cunning shaver, a barber from the west,
Of all the people e'er he shaved, did Thronley*   A: *sic*, B: Thornly
    men the best.

CHORUS.

He is a cunning shaver, a barber from the west,
Of all the people e'er he shaved, † did Thornley*   B: he; Thornly
    men the best.

He shaved* them at Hartlepool, he shaved them at   B: shav'd
    Seaham,
But when he went to Sunderland he shaved by
    steam;
He shaved them at Cleadon, he shaved them at
    Shields,
Then went unto Newcastle and shaved in the
    keels.

O, poor Tom the shaver! you have lost all your
    store,
By playing at the card-table, you must shave for
    more;
He shaved them at Bedlington, he shaved them at
    Blyth,*   B: Blythe
Then took a trip, all in a ship, with cash from the
    Beehive.

He shaved them on the Tyne and Wear, he shaved
    them on the Tees,
And on his passage to Brazil, he shaved them on
    the seas;
He shaved at Newcastle market, he shaved in the
    shops,
And when he came on the Quayside,* he shaved   B: quay side
    some mutton chops.

Now for your cheating Thornley men, you never
    will have peace,
You have just another class to shave, that is the
    new police;
You met a woman on the road, and said "we'll
    have a glass dear Bella,"
The reckoning she had to pay, and you stole her
    umbrella.

Its oh! poor Tom the shaver, what can you get to
    do?
You're forced to come to Thornley to join the
    black-leg crew;
Now, Tom, I'd have you to repent, while on this
    earth you dwell,
⌊If this wicked course you do pursue, you'll have
    to shave in h—l.⌋

B: Lest, when old death has shaved you off, you should not fare so well.

Print. **A:** NCL 1844. **B:** Wigan 58.   **A:** Decorative border. No colophon [Dodds]. See also Wigan 109 (301). **B:** No colophon [Dodds]. Published above *The Miner's Complaint* **(61B).**
    Probably from early February 1844.

63. THE UNION KNOT.
Adapted to the Air of "Auld Lang Syne."
Written for the Miners' Advocate.

Come, let us make a Union Knot
    Round every heart to twine,
When carried to the Miner's cot
    It may his cause combine.
The first is *"England's bonny rose,"*
    Then *Scotland's thistle's* seen;
The twain will heal a Miner's woes
    And make his heart serene.

Truth, like a rock of adamant,
  Will ever stand secure;
The Union, like the *shamrock-plant*,
  For ages will endure!
The valiant hosts for liberty
  Are neither cold nor bleak –
Firm in the bands of unity
  With the *Welchman and his leek.*

Divided interest sinks itself,
  And good must fail to do,
As he that journeys without pelf
  Will soon find cause to rue.
But when together men are bound
  In sacredness of love,
Then strength is trebly stronger found,
  A safeguard sure to prove.

Thus, brethren, you will plainly find
  Success will cheer your lot,
For if you love sweet liberty
  Then wear the Union Knot.

East Holywell, Dec., 1843.   THOMAS NICHOLSON.

Print.   *Miners' Advocate*, February 10th 1844, p. 48.
    A piece with this title was mentioned in the *Advocate*, January 27th 1844,
p. 40., sent by 'W.S.N.' Nicholson also wrote 78.

64. ACROSTIC.

J oy lifts the dancer's merry feet;
O n every maiden's lip the smile
H overs, like light on roses sweet,
N ow happy swain regale the while.

H ail to the bride – the bridegroom hail!
A ll pleasure crown thy wedded lot!
L et not a shade of woe prevail,
L et none *untie* thy "Union Knot."

February 5, 1844.   J.P.R.

Print.   *Miners' Advocate*, February 10th 1844, p. 48.
         The initials are those of Joseph Philip Robson.

65. THE COAL KING!

Away with the king of the bright black coal!
    On a throne in his hall of pride
He laughs at the wail and the Miner's tale
    As he sits by his gem-deck'd bride.

Away with the king of the bright black coal!
    For his wealth in profusion lies;
His coffers unfold his heaps of gold
    While the slave who gives them dies!

Away with the king of the bright black coal!
    For his feast of joy is spread;
And the revel and song the gay hours prolong
    While his slaves are starved and dead!

Away with the king of the bright black coal!
    For his heart of the flint is formed;
For the shriek and cry of man's agony
    His callous breast ne'er warmed!

Away with the king of the bright black coal!
    For his revel and song are o'er;
The dream of his pride, like an ebbing tide,
    To his soul will come no more!

Away with the king – for the bright black coal
   Hath changed to an *iron stone*,
And his slaves are *free* as the bounding sea,
   And he falls with his falling throne.

Print.   *Miners' Advocate*, February 24th 1844, p. 56.
   No author's name is given, but the style is reminiscent of Robson's.

66. LINES TO THE MEMORY OF MR. B. PYLE.

Grim Tyrant! when will thy envenom'd darts
Cease to destroy the best of human hearts?
When will thy vulture-appetite be stay'd?
When will thy restless scythe at peace be laid?
Alas! again we mourn thy victim low;
Again the sympathetic tear-drops flow
For him, who like a patriot martyr bled,
And wasted life that freedom might be fed!
Departed shade! if we thy grave could crown
With amaranthine flow'rs of bright renown;
If we, in grateful accents, could bestow
All thou dost merit – yes, and all we owe,
Thy epitaph above thy head should rise,
Proclaim our sorrow, and thine energies;
Thy labour ceaseless for thy fellows' good;
Thy loss lamented, and our gratitude!
Foe to oppression, friend to honest toil,
For ever honour'd be the grave of PYLE!

Newcastle, Feb. 19, 1844.   J.P.R.

Print. *Miners' Advocate*, March 9th 1844, p. 64.
   The initials are those of Joseph Philip Robson.

67. LINES, WRITTEN ON SEEING THE WEST MOOR EXPLOSION IN THE 'MINERS' ADVOCATE.'

Relentless death, untimely to destroy
This early hope, and crush the rising joy.
Lamented men, how swift your minutes flew;
Weeping, how soon you take your last adieu.
Yet why mourn we, their dying pangs are o'er –
Their souls are landed on a safer shore.
And tho' beneath the earth their bodies lie
Their souls unfettered springs* into the sky,   *sic*
And joins the harmonious chorus of the blest
In realms of bliss and everlasting rest.

Framwellgate Moor Colliery, Feb.17th, 1844.   JOHN WALL.

Print.   *Miners' Advocate*, March 9th 1844, p. 64.
    Perhaps this was the same John Wall as the one-time Independent Methodist turned Primitive Methodist, described as 'an ardent sunday schooler before "he was led away by evil companions,"' mentioned by Colls, *The Pitmen*, p. 175.

68. THE TRAPPER-BOY'S* DREAM.

Written Expressly for the Miners' Advocate.*   **B&C:** *line omitted*
By the Author of the "Miner's Doom."*   **B&C:** *line omitted*

Silence was in the lowly cot – the Trapper-boy   **C:** *lines split in two, and second*
    reclined*   *half indented*
Upon his clean, tho' humble couch, prepared by
    mother kind;
And near him sat the matron form, as fearful to
    molest
The slumber that* she though[t]* partook of   **C:** *which, thought*
    dreaming and unrest.

For see! he starts – he mutters words breath'd*   C: breathed
    from his lips of fear,
And drops of sweat upon his brow like shining
    beads appear.
And now he lifts his trembling hand – he holds
    his burning brow;
"Save me, oh, save me!" loud he cries – he wakens
    wildly now.
"Oh mother, such a dreadful dream! a cup of
    water, pray!"
How eagerly he takes the draught – his cheek is*   B: as
    cold as clay.
"Oh what a dream! I would not sleep⌊to see   B: again to see
    again⌋ that sight
For all the gold that earth contains – oh, horror
    and affright!
I thought that at my post I sat, upon my duty
    bent,
When suddenly there came a sound as if the mine
    were rent;
And then the earth rock'd* to and fro – I strove   C: rocked
    for help to call,
For o'er my head a mass of coal hung ready for to
    fall!
It sway'd *– it tottered – still it hung, as held by   B&C: swayed
    secret power,
And as I gazed such horrid faces seem'd* on me   C: seemed
    to lower;
Grim demons look'd* with scowling eye, and   C: looked
    nearer then they came –
They smote me – dashed me to the earth and
    turned my heart to flame.
I felt my bones were ground to dust, my carcass*   B: carcase
    mangled lay;
My head I found was crushed – the brains were
    mingled with the clay;
And yet the state of sense was left, the terror of the
    heart
Was vivid, and I thought how blest if I from life
    could part.

I saw as 'twere* without my eyes, and reasoned   C: 't were
    without brains,

I felt a death that dying man ne'er felt in worst of
    pains;

⌊And without⌋ tongue a voice I found and called   C: Without a
    on God to save –

Oh, mother, did I ever think so earnestly to crave!

God heard me, and I dream no more – but do not
    let me go

Again within the dreary mine – I'm warned to
    shun the blow!

You weep, my mother, and I know what you
    would wish to say,

That I am foolish to regard a dream that fades
    away!

Oh, do not weep and I will chase this vision from
    my brain,

'Tis for you mother – we are poor – I go to work
    again."

'Tis done – and he obeys the dictates of fond love,

*For 'tis alone by sacrifice affection we can prove.**   B: *no italics*

'Tis done – and now the shapeless ⌊body rests⌋ on   C: form reclines
    that same bed

Where late it dreamt – from which it rose – on
    which it lieth dead,

Proclaiming to the selfish world, that labours to
    destroy,

The better feelings of the poor – *This was a*   B: *no italics*
    *Trapper-boy!**

Newcastle, February 27th, 1844.*   B & C: *line omitted*

Print.   **A:** *Miners' Advocate*, March 23rd 1844, p. 72. **B:** Picton. **C:** Robson, *The Monomaniac*, pp. 226–29. **B:** Broadside. Colophon: Printed at the Miners' Advocate Office, Sun Inn, Side [ie by Dodds]. Lloyd, *Come all ye bold miners*, (1952), pp. 75–76,135, subtitled the piece *The West Moor Colliery Explosion*, put the text into four-line stanzas (except for the final one, which contains six lines, because the equivalent of two lines is missed out), changed many of the lines and generally recast the whole piece, but noted that his text was 'Communicated by J.S.Bell, of Whiston, Lancs, "from a leaflet on *The Dreadful Explosion at Westmoor Colliery*, April 3rd, 18?, in which ten were killed, including four boys"', so he may have relied on **68B**. Lloyd, *Come all ye bold miners*, (1978), pp. 158–59, published a similar highly-mediated version of the piece, with the same subtitle. However, he did not mention J.S.Bell.

Lloyd, *Come all ye bold miners*, (1978), pp. 349–50, supplied a date of 1845, placed the colliery at Killingworth and suggested that the gas 'was ignited by the candle of a little boy who was allowed to proceed before the men'. A was later claimed by Joseph Philip Robson (see C). B mentions April 3rd. *Dreadful Explosion at the West Moor Colliery* begins with a brief account of a disaster for which Robson's poem seemed an obvious tail-piece:

It is our painful duty to record another of those awful calamities, alas! too frequent in these mining districts, viz., a colliery explosion, has taken place, by which many families are plunged into the deepest sorrow destitution and distress. This melancholy catastrophe took place on Thursday the 3rd, Instant, at West Moor Colliery, and by which ten of our fellow-creatures were hurried at a moment's warning, form [*sic*] time into eternity.

In the fatal list of the unfortunate suffers, were to be found husbands, fathers, sons, and brothers. The consternation and despair into which the village was thrown by the dreadful occurrence may be conceived but cannot be described – wives weeping, in the bitterest anguish, over the lifeless, blackened bodies of their husbands – mothers over their sons – and relations over their friends, all refusing to be comforted!

This melancholy occurrence took place on Thursday afternoon, April 3rd, between 5 and 6 o'Clock; it appears that the pit had been off work, and the unfortunate individuals had just gone down to resume their toil, when the awful catastrophe took place, and swept them instantly into eternity.

List of the Sufferers.

William Sharp, married, left – children.

John Sharp, do. do.

R. Hall, deputy, unmarried.

P. Tweedie, do.

Thomas Thompson, married, 4 children.

John Gray, unmarried.

Matthew Thompson, boy.

———, Mouter, do.

T. Stewart, do.

John Hindmarsh, do.

69. THE PITMAN'S HYMN.

The christian collier rises soon,
   With glory in his soul,
He prays he might be spared till noon,
   While working at the coal,
Then to the pit the collier goes,
   To earn his daily bread
He may be killed for ought he knows
   And go to Christ his head.

When he goes under the dark shade
   To labour with his hands,
He cries up to his living God,
   While Jesus with him stands
He basely prosecuted is
   By proud and cruel men
Though grace divine he does not fear
   But prays for them again.

While some doth swear on his right hand,
   And on his left as well,
He prays to Jesus that has died,
   To save their souls from hell
Though floods of troubles roll along,
   The colliers peaceful breast
The love of Jesus is his song,
   He on that rock doth rest.

And when the colliers work is done,
   Then to his home he goes,
His christian feet are swift to run,
   Where milk and honey flows,
The word of God is his delight,
   While he is at his home,
He loves that God whose power and might,
   Hath brought him there again.

And what instruction he has given,
  To all his dear family;
He earnestly solic[i]ts heaven
  Their souls may never die.
But live to God while in this world,
  And feel their souls forgiven,
And never into hell be hurled,
  But reign with Christ in heaven.

Print.   Wigan 115. Broadside. Woodcut. Colophon: T. Dodds, Printer, 77, Side. Printed alongside 70A. For another copy of *The Pitman's Hymn*, see Bell 12/475.
    Possibly from early 1844.

70. THE RANTERS'* SHIP.

B: RANTER'S

The Ranters's Ship along is sailing.
  Bound for Canaan's peaceful shore;
All who wish to sail for glory
  Come, and welcome, rich or* poor.

B: *all verses numbered*; A: *sic*, B: Ranter's

B: and

    Glory! Glory! Hallelujah!
      All her sailors loudly cry;
    See the blissful port of glory,
      Open to each faithful eye.

Thousands she has* safely landed,
  Far beyond this mortal shore,
Thousands now are sailing in her,
  Still there's room for thousands more,
    Glory; Glory; † &c

B: hath

B: Hallelujah!

Waft along this noble vessel.
  All ye gales of Gospel grace,
Carrying every faithful sailor
  To his heavenly landing place,
    Glory, Glory, † &c.

Their sails are filled with heavenly breezes   B: Hallelujah!
  Sweetly wafts the ship along;
All her sailors are rejoicing. –
  Glory, bursts from every tongue,
    Glory, Glory, † &c;

                                                 B: Hallelujah!

Come poor sinners get converted,
  Sail with us through life's rough sea
Then with us you will be happy –
  Happy through eternity.
    Glory, Glory † &c.

                                                 B: Hallelujah!

Print.   **A:** Wigan 115. **B:** CULM 16/741. **A:** Double broadside. Illustration. Colophon: T. Dodds, Printer, 77, Side, Newcastle. Printed alongside 69. **B:** Double broadside. Two illustrations. Colophon: G. Walker, Jun., Printer, Silver-Street, Durham. [185]. Published alongside *A Jubilee Hymn*.

Possibly from early 1844. Walker's c.1837 *List of Songs* stops at No 181, but Hunt, *The Book Trade*, pp. 92–93, gives a Sadler Street address for him only between 1846 and 1859.

71. THE COLLIER BOY.

Yon starry light that rules the night
  In yonder distant sky,
It sheds its bright and bonny light,
  On thee my Collier Boy!

In silent flight o'er hills at night,
  For rights with alloy;
It ne'er ask'd who wander'd past,
  But lit my Collier Boy!

For all yon viewer scourges the hewer,
  And robs him of his joy;
It shines as free and bright on thee,
  My honest Collier Boy!

Away, away from light of day
  To your toilsome labour hie,
And take the view of freemen now,
  My gallant Collier Boy!

Away, away, no longer stay,
  For freedom live or die;
The heart that's true shall have its due,
  My brave young Collier Boy!

Away my brave forsake thy grave,
  Forget each slavish tie;
And raise a light an English night,
  Be free my Collier Boy!

Be free, be free, and let them see,
  That Heaven's laws defy,
Their Baal shrine shall ne'er be mine.
  My own young Collier Boy!

Thy father's gone, then on my son,
  My heart shall beat with joy,
To see the foe in death laid low,
  My own dear Collier Boy!

Print. Wigan 106 (304). Broadside. Decorative border. No colophon [Dodds].
    Probably from early 1844. Robert Lowery wrote a poem with this title
(Harrison & Hollis, *Robert Lowery*, pp. 240–41).

72. [THE EXPLOSION.]*

	B: *title supplied*
† What is this which* strikes my ear	B: Lo!; that
most awfull* is the sound I hear	B: awful
† listning* to the rolling sound	B: While; list'ning
⌊I hear it comes from under⌋ ground	B: Rising from the trembling
<?>* lo* the flame and* smoke ascend	B: *omitted*; See; &
⌊the awfull shock the structers rend⌋	B: And awful shocks the structure {rend}
† fragments in confusion fly	B: Huge
the awfull* scene obscure* the sky	B: dreadful; obscures
† soon the dreadfull* news is spread	B: And; thrilling
† the pit has* blasted all are dead	B: "; hath
now the wifes* distracted runs	B: wife
to seek ⌊their husbands and their⌋ sons	B: the husband & her
† each mind ⌊is; then filld⌋ with despair	B: Then is; fill'd
some wring their {hands} ⌊and tear⌋ their hair	B: & rend
⌊the shricks most dreadfull is⌋ to hear	B: Wild shrieks arise most sad
⌊while some more silent⌋ drops the tear	B: The silent mourner
but see the consenting* fair one stands	B: hapless – *long 's', here and elsewhere*
⌊she heaves the sigh⌋ she wrings her hands	B: The sigh she heaves,
the crimson on the* cheek turns pale	B: her
⌊and all her facultys do faill⌋	B: Her faculties & senses fail;
but nature ⌊kind gives some releif⌋	B: lends her heart relief
A flood of ⌊tears gives vent to⌋ grief	B: sorrow vents her
⌊and then⌋ in broken accents hear her say	B: *omitted*
⌊sab sab⌋ sabbath next for wedding day †	B: 'Sad; '
⌊but O she cries my prospect;s⌋ fled	B: All pleasing prospect now is
† my darling spouse is lying* dead	B: Alas; *omitted*
he;s gone to join his kindred clay	
and as she speaks she faints away	
another ⌊prospect strikes⌋ my view	B: scene comes [*altered from* cones] to
a group of men all* dresst* in blue	B: and; A: *long 's', here and elsewhere*, B: dress'd
and minor* slaves do* them attend	[B: miner's; with
when down the pit they all descend	
the miners then* both far and* near	B: now; &
in ⌊numbers on⌋ the hill appear	B: throngs upon
⌊enquiring then what must⌋ be done	B: And eager ask what can
when in obedience swift they run	
then* mark the banksman* with his eye	B: And; bankman
⌊upon the rapper fixt close by⌋	B: Fix'd on the rapper lying nigh,

and as it moves then* hear him say   B: I

there;s* something on come bend away   B: There's

and now begins the tragic scene

wives mothers sisters swe{e}thearts scream

and when to bank the corpse* do* come   B: corses; *omitted*

to ⌊claim their own each trembling⌋ run   B: claim⟨his⟩ {their} own, behold them

⌊but when the corps is viewed there;s none   B: The corp{s}e is seen – but none can claim
     {claim}can⌋

nor yet the mangld* body name   B: mangled

⌊some buttons they take⌋ from the clothes   B: They take some buttons

and ask if any* one those* buttons knows   B: *omitted*; these

⌊the buttons then are passed round⌋   B: Examined well they're pass'd around,

and ⌊soon an owner then is⌋ found   B: then the hapless owner's found,

A mother cries those* are my sons*   B: they; Son's,

to ⌊get him in her arms⌋ she runs   B: clasp the corse in haste

⌊but some kind friend steps in betwen*   B: between

⌊to take her from the shocking⌋ scene   B: And bears her from the deathful

and lends her arm to lead* her home   B: With gentle aid he leads

⌊when to the door the corps do⌋ come   B: And slowly corse & bearers

now strangers flock to view the scene

⌊and females help the same ⟨?⟩ to⌋ clean   B: The lifeless form the females

⌊they strip the clothes⌋ wash hands and* face   B: The clothes they strip; &

⌊but still no⌋ features can they trace   B: Still no known

The coffin;s brought the corpse put in*   B: The coffin's brought – the dead is laid
†   B: In humble sleep of death array'd

A tuft of hair ⌊in paper pain⌋   B: is cut away
†   B: For memory of another day

and in the drawer ⌊is put away⌋   B: safe it lies

for ⌊to look at some other day⌋   B: other times & other eyes

* ⌊again unto⌋ the pit † I turn   B: *indented* ; Now to; again

each object ⌊viewed it makes me⌋ mourn   B: makes the bosom

† coffins upon coffins pild*   B: There; pil'd

some for the father some the child

⌊when down the pit they do them⌋ send   B: Which – *altered from ? –* quickly down the pit they

enough to make* the rocks to rend   [B: cause

so* when each body then* is found   B: For; there

its* closely coffind* under ground   B: 'Tis; coffin'd

take of* the shoes pull ⌊of some⌋ hose   B: off; off the

or* other fragments of the* clothes   B: And; their

and give them to the gazeing* throng   B: gazing

to* See to whom they do belong	B: And
* but ere they all the bodys* find	B: *indented*; bodies
they something* meet which* pain the mind	B; *omitted*; with sights that
for as they make ⌊their way inby⌋	B: advances nigh
A flame of fire ⌊they do espy⌋	B: is seen to fly.
and ⌊then they Quickly make⌋ away	B: quickly then they haste
⌊it would be dangerous for⌋ to stay	B: Twere death a moment more
then ⌊right outby⌋ they run with dread	B: hastily
the pit;s* on fire the news is spread	B: pit's
and when* to bank ⌊they all do⌋ come	B: as; with fear they
⌊they then consult what must be done⌋	B: Consult in whisper's on their doom.
and* soon they all in one agree	B: But;
to close the shaft* immeadiately*	B: *altered from* ?; immediately!
† buntons+ then* and † planks ⌊do come⌋	B: Then; *omitted*; strong; come on
and soon the scaffold;s* fixt and* done	B: scaffold's; &
with full four foot* of temperd* clay	B: feet; tempered
and water lest it pine away	
⌊then full eight weeks and⌋ sometimes more	B: Eight weeks relapse &
or* they the mine again explore	B: Ere
and when the pit they do* go round	B: dare
⌊and all the putrid bodys*⌋ found	B: Then every putrid corse is; A: *altered from* bodies?
⌊they are coffind⌋ close and* sent away	[B: They're coffin'd; &
and each interd* without delay	B: interred
and here doth* end this mournfull* scene	B: I; mournful
the pit is now both safe and* clean	B: &
the coroner has* verdict past	B: hath
⌊it was by accident⌋ the blast	B: That <u>accident</u> produced
the case I have examiend* through	B: examined
the Overman and* Viewer too	B: &
⟨the gas was small⟩*	B: *line omitted*
and all the witnessess* declare –	B: witnesses
the gass* was small but strong the air	B: gas
so gentlemen you all may see	
what was observd* by Mr B	B: observed
the fact so plain needs no debate	
we all ⌊must be subject to⌋ fate	B: {must} bend to stubborn
the scriptures they explicit are	
how god ⌊does watch each numberd⌋ hair	B: hath numbered every
and while we such disasters see	
⌊they all must⌋ come by heavens* decree	B: We know they; Heaven's

so Gentlemen*⌊its left with⌋you
to pass A sentence just and* true
you ve* heard the witnessess* declare
how each⌊engagd did take due⌋care
so choose A foreman and* withdraw
be in accordance with the law
and if you think theres* one to blame
you have full power⌊the same⌋to name
the jury then withdrew one* hour
to do the best lay in their power
and when⌊again they did come in⌋
the foreman did* his speech begin*
† well sir this is A serious case
⌊and we each witness close did trace⌋
⌊we searched them through⌋both pro and* con
but⌊find the blame attachd⌋to none
and now* we are convincd* at last
⌊it was by⌋accident † the blast
no human prudence can forsee
⌊what is wrapt up in⌋destiny †
* the Coroner then* made his address
* and turning to the witnessess*
⌊'sirs you might⌋think I was severe
but † points⌊like those they must be⌋clear
⌊you know we swear for to be⌋true
and allways* strive to* Justice do*
lest⌊some poor man should get⌋the blame
and⌊so be slandered in his⌋name
but* gentlemen⌊it pleaseth me⌋
⌊to see we all in one⌋agree
but then⌊the fact it⌋is so plain
⌊no spark of dout there can⌋remain
⌊now gentlemen I do thank⌋you
⌊you {ha}ve⌋done your duty⌊just and⌋true
but one thing⌊more for such the plan⌋
⌊you now must⌋fix the Deodan*++
and you must strive to moderate* be
⌊but still we cannot⌋set them free
the accident has been* expence
⌊you may the deodan condence⌋

Notes:

A: *altered from* Gentleman;
B: it is for
B: &
B: You've; witnesses
B: engaged used every
B: &

B: there's
B: that man
B: an

B: returned had every man
B: thus; began
B: "
B: Each witness'd word has had its place
B: And well we've search[ed]; &
B: blame we find attach'd
B: here; convinc'd
B: That; produced

B: The workings of our; "
B: *indented;* omitted
B: *indented;* witnesses
B: 'You might, Sirs,
B: serious; I wish to
B: Our oath is pledged for justice
B: thus we; for; due;
B: innocence should bear
B: Slander blast his honour'd
B: And; I love to see
B: A jury such as this
B: {the} matter
B: How can a Spark of doubt
B: I tender, Sirs, my thanks to
B: You've; well &
B: yet, which must be {scanned}
B: Which is, to; Deodand.–
B: mod'rate
B: Yet not of all to
B: caus'd
B: Yet you the fine may still condense:

such things as those* have practised been	**B:** these
such things ⌊I have both⌋ heard and* seen	**B:** you all have; &
⌊and often has my ire been rousd⌋	**B:** Tho oft[en?] hath my ire aroused
to hear both God and* man abusd*	**B:** &; abused

+A: *transverse pieces of wood placed in the pit-shaft to which the guides for cages were attached.*

++A & B: *a fine; originally a forfeit to the Crown for religious or charitable use for having caused a human death.*

Manuscript. Picton. **A:** Hand: William Hammond? **B:** Hand: William Daniells. Published by Lloyd, *Come all ye bold miners*, (1952), pp. 72–74, 135, as *The Wallsend Explosion*, an 'edited version of a text from J.S.Bell, of Whiston, Lancs., who says "This ballad appears to describe the Wallsend explosion of 1835"'. This is probably the most mediated text in Lloyd's book. Lloyd, *Come all ye bold miners*, (1978), pp. 154–57, 349, indicated that his text was found by 'J.S.Bell' 'as a manuscript in the Picton Library, Liverpool', though it is unclear which of the two manuscripts is being referred to. A letter to the Editor from the Director of Libraries and Arts of Wigan County Borough, dated January 22nd 1973, mentions a piece with this title, gives William Hammond as the author, quotes the first line and supplies a date of March 6th 1844. When I first visited the Library in 1984 the text was missing, and a search in 1985 also failed to unearth it. Hammond is referred to as the author in C & R, *The Miners' Association*, p. 202.

Probably published early in 1844 as part of the preparation for the strike though it is highly likely that the piece was written earlier. A note in the *Advocate*, December 30th 1843, p. 24, reads: 'Received the poem entitled "the explosion" by our friend Mr. W. Hammond – he has our thanks'. Hammond also wrote **54** and **55**. 'Mr.B.' probably refers to John Buddle, a nationally-known figure in the coal trade who died in harness in 1843, but who seems not to have been above lying to a Parliamentary Committee, let alone a Coroner, especially if this meant a lower fine for his employers (Welford, *Men of Mark*, Volume 1, pp. 425–31). Lloyd, *Come all ye bold miners* (1978), p. 349, insisted on the 1835 date and the Wallsend provenance, and referred sympathetically to a 'John Biddle'. For deodands, which were abolished in 1846, see Gittings, *Death, Burial and the Individual*, pp. 66–67.

73. THE PITMEN'S DISGUST TO THE MONTHLY BOND.

Ye Miners all both great and small,
   I pray you give attention,
And with me don't agree
   To that diabolical invention.

The monthly bond I mean to say,
   Which at Derwent was suggested,
And thro' the colliery found its way
   To the Coal Office to be discussed.

There the great Sanhedrim sits
   In council to devise this plan,
The monthly bond says one is it
   That will dissolve the Union.

Poor mortals themselves deceive,
   Thinking that should be the case,
For it has cemented us we believe,
   And increased our Union on a space.

But we are aware what will occur,
   If that on us they should enforce,
There'll be no money but truck store,
   And likely we will get the worse.

Besides our men will have to walk
   If they incur the least displeasure,
And through the country they may talk,
   Without relief in any measure.

Should we agree to that infernal thing,
   We with our families shall lament,
It will misery and destitution bring,
   In finding houses and paying rent.

On us they will the fines enlarge
   Should we submit unto this plan,
Of every comfort we will be debard,
   Of our rights as labouring men.

But we will never more be gulled,
  Or wronged or cheated by those knaves,
But have our liberty to the full,
  And not submit to be their slaves.

Servants we intend to be,
  Our rights of labour to defend,
And things that's wrong which we see,
  In future we intend to mend.

Print. NCL 1844. Another copy is Wigan 109 (301). Broadside. Decorative border. No colophon [Dodds].
  Probably from March 1844.

74A. A CALL TO THE MINERS OF GREAT BRITAIN

Vrs 1.. Britains, Where your once boasted bravery
            Can You tamely Sit and See
          Cursed oppressors* with their bonds of Slavery   *long 's', here and
          Trample down your libety –   elsewhere

2,..   When You have ga{i}ned the good will of the Publick
            Would you give in to the tyrants call
          and give them the {boast} of their Self Praise Republic
            Bel[i]eve me my Brothers we must Surely fall

[3]   Have we as Strangers ⟨and⟩ to valour and courage grown
            Scorned by other Trades a round
              Freedom is all the Poor Englishman can call his {own}
            Their monthly bonds is but an empty Sound

[4]   Remember for ever the banishment of Frost
            the imprisonment of Feargus and others
              and these are the men let us be gain'd or be lost
              that we have a right to claim as fathers and brothers

[5]   See the Policemen Strut,, with Insolence
           arm'd. with Cruelty and Power
       See them like Tyrants, exulting on ouer impotence
           See them exert Tyranical Power

[6]   See How the Petty Majestrates Spurns at Mr. Roberts
           and casts all the trouble on him they can
       but I tell you they are only a Set of house Lubberts
           When they come in contact with an honoust man

[7]   Say: How long Shall the Majestrates and V{i}ewers {authority}
       Rule the Land without controul
       Rise like Men, Join the Great Majoriety
       and Scourge the Tyrant from Pole to Pole

[8]   All You that wishes Your Countries welfare
       Nows the day to lend your help
       And if You let this Pass and dont look out for a fulshare
       You may make your selves content with Scilly*   skilly; heavy boiled
           and water Whelp*   dumpling

74B & C. A CALL TO THE MINERS OF GREAT BRITAIN.

1*   Britains! wheres your boasted bravery?   C: *no verse numbering*
           Can you sit unmoved &* tame: C: *and*
       And behold the bonds of Slavery,
           Shackle your's and Freedom's name!

2   When by public voice the rank you join,
           Would you heed the Tyrants call?
       Would you leave the grand united line,
           Like* a treach'rous Brother fall!?   B: *altered from* And

[3]   We to Strangers Kindness* now are bound, B: *long 's', here and
           Never let us merit scorn;   elsewhere*
       Freedom is a glorious fertile ground,
           Monthly bonds are quickly torn.

[4]   Think on Frost forever* banished far,   C: for ever
            Imprisoned Feargus with all others,
        That have nobly fought the patriot war,
            Let us claim them as our brothers!

[5]   Policemen may strut with insolence,
            Armed with ignorance &* power –   C: and
        Tyrant-like exult in impotence
            Still they only have their hour!

[6]   Petty magistrates may Roberts Spurn,
            And beset him if they can;
        He will treat them with a* noble Scorn   C: omitted
            And he'ill* baffle every Man!   C: he'll

[7]   How long shall Viewers and the Magistrates,
            Rule the land without controul?
        Britains rise and catch the Sinking States,
            ⟨And⟩* Let them see you have a Soul!   C: omitted

[8]   You that wish your injured Cause to save,
            Now's the day to look for aid;
        Let this pass and freedom finds a grave
            Rouse, ⟨and⟩* be firm and undismay'd.   C: omitted

A & B: Manuscript. **C**: Print. **A & B**: Picton. **C**: NCL 1844. **A**: Hand: William Roxby? **B**: Hand William Daniells. **C**: Broadside. Decorative border. No colophon [Dodds].
    Probably from March 1844.

75. THE COAL OWNERS' VEND, AND THE MINERS' UNION.

Cheer up, cheer up, my fellow men, don't let your spirits fail;
Our support will be coming in from Scotland and from Wales;
The miners throughout England they will your course*   B: cause
    maintain,
Because it is a noble one – your former wage to gain.

The last four years we know full well, our wages have come
    down,
As far as twenty-five per cent, five shillings in the pound;
The cause of this we do not know, but we feel the effect
We're meanly fed and poorly clad, and treated with disrespect.

Our masters say we might have earn'd, more money the last year
But live and let our Neighbour live this is the course we steer;
Had we not restricted ourselves that each might have a share,
One-fourth of us would paupers been to live on Workhouse fare.

I wonder how the masters can find so much fault with men,
For joining in a Union themselves for to defend;
These twenty-seven years or more they've had their monthly
    Vend,
For to keep up the price of Coals, which they to market send.

Had we not join'd in Union, our labour to protect,
The Workhouses would all been full throughout the coal district;
The Farmer, Butcher, Shopkeeper, and all that pay poor rate,
The Miller and the Brewer they would been in a sad state.

In eighteen hundred and twenty-nine, their monthly Vends
    they broke,
Away they went at Railway-speed, each Colliery had their stroke,
The Markets they were overstocked, the price of Coal came
    down,
Then to their monthly Vend they flew, their prices to bring
    round.

If Union be so heinous they have themselves to blame,
By setting the example in beginning the same;
They join'd themselves in Union, their capital to protect,
Our labour is our capital which we must not neglect.

The case it is so very plain, a child may understand,
The Owners have their Union, the same as working men;*   B: working-men
The sauce thats* good for gander, will not be bad for goose,   B: that's
I hope the wings of Union, will not one feather lose.

Now to conclude and finish these few lines I have penn'd,
Success to Mr ROBERTS, he is the [m]iners* friend;   B: Miner's
Success attend each Union man* where ever he may be,   B: Union-man
Bad luck attend each Blackleg, our greatest enemy.

Fairplay's a Jewel.

Print. **A:** Wigan 116 (verso). **B:** Wigan 111 (299). **A:** Broadside. Colophon: W. Ainsley, Printer, Durham. **B:** Broadside proof? No colophon [Dodds].
    Probably published on or near April 5th 1844. For William Ainsley, see Hunt, *The Book Trade*, p. 1. Compare Colls, *The Collier's Rant*, pp. 221, 330 note 65.

76. THE MINERS' FRIEND.

Dear shades of my Fathers! sad thoughts now oppress me,
    When I think on the times when you lov'd and were free;
Now your descendants are bound down by tyranny,
    To keep us in slavery our masters agree.

But by the Almighty that rules the Creation,
    We swear that no longer their fetters we'll wear;
And let them give ear, 'tis the voice of a Nation!
    Let justice take place, and let tyranny forbear.

'Tis true that the curse to labour hath bound us,
    All we want is to labour and work for our bread;
That all may live happy and free that surround us;
    That all may be clothed, and that all may be fed.

But altho' our labour brings wealth in profusion,
　　To our masters that they may in luxury live;
Their sordid minds cling to the phantom delusion
　　That we are beholden to them what they give.

But we know our just rights, and we now will maintain them,
　　Return the great blow they have aim'd at our heads;
With those evils we'll grapple while evils are in them,
　　Or for principle perish as martyrs have bled.

Then cheer up brave Miners, the day's not far distant,
　　When victory will crown us in this our just cause;
Let your hearts and your voices respond now this instant,
　　And the world while admiring will give you applause.

　　　　Framwellgate Moor.　　　　　　　　W. JOHNSON.

Print. NCL 1844. Broadside proof. No colophon [Dodds]. Another copy is in
NRO 3410/Wat/1/27. Bell 12/257 and Wigan 108 have decorative borders.
　Probably published in early April 1844. William Johnson also wrote 76.

77. [THE MINERS' GRIEVANCES]*

B&C: *title supplied*

1* A voice it* hath ⌊gone through⌋ the † breadth
　　of the land

B&C: *no verse numbering;
omitted;* sped thro'; wide

　　That the tyne wear and tees they* are* all at a
　　stand

B&C: men; were

　　The miners have struck for ⌊they have been
　　opprest*⌋

B&C: they've long been
oppress'd, **B:** *long 's', here and
elsewhere*

　　And ⌊nomore thay will work til⌋ their wrongs
　　⌊ar redrest⌋

B: no more they ⟨'ill⟩
{will}work {till}, **C:** they will
work till; **B:** be redressed!, **C:**
be redress'd

2* For ten years or more we have* been regular   C: *no stanzas*; B&C: we've
   slaves
  Bound down by our masters the greatest of
   knaves
  But no longer weel* bear it, ⌊for now we are⌋   B: we'ill, C: we'll; B&C: but,
   free   vow to be
  For right will* beat might, that our masters will   B&C: shall
   see

3 ⌊Nomore thay⌋ will get us to work by the fines   B&C: No more they
  For the ⌊splent and foul coal⌋ that we get in   C: splint and foul-coal; B&C:
   their* mines   the
  And the word ⌊seperation wont⌋ stand in our   B: separation, C: "separation",
   bill   B&C: won't
  For ⌊boath roundy⌋ and* small in the tub we   B&C: both round; B: &
   will fill

4 For* their measures and steelyards* weel* do   B&C: *omitted*; B&C: steel-
   them away   yards; B: we'ill, C: we'll
  ⌊For by them they have rob'd⌋ us for many a*   B&C: By such things they've
   long day   robbed; B: many'a
  ⌊We will work by the weight⌋ now for it* is our   B&C: By the Weight we will
   will   work; such
  That* a just beam and ⌊s[cal]e it do⌋ stand on   B&C: And; scales, let them
   the hill

5 Now* nomore* in the morning at one we will   B&C: *omitted*; No more
   rise
  Nomore* leave our homes til* the sun meets our   B&C: No more; till
   eyes
  † The ten shilling* smart we will have it is true   B&C: And; Shillings'
  ⌊So that they may⌋ keep the place safe where we   B&C: And then let them
   hew

6 ⌊Nomore in their mines we will work⌋ without   B&C: No longer; B: we'ill, C:
   air   we'll; B&C: work in the mines
  ⌊For ⟨But⟩ to have ventilation weel⌋ make it our   B&C: Ventilation, B: we'ill, C:
   care   we'll B&C: have and, B: we'ill,
        C: we'll
  Two shafts they may sink, for the down and*   B: &; B: up cast, C: up-cast
   upcast*

⟨And [round?]⟩*   B&C: *omitted*
To prevent the † hydrogen from* making a blast   B&C: strong; *omitted*

7 Then the neuk* of the putters* is to* far to run   C: rank; B&C: putter; too
   But* I know that* sixty yards † neuk* will be   B&C: For; *omitted*; of the C:
   won   rank
   ⌊In stead⌋ of twelve hours then the Boys shall   B&C: And instead
   have ten
   ⌊That they may gain knowledge before they   B&C: To gain useful
   are⌋ men   Knowledge and walk as good

8 Now the gaurantee* clause I think* it will do   B&C:guarantee; fain hope
   ⌊Thats the⌋ fifteen a week when we go down to   B&C: That is
   hew
   Eight hours and ⌊nomore we will⌋ stop in the   B&C : no longer, B: we'ill, C:
   mine   we'll B&C: fears
   And then come to bank without fear* of a fine

9 The* five shillings a* week I* think ⌊its to⌋ small B&C: *omitted*; B&C: per; B&C:
   For the ⌊widdow and famely that lowses⌋ their   we all; B & C: it too
   all   B&C: Widow and Children
                                                        when losing
   A coffin for those ⌊that is killd we do⌋ crave   B: who ⟨may⟩ {are}, C: who
   ⌊The five Pounds to bring him⌋ with mence ⌊to   are, B&C: Killed, we now
   his⌋ grave   B&C: With Five pounds to lay
                                                        them; in the

10 Now look at the dangers that* we * undergo   B&C: *omitted*; all
    While we work for our bread in the caverns
    below
    The rope it* may* † break ⌊the stone it may⌋   B&C: *omitted*; B: {may}, B&C:
    kill   soon; B&C: and the falling
                                                        stone
    And the ⌊bursting of waters the pit it may⌋ fill   B&C: waters burst forth and
                                                        the pit quickly

11 ⌊The gass*⌋ may ignite in the mine when were*   B&C: Then the Gas; A: *long 's'*;
    under   B&C: we're
    ⌊And cause subteranious lightning and⌋   B&C: Then flashes the
    thunder   lightning and roars the dread
    The* choke damp* ⌊it spares none thats left in⌋   B&C: Then; C: choke-damp,
    the mine   B&C: unsparing flies hot thro'
    ⌊Those things often hapen in⌋ tees wear and   B&C: Then happen the
    tyne   horrors on

12 Now you se* what we want and I think you   B&C: see
     will say
   That the* miners are asking nought out of the B: {the}
     way
   Then haste to the rescue, help the* sons of the B: {the}
     mine
     † Cheer on* the brave lads of the Tees Wear   B&C: And; *omitted*; B: &
     and* tyne.

Framwellgate Moor   Wm. Johnson* B: 'Wm.Johnson'

A & B: Manuscript. C: Print. A & B: Picton. C: Wigan 107 (303). Hand: William Johnson. B: Hand: William Daniells. C: Broadside. Decorative border. No colophon [Dodds]. See also Bell 12/255. Lloyd, *Come all ye bold miners*, (1952), pp. 89–90, 136, published a version 'Communicated by J.S. Bell' and 'From a MS, crediting the authorship to William Johnson, of Framwellgate Moor', which seems to rely at key points on the broadside text. Lloyd, *Come all ye bold miners*, (1978), pp. 244–45, 357, though without mentioning J.S. Bell, supplied a similar text as taken 'From a broadside, no imprint, undated (but evidently 1844), in the Picton Library collection' and claimed that 'Another version, with some alterations, is among a manuscript collection in the Wigan Public Library'. No such Picton broadside or Wigan manuscript collection can now be traced. See also C & R, *The Miners' Association*, p. 201.
   Probably written and published in early April 1844. A has a manuscript note, 'Mr Dodds'. William Johnson also wrote 76.

78. ACROSTIC.

T hou tyrant, see the Miners' glass displayed!
H ere poverty, and want may be surveyed,
E nshrouded long, now bursting from the shade.

M iners, your wrongs have taught the mighty press,
I n language bold, that they must have redress;
N o bribe, no oily promise shall prolong –
E nslaved we are, but we must break the thong!
R uled by a despot we can never toil,
S ense bids us cease and freedom spurns the soil.

A n able *Advocate* we have, whose hand
D reading no labour, every foe can stand!
V ouches afar of all good who rules the sky.
O h bless our cause of truth, humanity!
C heer our true friends with union's sacred song,
A nd teach mankind the shame of doing wrong!
T each them to live that in a future state
E ach deed may prove – a glorious advocate.

East Holywell, March 2nd, 1844.   THOS. NICHOLSON.

Print. *Miners' Advocate*, April 20th 1844, p. 88.
    Mentioned in the *Advocate* of March 9th 1844. Thomas Nicholson also wrote **63**.

79. PATRIOTISM.

The noble patriot scorns to plant a root
But that from which proceeds the freshest fruit;
For thus he reasons – If I reap the gains
Of other predecessors' honest pains
It is unfair – for every man should be
The keeper of his treasured industry!
Should every age but serve its turn and take
No thought for future times it soon would make
A bankrupt world, and thus entail a curse
From age to age, and grow from bad to worse.
Our christian predecessors careful thus
Have left a better heritage to us.
Christ's precious truth, concentred in their blood,
Revealed the price for which they nobly stood!
What they have given, will they alienate
From us, their children, such a fair estate?
We reap their well-set seed, which ne'er can fail,
But be transmitted by a just entail!
For shall the line of honour cease to live,
Or future ages execrations give,

And blast our names, and blot them from the page
Bright with the deeds of freedom's heritage?
Let pity move us, let us muse upon
Our children's fate when we are dead and gone:
Shall they, deluded, darkly grope while we
Quench the fair star of glorious liberty?
Shall it be said of us, in years to come,
That we immersed their minds in slavery's gloom?
Shall it be said, that, traitor-like, we gave
From Judas hands the annointed sent to save?
Oh, let us cherish *patriot thoughts* and give
More good to future days than we receive.
Then grateful hearts will beg of Heaven to keep
Our memories green when we in dust shall sleep.

Bo'ness, Linlithgowshire, Scotland.   GEORGE COWIE.

Print. *Miners' Advocate*, May 4th 1844, p. 96.
    Mentioned in the *Advocate* of April 6th 1844 – 'it shall be inserted in an early number'.

80. THE MINERS RIGHTS*   B: THE MINER'S RIGHT.

1 On the eighteenth of march eighteen hundred †   B: and
        forty three
    the pitman* of the tyne and ⌊weare was⌋ bound   B: pitmen; Wear were
        down to slavery
    ⌊Cors the tyarnt coall vewour that lives by his   B: CHORUS The tyrant coal
        pray⌋   viewer that lives by his prey
        Right shall beat might and drive ⌊tyrney a way⌋   B: tyranny away
            thaye* have turned the poor pitman head   B: They; pitmen headlong;
                long* to the Dore*   door
                this is thare* last shift for thay* can dow*   B: their; they; do
                    no more

2 But now the {word} is spread through the   B: breadth
        breath* of our land
    that the tyne weare* and tees men are all at a   B: Wear
        stand
      * the tyarnt coall vewour that lives by his   B: The tyrant, &c. *only, after*
                    pray   *this and every other verse*
        Right shall beat might and drive tyrney a
                    way
        thay have turned the poor pitman head
                    long to the Dore
          this is thare last shift for thay can dow
                    no more

3 The Kekers*+ and banksman* thay dow* us   B: keekers; banksmen; do; no
        noo* good
    for ⌊thay lay out⌋ and set out* the fift* part of   B: they lay-out; set-out; fifth;
        ou* tubs   our
    the ⌊vewours thay⌋ have all the [?]st* at thare*   [B: viewers they; rest; their
        command
    the pitman* supports them as † understand   B: pitmen; I
    the tyarnt coall vewour that live by his pray
    Right shall beat might and drive tyrney a way
    thay have turnned the poor pitman headlong to
        the Door
    this is thare last shift for thay can dow no more

4 ⌊Nither laid ought⌋ nor set out* shall stand in   B: Neither laid-out; set-out
        our bill
    for both round and small in the tub we shall fill
    Eight ours* and no {longer} will* stop in the   B: hours; we'll
        mine
    then we will come to bank without fear of a fine
    the tyarnt call vewours that lives by his pray
    Right shall beat might and drive tyrney away
    thay have turned the por pitman hedelong* to   A: *altered from ?*
        Door
      this is thare last shift for thay can dow no
                more

5 The ⌊garnte {guarantee} clas i fain⌋ it will dow*   B: guarantee clause I find; do;
     that*   omitted
  is fifteen a* week when we go down to huwe*   [B: per; hew
  and instead of twelve hours the boys shall have
     ten
  to gain usefull* knowledge to make them walke*   B: useful; walk
     like {good}*men   B: omitted
  the tirant Coall vewour that lives by his pray
  Right shall beat might and drive tyrine a way
  now thay have turned the poor pitman out to
     the Dor
  this is thare last shift thay can dow no more

6 The miners have struck ‹till their›* for they ve*   B: omitted; they've
     long been oppress[t?]*   B: oppress'd
  and no more will they work till theirs* wrongs   B: their; redress'd, A: long 's',
     be redressed*
  then cheear* up brave miners and stand man to   B: cheer
     man
  for Roberts and Beesley will dow* all they can   B: do
  the tyarnt call vewours that lives by his pray
  Right will beat might and drive tyriney way
  and thay have turned the poor pit man to the
     Door –
  this is thare last shift thay can dow no more

7 Now you see what we want and i think you will
     say
  that the miners are asking nought out of the way
  come all you good frinds* help the sons of the   B: friends
     mine
  and cheare* the brave of* {?} lads * tees weare*   B: cheer; omitted; of; Wear
     and tyne
  the tyart call vewiours that live by thar pray
  Right will beat might and drive tyurney away
  and thay have turnd the poor pitman to the Dor
     this is thare last shift thay can dow no mor

Winlaton   James Purdy*   B: James Purdy, Winlaton.

+ *pit-bank overlooker or inspector of coals: the word 'keek' also means to look slily*

A: Manuscript. B: Print. A: Picton. B: NCL 1844. Another copy is Wigan 112 (298). A: Hand: James Purdy, with changes by William Daniells. B: Broadside proof. No colophon [Dodds].
    Probably published early in May 1844 – see also **107**.

81. A NEW SONG ON THE PITMEN'S GRIEVANCES. BY JANE KNIGHT.

Come all kind-hearted Christians,
    And listen to my song,
Such times in Durham ne'er were known
    And yet to last so long;
Our wives and children are turned out.
    And camping out of doors,
Which causes us to wander,
    And your charity implore.

'Twas on the 5th of April,
    That was the very day,
Our Leaders had appointed
    Our Tools to bring away.
Until our wages are advanced,
    We must work no more;
Which causes us to wander,
    And your charity implore

Our Masters are hard hearted,
    Our Wages they'll not rise,
They will not hear us speak a word
    Our wants for to appease,
Unless our Union we will break,
    And Roberts own no more,
Which causes us to wander,
    And your charity implore.

Ye Black-legs of Wingate,
  I would have ye mind your ways,
You follow Christ for Fishes,
  And then for Gold betray,
Ye have sold us all for silver,
  And what can ye do more;
Which causes us to wander,
  And charity implore.

Here's a health to Mr. Roberts,
  And long may he reign;
Likewise all other gentlemen
  Who do our rights maintain,
Before our Union we will break,
  And Roberts own no more,
We're resolved for to wander
  Upon some distant shore.

Print. NCL 1844. Broadside. No colophon [Dodds]. Lloyd, *Folk Song*,
pp. 346–47, and Lloyd, *Come all ye bold miners*, (1978), p. 261, rearranged the
stanzas into four lines and made other alterations.
    Probably published in early May 1844. Lloyd, *Come all ye bold miners*,
(1978), p. 358, dated this piece 'July 1844', but by that date the evictions were
almost complete and serious resistance had been crushed.

82. A NEW SONG.

Come all you Colliers in this place,
  And listen to my song;
And {we'ill} <we will>* show <?>* {the} Viewers   B: We'll *omitted*
      {that they} have
  Done us, poor Miners, wrong.
They have oppressed* us very sore,   A: *long 's', here and elsewhere*
And that we truly know;*   [B: *every other line indented*
They've tied a knot they cannot loose,   *throughout;*
  They've struck the fatal blow.

Chorus.
Now is the time our wrongs to prove
    While we in chorus join;
Long may the Union flourish still
    On Tees, on Wear and Tyne!

The monthly bonds they offered us,
Have forced <?>* us now to strike;   **B:** *omitted*
Six weeks now idle we have been,
Which Owners do not like.
And if we go to work again,
We vow {to have} our rights, <to have>*   **B:** *omitted*
The Six cwt* Tub we will regain,   *le* hundredweight
And no more <u>Sevens</u> or <u>Eights</u>.

Our price they lowered* from time to time,   **B:** lower'd
Which to our grief we know:
We'll ne'er forget their bounteous deeds
    Wherever we may go.–
They're bet this time they all confess
    Our Union's spread so far:
Against us they've combined for long
    Now, Sirs, we're on <u>a par</u>.

The Blackleg-men, have proved untrue
    And sought for rest &* ease: **B:** and
They've undermined their fellow men,*   **B:** fellow-men
    Their Masters for to please.
    They hope for favors* after this,   **B:** favours
And how they hew away!
But the time is coming fast, my lads,
    When they will rue the day!

There's one thing we have vowed to do,
    That is to Keep the Peace;
And not to trouble any foe,
    But friendship to increase
Thus Roberts has exhorted us,
    By his advice we go:
He never led us <u>yet</u> to wrong,
    And never will we Know.

To Tyrany* he is a foe   B: tyranny
   A friend unto the Poor,
From London he has brought a law
   Which will our rights secure –
He let the hapless pris'ners free
   The Country stood amazed:
The Masters they were panic struck
   And nearly all went crased.*   B: crazed

Now to conclude a Collier's Song
   No more ‹Ive Ive›* {Ive}* got to say,   A: *sic*, B: *omitted*; B: I've
Our Union shall be proved the first
   For we will have the sway.
Now Brothers all, I pray beware,
To each stand firm &* true   B: and
And let us show ‹to›* {that} rising years   B: *omitted*
   Depend on {what} we do –

                      B: JOHN ATKI[NSON.]

A: Manuscript. **B:** Print. **A:** Picton. **B:** Wigan 112 (298). **A:** Hand: William Daniells **B:** Broadside proof? No colophon [Dodds]. Lloyd, *Come all ye bold miners*, (1952), pp. 97–98, 137, printed a version in four-line stanzas, with a title of *Come All You Colliers* and without the two stanzas found on a separate sheet, as from a 'text communicated by J.S. Bell' 'from a miner's manuscript'. Lloyd, *Come all ye bold miners*, (1978), pp. 250, 357, retained the new title, stanza-form and truncated text, but described the source simply as 'From a manuscript in the Picton Library collection'.
   Six weeks of the strike ended on May 16th 1844.

83. LINES ON THE DEATH OF ROBERT CARR.

Lamented Carr! how sudden was your death!
When the grim monster came to stop your breath
You breath'd not in the mine – your glass was run,
Destined brief space to feel the glorious sun
That brightly shone above your fated head.
Loud blew the wind – the winged arrow sped.
Uncertain life! oh, may we ready stand
For death prepared to sit at God's right hand.

Framwellgate Moor Colliery.   GEO. PATTERSON.

Print. *Miners' Advocate*, May 18th 1844, p. 104.

84.   THE MINERS' MOTTO.

WRITTEN FOR THE MINERS' ADVOCATE.*   **B&C:** *omitted*

"Let us live by our Labour" – and never forget,
    Tho' our destiny weaves us a troublesome chain,
When the worth of our labour is generously met
    The pleasure will balance the weight of the pain!
'Tis oppression that only can injure the peace,
    And rob the young heart of its joy and content;
For who would be happier, were tyrants to cease
    To laden the back overburden'd* and bent?   **B&C:** overburdened

We care not for riches – our children supply
    Every treasure of price with affection and love;
And we care not for honours, the great and the high –
    The *honours we** sigh for, is *faithful* to prove!   **C:** *no italics throughout*
Yes, faithful to *all* who like *men* and not *slaves*,
    Shall hold us (tho'* humble in station) to be;   **B&C:** though
But when, by hard grinding, they* treat us as knaves   **C:** the
    Our bosoms are roused and we vow to be free!

We are lowly! but shall we be spurned by the great?
　　Omnipotence honours the rank of the *soul,*
And heeds not the mock'ry of splendour and state,
　　But weighs *the kind feelings* of man as a *whole!*
We are men, and possessed of God's image and spirit,
　　In the eyes of our Maker as great and as high,
As the butterfly creatures that soar without merit,
　　Tho'* winged, but poor *worms* that with　　　　B&C: Though
　　　　maggots must lie.

Then blame not the Miners who wish to secure
　　The *right of the workman** – *the worth of his toil;*　B&C: workmen
Who shrink not from danger nor death to procure
　　Teeming coffers of gold from the womb of the soil.
Let our masters proclaim us the rudest of men,
　　Let them scurrilous epithets foolishly give;
But, oh, let them *never withold what we gain –*
　　"For we live by our labour – we labour to – live!"

J.P.ROBSON

Print. **A:** *Miners' Advocate*, May 18th 1844, p. 104. **B:** Robson, *The Monmomaniac*, p. 238. **C:** Ross, *The songs of the Tyne*, No.8. For Ross' songbook, see Thompson, *Newcastle Chapbooks*, p. 73.

85. THE COLLIERS' APPEAL TO THE COUNTRY, BY R. HOLDER.

Good christians all to me draw near before I go
　　　　away,
And lend a kind attentive ear to what I've got to
　　　　say;
And when I've read you these few lines my paper
　　　　does contain,
I hope in love your tender minds will let me
　　　　favor* gain.　　　　　　　　　　　　B&C: favour

I come to plead the Collier's cause, these poor
    enslaved men,
That venture through earth's flinty jaws in[to a
    lonesom]e den;
There they toil hard all the day long and thro'
    [dark ca]verns run,
Without one feeble glimmering ray, of day lig[ht
    o]r the sun.

When boys at six years old – early in the morning
    rise,
In winter trudge through frost and snow with
    bitter moans and cries;
Then down a pit nine-score* yards deep these   **B&C:** nine score
    poor lads have to ride,
And on some narrow burrs* they creep with   ?planks
    danger on each side.

To fetch you coal it is too true these little boys
    have gone:
But oh! the weeping mother view, when she has
    lost her son.
How many little boys are kill'd, within these pits
    I've known,
To sufferings great their bodies yield, in blooming
    youth cut down.

And if each precious life is spared till he grows up
    a man,
Thro' hardships crooked some are made, and look
    both pale and wan;
And as these lads grow up in years, like slaves they
    thus are train'd;*   **B&C:** trained
What marks their mangl'd bodies bear – 'tis few
    escape being lamed.

And view those pits where they've to work, so
    deep with safety lamp,
Where foul air lights and at a stroke they're killed* **B:** kill'd
    by fire damp;

In sulphurous blaze their flesh is burnt – just in
     their bloom cut down,
Their mangl'd* bodies are so bruised you scarcely   B&C: mangled
     could them own.

Some pits the water does burst in and drowns the
     colliers all;
Others are lam'd and crush'd to death by heavy
     stones that fall;
And some when riding up the shaft the rope
     sometimes has broke,
The colliers to the bottom dash'd – this world
     clos'd at a stroke.

In winter early in the morn these colliers leave
     their wives,
To get good coal to keep you warm they venture
     much their lives;
Also their little children dear, their harmless babes
     to feed,
Yet colliers they are prest severe some help from
     you they need.

No Indian slaves, transports abroad, nor all the
     men of war;
No men on earth are used so ill as the poor colliers
     are;
They'll gladly go and venture still for you to have
     a fire,
And all they want or what they crave – "the
     labourer's worth his hire."

By weight their* masters sell you coal, but colliers   B&C: the
     they compel
To work by measure, so much a corve, which does
     not suit them well;
These corves the masters oft enlarge and make
     them a great size,
Which does increase the colliers'* work, and then   B&C: collier's
     pull off their price.

For eleven or twelve long* hours a day they're   **B&C:** *omitted*
      working under ground,
And only earn ten shillings a week through all the
      country round;
They're so screw'd down that they can't live,
      they're fast on every side,
O Britons won't you them relieve – better for them
      provide.

When the Israelites in Egypt were by Pharaoh
      'prest severe,
With heavy burdens day by day too much for
      them to bear,
Then God a Moses did prepare to set his people
      free,
And drowned Pharaoh and his host when crossing
      the Red Sea.

Lord, let a Moses rise again the colliers to release,
And free them from the tyrant's hand and bid
      them go in peace;
'Tis not the colliers thus alone, but view the
      country o'er,
Look at the starving multitude how masters press
      them sore.

Such acts they will not stand the test when called
      to the bar,
When every secret action speaks, then tyrants you
      will fear;
But he that's cloth'd and fed the poor or lent a
      helping hand
The Lord will recollect the deed when he does in
      judgment* stand.   **B&C:** judgement

'Tis hard within a christian land, poor men to be
      thus used,
For if they speak or want what's right they're
      turn'd off and abus'd.

Now is their masters thus to press and keep their
    workmen down,
And not a single word be said or to the country
    shown?

Yes, let their deeds be spread abroad so far as
    Britons reign,
Till every master does begin to give what's right to
    men;
I'd have the masters well to live and let the men
    live too;
But fortunes great they want to save by screwing
    men so low.

Now in two days men work as much as formerly
    in three,
And won't you lend a helping hand to ease their
    misery;
We sing, ⌊that "Britons shant be slaves,"⌋ and   B&C:"That Britons shan't be
    still old England's full,   slaves,"
Of worse than slaves, and tyrants try the nation
    thus to gull.

Now to conclude my tale, kind friends, and bring
    it to an end,
I hope you'll view the collier's cause and try them
    to befriend;
But mark what the old proverb says, "a friend in
    time of need,
He that his neighbour doth befriend he shall be
    blest indeed."

Print. **A**: Wigan 52. **B**: Bell 12/254. **C**: Wigan 52 and 52 verso. **A**: Broadside. No colophon (Dodds?). **B&C**: Broadside. No colophon (Dodds?). Both broadsides begin with a prose statement. That given here is from **A** (with one apparent misprint from **B**):

    The evils of which the Colliers complain are: – First, – Reduction has been made in their wages to a very great extent, so that they and their families are perishing for lack of food. Secondly, – A great addition has been made to their day's work, without any corresponding advance per day to their wages; the reverse indeed, is the case, for they have now as much coal to get in *two days, as formerly in three days*, when steam was not so generally used, the corves or waggons which they fill with coal in the pits having been enlarged from year to year, even from month to month, without the consent of the colliers. Thirdly, – Ten or twelve shillings a week, which is the pay for the majority of the colliers, is not sufficient to maintain themselves and families, and pay those expenses consequent upon becoming householders. Fourthly, – They are obliged to work in water, or in such damp places that they are subject to rheumatism, and all sorts of complaints. Fifthly, – On account of the narrowness of the places, they have to crawl to and fro in the tunnels like beasts of burden. Sixthly, – They are obliged to work naked or nearly so. Seventhly, – The masters, though always selling to the public by weight, compel them to get the coal by measure, or so much per corve. By enlarging the corves they have considerably increased their day's labour; formerly the masters did not enlarge the corves as they do now, for if they had the public would have got the benefit of it, but now that they sell coal by weight, they get all the advantage themselves. Eighthly, – The masters have discharged and left destitute some of [**B**: o] the delegates the colliers had chosen to represent their grievances, in order to intimidate, frighten or terrify them from further attempts at improving their condition, and that of their families. Ninthly, – On account of having so much work to do, they cannot attend to the necessary precautions, and by this means thousands are killed, lamed, burnt, or scorched alive, &c. Tenthly, – Their employers use defective machinery to draw them up and let them down into the pits, and do not ventilate and drain the mines as they should for the preservation of health and life.

One of the Wigan copies has a note in Dodds' handwriting, '1000 May 25 1844', presumably indicating the print-run. A manuscript note on **B** indicates it was 'Bought 28 May 1844 price 1d'. A note on one of the other Wigan copies (in apparently identical handwriting, suggesting deliberate multiple purchasing) indicates it was 'Bought 28 May 1844'. **A** has been folded neatly three times, and was evidently copied by Dodds using a very similar format and type-face.

86.   SONG.
TUNE, – "The Brave Old Oak."

Away wi' the knave, the lying knave,
   Who hath gulled* us "victims" long –   tricked
Wi' *his* off-puts *we've* "hungry guts,"
   And now he wants a song!
There's *fear* in his frown, as the cash gets down,
   And "the last in the Bank" runs out;
While the "Wire-rope" "smarts" wi' the Thornley
     "quarts,"

And the trial's "up the spout."
   Then away wi' the knave, the lying knave,
     Who hath gulled us victims long –
  Wi' *his* off-puts *we've* "hungry guts,"
     And now he wants a song!

In the days of old, 'twas glad to behold
  Each pitman happy and gay –
No work we refused, we were not "abused,"
  And made our money "like hay."
On our pay-day, with revelry gay,
  We sang in the blithest strains;
Each *drank* his"quart," and was loth to part,
   But nought o' that now remains!
     Then away, &c.

We had then rare times, when the Christmas
     chimes
  Were a merry sound to hear,
And the "singing hinny"* sung, as the girdle   a rich, kneaded cake
     hung,
  Our canny auld wives to cheer.
Now this knave hath the sway – we must obey,
  And a ruthless king is he;
But we'll send him t' th' South, and that'll stop his
     mouth,
  And right happy again we'll be.
     Then away, &c.

AN OLD PITMAN.

86. Print. NCL 1844. Unidentified newspaper-cutting. See also C & R, *The Miners' Association*, p. 150.
   The seventh week of the strike ended on May 23rd 1844.

87. AN ADDRESS TO THE MINERS.

Awake, ye sons that work the mine,
Ere youthful vigorous years decline,
 And ages feeble ray
Destroy the spirit, force, and power,
In which we gladden at this hour,
 The zenith of our day!

Too well we know we are oppress'd,
But as by Union we are blest,
 'Twill remedy this ill.
Come, then, and join the numerous band,
And drive oppression from the land,
 By our united skill!

Had we no evils to redress,
Our plaints and cries would soon be less,
 And enmity would fail.
Each in turn would blessings share,
And they who gave, could always spare,
 Their source would never fail!

But oh! how chang'd and sad the case,
When we survey a brother's face,
 Behold want pictured there:
No future hopes illume his smile,
For all his labour and his toil
 Is bordering on despair.

And yet the finer mould at home,
His flesh of flesh, his bone of bone,
 Feels agonizing pain
When mournful voices round her cry,
"We faint for hunger, we will die,
 We cannot here remain!"

Is this the case? then, God, with me
Link fast the chain of liberty,
   And bind us one and all.
Break thou the bonds of tyrant sway,
And turn their swords to rods of clay,
   And make oppression fall.

Let Union then display her power,
And let us triumph in that hour.
   When summoned to the field
To combat with malignant foes,
That will, with Union, interpose,
   And die before we yield.

Let our united strength come on,
Like youthful David's single stone,
   That slew the Philistine.
Let gather'd force subdue the foe,
And lay our proud Goliaths low,
   For such a wish is mine.

DAVID MOFFAT.

Stobhill, near Dalkeith, Scotland, May 25th, 1844.

Print. *Miners' Advocate,* June 1st 1844, p. 116.
   The *Advocate* of March 23rd, 1844, p. 72, indicated that Daniells 'Received
the poetry from friend Deans, Dalkeith, which shall have an early insertion'.

88. THE FAMISHING MINER.

Before the rulers of his Fate,
   The Miner humbly stands;
He cheek is wan, his eye is sunk,
   Toil-hardened are his hands.
Care-worn his face, and deep the stamp
   Of sorrow and despair;
Tho' blasted be his faded form,
   A heart is beating there!

A heart, that, spite of human foes,
   Is true to Nature's ties;
That swells whene'er he dares to think
   Of this life's destinies!
For to the Molochs of the land,
   He oft hath made appeal;
Give, give to me my "daily bread" –
   But no! their heart is steel.

The wife that to his manly breast,
   In hopeful youth he clasp'd,
Must sink beneath the deadly blow,
   By stern starvation grasp'd!
His children clinging to his knee,
   Have begged of him for bread;
And in the bitterness of soul,
   Sobbing, he hangs his head.

His brother worms feast sumptuously,
   Their lands are broad and fair,
Of want and wretchedness like his
   Why should the wealthy care?
Stern were the laws, which hist'ry tells,
   Old Draco wrote in blood;
But sterner still must be the code,
   That robs the poor man's food.

How long shall toil, without its meed,
   Be all his earthly doom?
How long shall life to Miner's* be,   *sic*
   A sunless – joyless tomb?
How long, how long! shall selfishness
   And Might o'er Right prevail!
Arise! ye Miners, at whose voice
   Stern Tyrant – Cowards quail!

Spital Tongues.   JAMES GORDON.

Print. *Miners' Advocate*, June 15th 1844, p. 124.

89. A NEW SONG BY WILLIAM HORNSBY

1 A Song I,ll* sing if you,l* attend, <&>* {and} pay B: *all apostrophes raised*; you'll;
     attention to my ditty,   *omitted*
   To these few lines that I have pen'd, to waste
     my time it is A pity;
   I sing of things in form of men, but they of men
     have not a feature,
   For God did never man ordain, to undermine* B: nudermind,
     his fellow creature.

2 At Shotton moor we have some tools, for men it
     is not fit to call them,
   They think that every one is fools, but mark &* B: and
     see what will befall them;
   Theres* some of them been much esteem'd,   B: There's; and
     both far &* near their name has sounded,
   But little have they thought or dreamed,* how B: dream'd
     their char<r>acter now is wounded.

3 There's one perhaps you know him well, A
    <u>preacher</u> was, perhaps youve* heard {him,}   **B:** youv'd
  For gain his principle did sell, for it the Lord
    will sure* reward him;   **B:** scre
  He has not kept the law so good, which we as
    well as him should go by,
  Do to thy neighbour as thou would, that thou
    would wish for to be done by.

4 Then <u>little Crooks*</u> has got A face, for every one **B:** *initials only, here and*
    that he does talk with,   *elsewhere*
  He has proved it since he got <u>A place</u>, and A
    <u>yard wand</u>*+ all for to walk with;   **B:** wan
  To act the Tyrant he knows how, but he had
    better stop his scoffing,
  Lest overboard we him should throw, then dirty
    tool what will come of him.

5 Then <u>Willy gape</u> A* <u>cockfield</u> man, he is A base **B:** o; and; treacherous
    &* treachorous* villain,
  To hurt us he'l* do all he can, but to do † good **B:** he'll; us; he's
    he is* never willing;
  A dirty useless* tool is he, he is always trying to **A:** *long 's', here and elsewhere*
    deceive ye,
  He should be drowned in the sea, he is not fit to
    live beleive* me.   **B:** believe

6 Then <u>Wardle tom's</u> next in the clan, for favour
    he'l* do ought that's dirty,   **B:** he'll
  To undermine his fell[ow] man,* but men like **B:** fellow-man; you
    these can never hurt ye;*
  False to his neighbour he has been, now mark
    &* see what will come on it,   **B:** and
  He'l* <u>rob his master</u>* twill* be seen, give him **B:** He'll; *no italics*; 'twill
    the chance depend upon it

7 And <u>ruff faced*</u> <u>Jack</u> did act his part, as well as   B: ruff-faced
    any that I've named.
  To work he never had the heart, for
  <f>{W}orthlessness he has been famed;
  He once was called a <u>bonny clock</u>, but like
    something that's* out of season,   B: *omitted*
 · The ⌊pendulum's <was>⌋ not worth a shock,* it   B: pendulum is; jot;
    was so short {and} ⌊that <was>⌋ the reason.   B: that's

8 Then plain face* <u>butes</u> so bad did show, when   B: fac'd
    to the Magistrates they took* him,   B: toyk
  He cried ⌊out stop to work I,l go,⌋ just as the   B: "stop, to work I'll go,"
    clerk was going to book him;
  † I cannot think to go to gaol,* although <the   B: "; jail
    Union> {resolved when} I did enter,
  But now I feel my strength to fail, for I have not
    the heart to venture.*†   B: enter; "

+ a coal-measuring-rod, ie an underground official's badge of office

A: Manuscript. B: Print. A: Picton. B: Wigan 111 (299). A: Hand: William Hornsby, with changes by William Daniells. B: Broadside proof? No colophon [Dodds]. Lloyd, *Come all ye bold miners*, (1978), pp. 232–33, 356, published a slightly amended version as *The Tools of Shotton Moor*, taken from 'a collection of (mainly) manuscript papers in the Picton Library, Liverpool'.

Probably from mid-June 1844. William Hornsby also wrote **57** and (probably) **107**.

90. [THE BLACKLEGS.]*   B: *title supplied*

Come sit ye down and hear the news
And screw your courage tight man *   B: *every other line indented*
And i,ll* tell you of that rattlesnake   B: *all apostrophes raised*
Poor Bob the Rechabite man

Now Bob he was a ploughboy*   B: *plough boy*
When ploughing was delight man
Twas then he came to Biggesmain*   B: *Bigge's Main*
And joined the Rechabites man

We thought he was a genius
With his buckles shining bright man
His looks did show the hypocrite
Poor Bob <?>* Rechabite man   B: *the*

Now when he came from Biggesman*   B: *Bigge's Main*
Twas* rather late at night man   B: *'Twas*
This hypocrite he did come hear*   B: *here*
The horses for to Keep man

Now when the horses they were nearly done
He was often on his prey man
And because he was a hypocrite
He gat* in the Rolleyway* man   B: *got; rolley-way, ie the horse road underground*

He stopped their* a good few weeks   B: *there*
But it was all in vain man
He had to take the pick it did his trick
Hewing at the Bankhead Crane man

He corved her in* at the right neuk*   *ie,* began hewing; B: *rank*
No vantage* could he make man   B: *'vantage*
He told it to the putter lads
That he had got a sore headache* man   B: *head-ache*

He quickly put up his gear
He buckled them so tight man
He thought it was a better plan
For to be on the Rechabites man

And then to bank poor Boby* came   B: Bobby, *here and elsewhere*
And home he went with speed man
Bella wrung her hands and gave a scream
That Boby he was dead man

She bathed his brow with vinegar
And laid him into bed man
She laped* him up in the cradletwilt*   B: lapped, *ie* wrapped; cradle
And bade him rest his head man   quilt

Then the docter* he was sent for   B: Doctor
A chap of noted skill man
The neighoubers* they were all called in   B: neighbours
Because Poor Boby he was ill man

The doctor he did soon appear
The day was now far spent man
Took out his watch and felt his pulse
He* could not find out his complaint man   B: But

The neighbours stood amazed
And stagnated to the brain man
Twas with the freight* that Boby gat   B: fright
Hewing at the Bankhead Crane man

She placed her hands <?> upon <?> † hips   B: her
I have gotten such a freight* man   B: fright
No more shall he hew down the pit
As long as their is* a Rechabite man   B: there's

He lay in bed for three long months
The nights were very dark man
Now he has broke the Rechabites
And gone to shifty wark* man   B: shift-work

Away to shift wark* boby went   B: shift-work
without either fear or doubt man
He stopped their* but as* short time   B: there; a
Untill* he was wrought out man   B: Until

The men they all felt for him
And pityed* his case man   **B:** pitied
If it had not been the union
He would had to left the place man

Now all the thanks that we have gat*   **B:** got
I'm sure it is* not our due man   **B:** it's
He has Broken up the Rechabites
And joined the Blackleg crew man

Now as you walk down Hebburn town
Only keep your eyes before man
And you will* see that bonney* ornament   **B:** you'll; bonny
It stands before the door man

Now twice a week she is* cleaning it   **B:** she's
And makes it shine so bright man
It is the case upon my word
Poor Bob the Rechabite man

There,s that Bonney* nursery before the door   **B:** bonny
Of puple* stones and chalk man   **B:** pebble
Fine Bella she does cock her lugs
All in the garden walk man

The people all* as they pass* by   **B:** *omitted;* **A:** *long 's'*
They look at her with spite man
They think upon the blackleg Knave
its* Bob the, Rechabite man   **B:** It's

But that happy day will come at last
When we will get our rights man
We will* think upon the blackleg Knave   **B:** We'll
As he did the Rechabites man

Now this is to conclude my song
I have got nothing more to state man
We,ll neer* forget that hypocrite   **B:** ne'er
Its* Bob the Rechabite man   **B:** It's

But that bonny day will come at last
When we will get our due man
We,ll think upon that hypocrite
Likewise the blackleg crew man

John Henderson

A: Manuscript. **B:** Print. **A:** Picton. **B:** NCL 1844. **A:** Hand: John Henderson. **B:** Broadside. No colophon [Dodds]. Lloyd, *Come all ye bold miners*, (1978), pp. 234–37, 356, retitled this piece *The Rechabite Man*, missed out stanza 23 and made various other changes. He cited 'a broadside, no imprint, in the Picton Library collection' as his source, yet his text followed the Picton manuscript version at various points. No Picton broadside of this piece has so far come to light.

Probably from June 1844. Lloyd dated the piece to 1835. According to Manders, *A History of Gateshead*, pp. 58–59, Rechabites did not begin organising on Tyneside until 1837. John Henderson's handwriting is similar to that of *The Roving Ploughboy* (**Appendix 1**).

91. A DIALOGUE BETWEEN HARRY HEARTLESS AND PETER PLUCK.

P. Good mornin Harry, how dis things luk now?
   A good way better than when aw saw thou,
   But yet aw guess, by that grave luk o' thine,
   Thou still dost murmur, and dost still repine,
   Aw really dinna understand sic folks;
   Ye're only easy under Tyrant's yokes,
    Freedom charms ye not, an if it only cost,
   A single hungry belly, 'twad be lost.

H. Nay Peter, thou's harder than thou ought to be,
   A coward aw never was, nor thought to be;
   But still if aw mun tell thee all my mind,
   How things should better luk aw canna find:
   The Maisters still are stiff, an men most dune,
   An blacklegs at wark – the fight's not yet won.

P. Nut won! that aw'l awn,* but it's nut lost,   own, admit
   It may last a few days, or a few weeks at most,
   An as for the blacklegs thou's talkin about
   Not being in the union, they could'nt come out.
   But what use are they te, the spiritless villains!
   If they'll swap us price, we'll mak punds for their
        shillins,
   An the few coals they hew are all mix'd wi' dirt,
   Yet they're dear as the best, man, keep up thy
        heart.
   The Maisters are stiff, aye as stiff as a prop,
   But props sometimes crack, when the stone
        starts to drop,
   And the Maisters though stiff will bend before
        lang,
   An when it dis cum it will come in a bang.

H. Wey Peter thou luks at it different fra me,
   A bright side o' the question aw wad like te see,
   But the viewers and shopkeepers all seem to
        'gree,
   To stop the bit credit, then what can we de?
   The straingers aw's flaid'll come down fra the
        south,
   An tak the bit bread that we hev fra our mouth,
   When there's just grund to hope man aw can
        hope,
   But now aw see nane, an we'd better give up.

P. Give up, Harry! never, as lang as there's reason
   To hope we can win, an it's not yet the season,
   To groan and despair, t'winge and to yield,
   It is'nt lost yet an we'll still keep the field.
   The Maisters are quakin, but wear a good face,
   To be rogues and luck rogues wad be a disgrace,
   What less can they de? it's nought but a fudge,
   And aw wonder Harry thou's sic a bad judge.

Thou kens's weel as me the last greet lang strike,
The Maister's behaviour was just the same like,
Ane thief the ——— aw'l not tell his name,
He said to the men they might all be gaun hame,
For what they were axin he never wad pay,–
They got all they ax'd for the very next day.
'Tis true the shopkeepers hae stopt the bit cridit,
But stop a short while an they'll rue that they did it,
We may yet win the day, then they're properly
          drawn,
When we get baith shopkeepers and shops o'
          wor awn,
Then let's keep our hearts up and help ane
          another,
An in every Unionest* luk at a brother.   *sic*

H. It's very strange Peter ne odds what it be,
About which we differ, we're sure t'agree,
Yet thou never flinches it's sure to be me,
Thou sees things se ready an niver a stammer,
Ane wad swear thou had studied baith logic an
          grammar.
A'l e'en tak thy advice and keep up my heart,
An niver till we get what we want will au* start. ɪ

P. That's reet Harry lad, we'll not flinch a peg,
We'll eat what we hev, an then start an beg,
We'll tell them plain stories what we hev felt,
For experience tells better than ony that's telt,
We'll tell a' the fines, a' the set-out, an laid-out,
O' the doctor, an house rent, an other things
          paid out,
O' the trifles that's left to get meat for our wives,
'Wor bairns an 'worsels to keep in 'wor lives,
An aw ken when they hear us, they'll give us
          their aid,
An help us to equal the other men of trade.

COMPOSED SOLELY FOR THE BENEFIT OF THE
   Men of Framwellgate Moor Colliery,
      By one of Themselves.

Print. Wigan 117 (295). Broadside. No colophon [Dodds].

Probably published in late June 1844. We know of three authors from Framwellgate Moor Colliery – William Johnson, John Wall and George Patterson – but the anonymous author of this text may have been a fourth.

92. MUNKWAREMOUTH TURN-OUT
Tune, – "Nae Luck about th' house."

Great George cam ridin' in his gig –
　　His horse did sweat and blaw –
Wiv fayce se white a' flaid wi fear
　　He cam frev Shiney-raw.
And mounted on his borrowed nag
　　Three-halfpenny Jack rode fast,
Ye'd said the deil was chasing him
　　An' it was near his last.

CHORUS.

So keep up your hearts, ye Miners brave,
　　Tho' ye're turned te the door
Wiv all yer sticks, and wives, and bairns,
　　Yet heaven will help the poor.

For mony a sin to poor Jack's charge,
　　In police-buiks is seen,
'Bout gas lamps broke, and knockers wrench'd,
　　Bruised heads, and blacken'd een.
The Pit-bairns a' cam out to stare –
　　The dogs cam out te bark!
The Viewer-bums heard poor folk's prayer,
　　Then said, "let's get te wark!"

Then cam the guard o' royal blue,
    All led by Captain Brown;
He wadna touch the pitmens' sticks,
    Nor help to pull them down.
Great George than spak te Noble Wade,
    "Bring bed-keys, if thou can!"
Wade said, "now, gang thysel, thou Bum!
    Te Heckelbairney gang."

So George, the Bum, and Ha'-penny Jack,
    Bill Redford and Tom Shiels,
Pulled down, and carried clocks and drawers,
    Beds, mugs, and traps, and creels;
Chalk pussey-cats, and chairs, and stuils;
    Claise-horse, and brush, and pan,
And out wiv pokers, skeels, and rakes,
    These nobil viewers ran.

A fair day's wage for fair day's wark,
    The Miners want te see.
Toil in the deep and dreary mines,
    Rewarded ought to be.
We hev ne house aboon our heeds –
    The sky's wor coverin',
Yet tho' we starve, we'll keep the peace,
    Wor rights we so shall win!

Print. Wigan 111. Broadside proof? No colophon [Dodds].
    Probably published late in June 1844.

93. A NEW SONG BY HENRY HOLLIDAY OF GREENCROFT COLLIERY*

B: A New Song *only*

1* Come all you* bold miners where-ever* you be
⌊one moment give ear & listen⌋ to me
i.ll sing you a song ⌊& not keep you long⌋
of our bold* la{w}yer Roberts that praiseworthy
man.

B: *no verse numbering*; ye; wherever
B: And give for a moment attention B: in the best way I can
B: brave

2 He is* a dread to all tyrants, where ever* he goes
they would ⌊rather by far⌋ take a bull by the nose
then ⌊have for to meet him &⌋ stand face to face
for ⌊as sure as they meet him he does them⌋ disgrace

B: He's; wherever
B: sooner by half
B: meet him in contest or
B: he baffles their wisdom and Shows their

3 At ⌊Courts where he goes he does them amaze⌋
and causes ⌊all people at him for to gaze⌋

he lays down the law ⌊so plain &⌋ so Clear
if he ⌊does get Justice we need never⌋ fear.

B: Court when appearing he gives them Surprize
B: the people ⟨the people⟩ to open their eyes
B: in a manner
B: gets what is just we have No Cause to

4 he is* so Calm and so steady o-er* stating a Case
and always stands up with a smile on his face
for to meet his oponents* he [n]ever is shy
⌊for if⌋ he gets Justice he'll* soon put* them by.

B: He's; when

B: o{p}ponents
B: And when; he; puts

5 he has been the best friend that ⌊eer we did see⌋
since ⌊he came amongst us in the North Country⌋
for to ⌊break down⌋ the ⌊tyrants in that he⌋ delights
and secure* to us miners our own legal Rights

B: e'er came to our aid
B: in the North Country among us he Staid;
B: conquer; tyrant he ever
B: give

6 ⌊Previous to his coming we were sore opprest⌋   **B:** Before he came to us we
   with unlawfull* reductions ⌊i am sure its no   sore were oppress'd – *long 's',*
   Jest⌋   *here and elsewhere*
                                                     B: unlawful; he had to contest;

   by the hand of oppression we ⌊were sore⌋   **B:** sore were
   abused

   till we rouse.d* from our slumbers & boldly   **B:** rose
   refused

7 we could not* get Justice before he came down   **B:** never
   which made the* Coal Kings on ⌊us for⌋ to   **B:** {the}; the Miners
   frown
   ⌊when we⌋ laid down our Case ⌊tho ever so⌋   **B:** Tho' oft we had; to them
   Clear
   ⌊we might as well held our toungs for they   **B:** Our voices were useless, the
   would not us⌋ hear   'Kings' would not

8 they have long had the* sway but ⌊we must⌋   **B:** their; we'ill now
   have our* turn   **B:** a
   for no longer ⌊wee-l ly down beneath them &⌋   **B:** beneath them we'ill
   mourn   patiently
   we'l* teach them a lesson they.l* long bear* in   **B:** We will; they'ill; keep
   mind
   and make them ⌊to treat us poor Miners more⌋ **B:** treat Miners more gentle and
   kind

9 ⌊we have⌋ gone forward like ⌊brittons &⌋   **B:** We've; Britons and
   taken the field
   and the* weapon ⌊Call.d truth we are   **B:** a; called Truth we're
   determined⌋ to wield   determin'd
   till our rights we obtain we will not † an inch   **B:** stir
   then stand to your Collours* brave men never*   **B:** colours; and ne'er
   flinch

10 A fair price for our labour is all ⌊we do⌋ Crave **B:** that we
   and with ⌊the assistance of god we are   **B:** God for our help we're
   determin.d⌋ to have   determined
   it must not be said that the miners gave oer.*   **B:** o'er
   and lost the great fight in the year forty four

11 ⌊what ever⌋ we do we must still keep the peace **B:** Whatever
   and abide by the law never mind the disease
   ⌊tho our minds they⌋ troubled about the Black **B:** Tho' we feel rather
   legs
   ⌊lets again get⌋ to work and we.l* give them **B:** Let us get once; we'ill
   the dreggs

12 so now ⌊to Conclude & to⌋ finish my song **B:** my bold lads I must
   i ⌊told you at first i would not keep⌋ you long **B:** hope as I promised I've; not
   here's a health to bold* Roberts [the] miners* **B:** brave; Miners' – *altered from*
   best friend   *Miner's*
   ⌊for he is a brave hero that god did us send⌋ **B:** And long may he live all
                                                  our Rights to defend! –

                    †   **B:** Heny. Holliday
                                                  Green croft Colly.

Manuscript. Picton. **A:** Hand: Henry Holliday. **B:** Hand: William Daniells.
Lloyd, *Come all ye bold miners*, (1952), pp. 95–97, 137, retitled this as *The
Ballad of Roberts*, as from a 'Text communicated by J.S. Bell…from a miner's
manuscript', though he evidently relied on Daniells' highly-mediated version.
Lloyd, *Come all ye bold miners*, (1978), pp. 248–50, 357, gave the source as
'from the Picton Library collection'.
    Probably published in late June 1844. A has a manuscript note, 'Mr. Thos.
Dodds'.

94.   THE COLLIERY UNION,
          A NEW SONG.*   **B:** *omitted*
    By Elizabeth Gair, Collier's Wife.

Come all ye noble Colliery Lads
    Wherever* you belong,   **B:** Where'er
I pray you give attention
    And you shall hear my song,
'Tis concerning of our Union Lads
    For they have prov'd so true,
They have stood fast, man to man,
    We must give them their due.

CHORUS. So stick unto your Union,
         And mind what Roberts say,
         If you be guided by his word,
         You'll surely win the day.

Little did the Masters think,
  That you would stand so fast,
They thought that hunger it would bite,
  You would give up at last;
But like the widow's Crouse* of Meal,   B: Cruise
  That never did run out,
The Lord did send them fresh supplies
  That served them round about.

      CHORUS. So stick, &c.*   B: *line omitted, here and below*

The Masters they divised* a plan   B: devised
  Their Union for to break,
It only made the Colliery Lads
  The firmer for to stick;
For when they thought upon the time
  That they'd been bit before,
Before that they would go to work,
  They would beg from door to door.

      CHORUS. So stick, &c.

Then for to get the Pits to work
  They have tried every plan,
Both Scotch and Irish they have brought,
  And every Countryman;
But all the coals that they have got
  Have cost them double pay,
Cheer up your hearts, ye Colliery Lads*,   B: Lad
  You're sure to win the day.

      CHORUS. So stick, &c.

Success to your commander,
  And Roberts is his name,
Since he has prov'd so loyal,
  We'll spread about his fame;
Cheer up your hearts, ye Colliery Lads,
  He'll not leave you alone,
After he has eat the meat,
  He will give them the bone.

    CHORUS. So stick, &c.

Let's not forget young Beesley,
  A man of wit possest,*   **B:** possessed
He's gain'd the Country's favor,*   **B:** favour
  For he has stood the test;
And let your day be e'er so dull,
  You'll see the rising sun,
For they will gain your victory
  Without either sword or gun!

    CHORUS. So stick, &c.

Print. A: Wigan 117. B: Wigan 58 (297). A: Broadside. Colophon: Henderson, Printer, North Shields. B: Broadside proof? No colophon [Dodds]. See also NCL 1844. Lloyd, *Folk Song*, pp. 347–48, published the first and fifth verses as four-line stanzas, and gave the chorus as two lines, from the Henderson exemplar, with other emendations. Lloyd, *Come all ye bold miners*, (1978), pp. 262, 358, published all six verses, though still in four-line stanza form, from an unlocated 'broadside printed by Henderson of North Shields'. See also C & R, *The Miners' Association*, pp. 108–9, and Challinor, *A Radical Lawyer*, p. 106.

    Lloyd, *Come all ye bold miners*, (1978), p. 358, suggested a date of June 1844, but referred to Beesley as 'an Accrington chainmaker'.

95. SONG OF THE OPPRESSED.

Hark the noble Pitmen's cause,
Thousands call for better laws;
Tyranny we do oppose,
   Death will not make us yield.

Onward, onward, to the fight,
We pledge our all for freedom's right;
Our rings we at the altar pledge,
   We pledge them to be free.

Let women's love and men's unite,
That God may bless us in the fight;
We onward will, our cause is right,
   And tyrants they must yield.

Tho' it may seem quite strange,
The blacklegs they there* way pursue,   *sic, ie* their
With soulless courage – dangerous crew,
   And blackguards guard their way.

G.A.

Print. NCL 1844. Broadside. Decorative border. No colophon [Dodds].
   Probably from late June 1844.

96. A SONG TO THE BLACKLEGS AND ALL THATS* NOT IN THE UNION

B&C: those

Vr.1..*Colliers: where's Your once* boasted Glory
   Where's your Manly Virtue flown
   Tho* renown in ancient Story
     While Your* Store
      as before *
   Freedom or Your Liberty* own

B&C: *no verse numbering; omitted*
B&C: The
B: you
B&C: *same line as above: five-line stanzas throughout*
B&C: Bondage

2..   England ⌊and Scotland for ages⌋ flourished
   ⌊While truth and⌋ Justice Propp.d.* their State
   But when Luxury was ⌊so much⌋ Nourished
     Freedom fled
     Ruin Spred*
   Such May.. False* be Your fate

B&C: hath with Scotland
B&C: When fair; propped
B&C: *omitted*
B&C: spread
B&C: haply

3..   ⌊Blasted are Your Selfish wishes⌋
   ⌊Bit by bit they [d]aily⌋ fall
   ⌊On thy Ruin.. by thy Hewing⌋
     ⌊Every⌋ Hour
      ⌊Reduce thy Powr⌋
   ⌊Faithless* Tyrant thoult. Surely fall⌋

B&C: Selfish wishes soon are blasted
B&C: By degrees they pine &
B&C: Hateful while their branches lasted
B&C: Now each
B&C: prunes the power
A: *long 's'*; B&C: Tyrants vanquished one, B: & all, C: and all

4..   Viewers lusting after Plunder
   on thy* impoverished* Vitals Prey*
   ⌊Honours Princepels torn has fled from thee⌋
     Virtue fails
     Vice Prevails
   Certain Signs of Quick decay

B&C: *omitted*; impov'rished; C: pray
B&C: Honor's links B: they're C: they've B: torn, C: turn, B&C: asunder

5..   Think!.. o* think let heaven inspire you
   Banish Avarice,* Pride and* lust
   Let ⌊your.. Commerade brothers Virtues⌋ fire You
     ⌊on Unions Ground⌋
     ⌊While unbound⌋ †
   Stand You May!.. or* fall You Must

B&C: oh
B&C: Av.'rice; B: &
B&C: a manly courage
B&C: While unbound
B&C: On Union's ground B: - ⟨still {while} unbound -⟩
B&C: but

       By William Roxby*

B: <u>Wm. Roxby</u>, C: W.Roxby.

A & B: Manuscript. **C:** Print. **A & B:** Picton. **C:** NCL 1844. **A:** Hand: William Roxby. **B:** Hand: William Daniells. **C:** Extract from a pamphlet, *A Dialogue between three Coal Viewers after being in search of men.* Lloyd, *Come all ye bold miners,* (1978), pp. 252, 357, retitled the piece *The Durham Strike,* gave 'Song to the Blacklegs and all those not in the Union' as a subtitle, and sourced his text as 'From a broadside, no imprint or date, in the Newcastle-upon-Tyne Public Reference Library'. No such broadside can now be traced.

Probably from late June 1844. William Roxby also wrote **46** and (probably) **74**.

97. [A NEW SONG]*   *B: title supplied*

Tune: – *Good conversation under the Rose***   *B: only*

[1]*Come all ye good people that live in this village,   *entire stanza in B only*
    And listen awhile to a tale that is true,
    Concerning the Miners that all are laid idle
    And swear* so to be till they get what is due.   *B: altered from ?*
    For what do we ask but our rights in all reason?
    To be paid for our labour is all we request;
    And we're certain to get it, if firmly uniting
    We show we are men when we're put to the test.

[2]*They've lowered our wages almost to   *line in B only*
        Starvation,
    By ⌊enlar⌋   *B: enla‹?›rging the Tubs and decreasing the pay;*
    We are worse us,d* than ⌊any other class of⌋   *B: used; other poor men in*
      the nation
    By* the schemes of our masters ⌊on us to   *B: For; oppress- long 's', here and elsewhere – night & day*
      o[ppr]ess⌋
    For ⌊30 years or more, they have been   *B: thirty long years they have battled*
      combined⌋ against us
    Till ⌊at last we have⌋ united our rights to   *B: now we're ; maintain*
      obtain*
    ⌊If we keep within the law, there is no one can *B: And if we steer clear of the law ‹in› there's no danger*
      harm us⌋
    Thus Roberts has ex{h}orted* us, again and   *B: told*
      again

[3] Ten weeks ⌊we have been idle, and no signs of⌋ agreement
  B: we've been idle and yet no

  And ⌊we vow for to stand other 20 weeks or⌋ more
  B: twenty weeks longer we'ill stand yet, and

  ⌊We,r surrounded with poverty and cannot find a friend⌋
  B: Tho we're friendless, and poverty starves all around us

  ⌊And our house taken from us,⌋ and turned to the door
  B: Tho we're houseless, deserted

  Like pilgrims ⌊we are wandering all over the Country⌋
  B: forsaken the country we wander

  ⌊seeking for subsistence where ever we do⌋ go
  B: For a scanty subsistence we miserably

  ⌊We are willing to put up with this for⌋ a season
  B: Yet we never repine, for we'ill suffer

  To Conquer ⌊our enemies we are sure for to do⌋
  B: the Tyrants that causes our Woe.

[4] They have ⌊promis,d for to give {us}all better wages⌋
  B: promised to give better pay for our labour

  If ⌊we will break the Union, and let Roberts go⌋
  B: the Union we leave and friend Roberts desert,
  B: But we know to our cost that

  ⌊To our grief we know,⌋ they oft have deceived us

  ⌊For their advise to us brings slavery and woe⌋
  B: So we will not regard the advice they impart

  But* we know our just rights and we ⌊now will⌋ maintain them
  B: omitted; vow to

  ⌊We will return the blow, they have aimed at our heads⌋
  B: And the blow shall fall harmless they aim at our head;

  With those* evils we,ll* grapple ⟨them⟩* while evils are in them
  B: omitted; we'ill; omitted

  Or for* principle perish as martyrs have bled
  B: from

[5] ⌊Now to conclude my song. Ive got little more to say⌋ — **B:** So now to con[cl]ude the true things I've been Singing

⌊We will drink⌋ a health to † Roberts ⌊where ever⌋ he be* — **B:** Here's; brave; wherever **B:** goes

He,s a friend to the ⌊miner likewise other people⌋ — **B:** Miners, a foe to oppression,

⌊He s ⟨value?⟩ equal is not known in th[?] Country⌋ — **B:** A Lion in contest a Lamb in repose.

Then Cheer up my lads, † the day is not far distant* — **B:** for; is fast coming,

When victory* will crown us, ⌊in this our just⌋ cause — **B:** Vict'ry; and honour our

Let your hearts and your ⌊voises respond now this instant⌋ — **B:** voices in chorus responding

And* the world ⌊while admiring yow will give yow aplause⌋ — **B:** Show; that admires – *altered from* admiring – {and} repeats the applause

Manuscript. Picton. Hands: **A:** ? **B:** William Daniells. Lloyd, *Come all ye bold miners*, (1978), pp. 256–57, 358, called this piece *The 1844 Strike* and supplied a text (evidently based on Daniells' highly-mediated manuscript version), as 'From a broadside, no imprint or date', but with no location. No printed text has yet been found.

The tenth week of the strike ended on June 13th 1844. A was folded.

98. AULD LANG SYNE*

B: *untitled*

Once compensations* bounteous hand
Lit* up the gloomy mine
And* lusture* lent our dingy band
In † days of Auld lang syne †

C&D: Compensation's
B: Let, C&D: Illumed
B: An; C&D: lustre
D: ";", *and throughout*

* With lightsome heart* and upright head
I brave,'d* the dangerous mine
But w{h}ither'd* are* all Joys and dead
Sin' days of auld lang Syne

B: *stanza three*; B: heat
B,C&D: braved
C&D: withered; C&D: now

* When right was* right and reason rul{e},'<d>*
Er,e* Masters did combine
To use qurt* pots to measure foul
⌊Bright days of⌋ auld lang syne

B: *stanza two*; B: stood; B:
ruled, C&D: rule
B,C&D: Ere
B&D: quart; C: ?girt, *altered to*
quart
C&D: That day was

Now dimly burns the gloomy* lamps*
And Harder boards are mine
And oft the blacken,d* brows* hung* damp
Sin* days of auld lang syne

C & D: feeble; B,C & D: lamp

B: blackend, C&D: blackened;
B,C&D: brow's; C&D: been
C&D: Sin'

⌊Sin <And> now⌋ the noble minded rank
Has* ⌊hatched the direful⌋ fine
We Scarce* dare send a tub to bank
Sin* days of auld lang syne

B: And now, C&D: And sin'
C&D: Have; B: grown handy
with, C&D: tyrant
C: scare

C&D: Sin'

And well⌊<theyve> Reductions rule theyve
        learn,'d⌋
They one with all combine*
To rob us of the Half we',ve* Earn,'d*
Sin* days of auld lang syne

B: Reduction rule theyve
learnd, C & D: Reductions rule
they well have learned
B: incline
D: we've have; B: earnd, C&D:
earned,
C&D: Sin'

But shall we thus in bondage bow
* In <fettring>* bonds* repine
And bid ⌊one final last adue⌋
To days of auld lang syne

A: *in margin*: <?>fetering; B:
fettering, C: fettring, D:
fett'ring; C&D: cords
C: a last & sad, D: a last and
fond, C&D: adieu

No Unions* Sun now sheds her* rays
⌊No Sun can brighter⌋ shine

D: Union; C&D: his
B: In lusture see her, C: <And>
[That], D: That, C&D: on our
prospects

She,'l* light the path to* Hapier* days
The* days of auld lang syne

B: She,'l<l>, C&D: To; D: of;
B,C&D: happier
B: To

⌊Each Man stand true⌋ nor quit your post
Ye sons of wear and* Tyne
We,'l* yet Enjoy the rights* we,'ve lost
Sin* days of auld lang syne

C&D: Then stand brave Men

C: &

C: We ill, D: We'll; B: right

C&D: Sin'

W..g..C*   J Matthews*

B&D: *omitted*; B: *omitted*, C:
'J.Matthews', D: J. Matthew

A, B & C: Manuscript. D: Print. A, B & C: Picton. D: Wigan 110 (300). A:
Hand: J. Matthews. B: Hand: J. Matthews. C: Hand: William Daniells. D:
Broadside. Decorative border. No colophon [Dodds]. Lloyd, *Come all ye bold
miners*, (1978), pp. 251–52, 357, retitled the piece *The Song of the 1844 Strike*,
excised stanza 4 (while following the stanza order from the B text), took
readings from other versions and located his source as 'a broadside, no
imprint or date. Author marked as "Anon"', from an unknown location. No
such broadside has yet been traced.

A and B are addressed to 'Mr Tho Dodds' and dated from Trimdon Colliery
on June 20th 1844. Inside, there is a note to 'Mr Doods': 'ple[ase] prent 400 of
this song and we will pay for them when we start. I am yours, Adam Murray'.

99. REASON'S CLAIM, OR THE MINERS' PLEA TO THE OWNERS.
By the Author of "The Miners' Doom," &c.

Men of Britain! now before you,
   Hear your ill-used slaves complain;
If as *suppliants** they implore you   **B:** *no italics, here or elsewhere*
   Let them not appeal in vain!
By the noble ties of duty,
   By the feelings *all* should know,
By the tearful eye of beauty
   List what they, poor Miners, show!

You are wealthy! God hath bless'd you;
   Let that blessing still descend;
Toil and want may ne'er have press'd you,
   Cause not want their toil to end!
They have labour'd from their childhood,
   Life's best days they spent for you;
Pleasures in the field* and wildwood   **B:** fields
   Seldom did their steps pursue.

When the weary world lay slumbering
   Their employment was renewed;
Ceaseless strokes their minutes numbering,
   Pale fatigue their limbs bedewed.
Still they murmured not, tho' toiling
   Death-surrounded – dangerous fate!
Never from their task recoiling,
   God they knew was good and great!

Poor they are – their station lowly,
   Still the *worm* unhurt may crawl;
There is nothing kind and holy
   That delights the *weak* to fall.
Oh, how heartless, then, denying
   Just reward for labour done;
For their sacrifice supplying
   Half the price their hands have won!

You have children – look around you!
  See them smiling at your knee!
Love with faithful wives has crown'd you,
  Greater treasures cannot be!
Should misfortune overtake you,
  Should the vulture hunger come,
And oppression rudely make you
  Dwellers in a cheerless home!

Children, famish'd, round you crying,
  Craving food you fail to give,
And your wife now pale and dying
  Prays you for her babes to live!
Can you hear it, still unheeding
  Nature's piteous, earnest prayer?
Can you see love's bosom bleeding
  And not pour truth's balsam there?

Scenes like this may be prevented,
  Hearts of hope may linger on,
And poor Miners toil* contented   **B:** live
  When the jarring strife is done!
What they ask – the simplest* reason   **B:** simple
  Shows the justice of their *plea*;
Let this be your *honest* season,
  Let their *claims* acceded be!

Men of Britain! you have granted
  Liberty to *Afric's* slaves,
Let the tree of right be planted
  By *your own home-circled waves*!
If there be a bounteous blessing,
  That the hand of heaven bestows,
'Tis the power of wrongs redressing,
  'Tis to soothe the suff'rers' woes.

As a mighty stream's divided
  By the hills and dales around,
Like a lazy snake it glided
  Till its meeting strength was found.
Then majestic march'd the current,
  Regular, and broad, and deep,
Then resistless pour'd the torrent,
  What can stay its bounding sweep?

Thus benevolence united
  Bids your scattered interests join,
And the stream divided, slighted,
  Roll in majesty divine!
Men of Britain! now before you,
  Hear your ill-used slaves complain,
They as suppliants now implore you,
  Let them not appeal in vain!

Print. **A:** *Miners' Advocate,* June 29th 1844, p. 123 (*ie* p. 133). **B:** Wigan 113. **B:**
Broadside. No colophon [Dodds].
    The broadside text is dated in manuscript as 'July 1844'. Henderson
Fawcett is credited with the authorship of *The Miners' Doom* (**102**), but,
confusingly, J.P.Robson wrote *The Miner's Doom* (**60**). This piece reads like
Robson's work. Fawcett also wrote **56**.

100. THE PITMEN'S UNION.
By William Walker Story and George Watson,West Rainton.
Tune: – "And a nutting we will go."

Keep up your hearts, ye noble boys,
  And ne'er let them go down;
For twelve long weeks we've stood, boys,
  And stand twelve more as soon;
But if that will not do, brave boys,
  Twelve more still we'll stand,
Unless that our employers
  Grant us our just demand.

For union we've tried, brave boys,
    And union we still will try;
And we'll stand by our union
    Until the day we die.

Roberts is our friend, brave boys,
    To us he has prov'd true;
He's defended our just cause, boys
    In courts of justice too;
He is a man of honour,
    The country well doth know –
He conquereth the Viewers,
    Wherever he doth go.

There is the Noble Marquis,
    Who sent for all his men,
To see if he could conquer,–
    But it was all in vain.
He tried every stratagem
    That was within his power,
And then he sorely threaten'd them
    To turn them to the door.

He sent for them a second time,
    But it was all in vain,–
The men would not resume their work
    Till they their rights did gain;
And when that he'd done all he could,
    And threatened them full sore,
He sent the Police and Overmen,
    And turn'd them to the door!

Print. NCL 1844. Broadside. Illustration. No colophon [Dodds?]. Lloyd, *Come all ye bold miners*, (1978), pp. 258–59, 358, gave a text 'From a broadside, no imprint or date, in the Newcastle-upon-Tyne Public Reference Library'.
    The twelfth week of the strike ended on June 27th 1844, so this piece will probably have appeared early in July. William Walker Story and George Watson of West Rainton were the only authors known to have composed together. Owen Ashton points out that William Watson of West Rainton was a Chartist.

101. A COPY OF VERSES REFERRING TO THE PREASANT STATE OF
THINGS. *   B & C: Verses on the present state of things

[1]*In the Year Eighteen hundred, &* forty & four,
    Some Clouds Without* watter,* did ⌊fulley appear,⌋
    They ⌊are Carred about of* winds for the Same,⌋
    ⌊Of Spreading oppression; a terrible Name,⌋

2   They:re* Like tree:s: that ⌊Withereth: Without fruit and twice⌋ dead
    † Wandering Star:s: as the Scripture,* hath Said,
    Rageing* waves of the: † Foaming out their own Shame
    Murmurs* complaining; ⌊and Searching for gain,⌋

3   They ⌊Seem to be flattering: themselves with welldone⌋
    Our* Notions and motives: are fineley* Spun,
    ⌊Their the Sordid Straithearted One Stick:s⌋ to his own,
    In spite* of ⟨a⟩ a principle* Because* he has None,

4   ⌊They Sacrifice wives: and Children Likewise⌋
    ⌊Religous duties: is Nought in their Eye:s:,⌋
    ⌊Deformity:s': hidous Pictture,⌋ is Seen,
    ⌊Sunk them, Below the Brute creation So⌋ mean,

1/1 B&C: *no verse numbers*, C: *no verse- structure*; C: and
1/2 C: with; B&C: rain; tempestuously lour;
1/3 B&C: were borne by the winds of Oppression – B: *long 's', here and elsewhere* – B: &, C: and,
B&C: Shame
1/4 B&C: And strayed, B: oer C: o'er, B&C: the skies like a, B: Meteior's C: Meteor's, B&C: flame.

2/1 B&C: *omitted*; are withered, and fruitless and
2/2 B: Like the; C: scriptures
2/3 B: Raging; Sea,
2/4 B: Murmur'ers, C: Murmurers; B&C: looking forth for a name!

3/1 B&C: flatter themselves that their deeds are well done
3/2 B&C: That their; B:⟨exquis⟩ ⌊cleverly⌋, C: cleverly
3/3 B&C: Strait-hearted and sordid each clings
3/4 B&C: lieu; B: pri{n}ciple; B&C: as

4/1 B&C: The women and Children are Cruelty's prize,
4/2 B&C: Religion's grand duties they coolly despise.
4/3 B&C: Deformity's horrible picture
4/4 B&C: Beneath the rude brutes they are abject, and

5 They hew and they Pu[t]* and they all undermine,
   For the Sake of ⌊a Smile: and⌋ a Selfish dising*
   ⌊They:l: Stand all the hissing that Nature⌋ Can give,
   Nay the Scripture itself <?>* Cannot make them Believe

6 ⌊That our allwise Creator:s: adopted⌋ a Plan,
   ⌊Of Love of Society, of: friendship⌋ to man,
   No* Reason, Or* Religion: ⌊Can make them to yield⌋
   ⌊From a worse condission than the Beast of the field⌋

7 ⌊They:l go Sculking about: Like hedgecreepers We See,⌋
   Their ⌊hellish desing: What Elce Can it Be,⌋
   For Want of ⌊Society is⌋ Not what i mean,
   But for want of ⌊humanity:s: Evry day⌋ Seen,

8 When ⌊infinite Wisdom: See:d: good to <?> let down⌋
   ⌊To mosses his will: & Commandments: to Own,⌋
   † The Bles,sed assemblies that ⌊join:d: in⌋ the Plan,
   We Read that their Love: was to God &* to man,

5/1 **B:** put, **C:** put
5/2 **B&C:** applause from; design.
5/3 **B&C:** They heed not the scorn that the honest
5/4 **B&C:** *omitted*

6/1 **B:** <Now our> The all wise Creator, **C:** The all-wise creature; **B & C:** exhibits
6/2 **B&C:** That Truth and firm friendship should bind man
6/3 **B&C:** But; *omitted*; **B:** still fail<s> to excite, **C:** still fails to excite
6/4 **B&C:** And a worse than Brute-manner they show to the sight.

7/1 **B&C:** They go prowling and sculking; like **B:** hedge creepers now, **C:** hedge- creepers now
7/2 **B&C:** design is infernal you all will allow,
7/3 **B&C:** Society's
7/4 **B&C:** Humanity evils are.

8/1 **B&C:** wisdom divine saw his own proper time,
8/2 **B&C:** He gave his commandments forbidding all crime;
8/3 **B&C:** And; followed
8/4 **B&C:** and

9   We Read of a Paul: who Sacrific:d* gain
     ⌊Likewise of a Zaccheus who join in the Same,⌋
     We⌊Read of a judas a trater⌋Behold,
     The* Numbers of⌊trators to day⌋in the fold,

10   ⌊Behold their the trator as he Passes⌋along,
     ⌊You may Read on his Countenance: a Bottom unsound,⌋
     But* the frown:s: of his Neighbour:s: he⌊cannot compare⌋
     ⌊To one Smile: from his master any time in the year,⌋

11   But* his master well knows that⌊a Bottom unsound⌋
     ⌊Will do him as much Service When his Back it is {turnd}
     ⌊As a⌋judas Who kiss:d:* his † master and Said,
     The innocent⌊Blood's I See i:v:⌋Betray:ed:,

12   The Candid the generous the⌊just and the⌋Brave,
     The masters Can trust:⌊When Sucspecting the knaves,⌋
     For they know that⌊one Corse of Nature thus Runes,⌋
     ⌊To deceive in their. Abcience if oppertunity:s: found,⌋

9/1 **B&C:** sacrificed
9/2 **B&C:** Of Zaccheus who knew, **B:** that, **B&C:** all riches were vain.
9/3 **B&C:** all know of Judas! but lo! **B:** & **C:** and
9/4 **B&C:** What; traitors are seen

10/1 **B&C:** You may soon tell the traitor when passing
10/2 **B C:** His count'nance is gloomy, his conscience is wrong;
10/3 **B:** Of <But>, **C:** Of; **B&C:** takes little Care
10/4 **B&C:** If his Master but smile on him speaking him fair

11/1 **B&C:** Tho'; his Slave can deceive,
11/2 **B&C:** Yet his work is performed and he makes him believe
11/3 **B&C:** And as; Kissed; **B:** good, **C:** good
11/4 **B&C:** blood I've sold, **B:** &, **C:** and

12/1 **B&C:** honest, **B:** &, **C:** and
12/2 **B&C:** but suspect every Knave;
12/3 **B&C:** the Nature of Mortals is vile,
12/4 **B&C:** Which watches occasion to dupe and beguile

13 ⌊But What Ear hath heard & Eye: it hath Seen
    ⌊Of the guilt that hath [?] Between⌋
    But the Servants and masters ⌊Soon with joy they Shall {sing}⌋
    † The winter is Past: and appear* the † Spring,

14* Then down with the ⌊flattering ⟨tatling?⟩ tatterling⌋ tribe,
    The Sound of the Sordid Shall Spread fare* & wide
    But* the wheat and* the tares: ⌊together musst⌋ grow
    ⌊Till the time of their ultermate overthrow,⌋

15 The ⌊wondering world {it} Enquire⌋ to Know,*
    How ⌊they Openley Can Pass from door to door,⌋
    When* they ⟨?⟩ know their ⟨appearing?⟩ appearance is
                                    ⌊enou{gh for}⌋ to Stain}
    And ⌊Suttle and tincture⌋ the Best of the men,

16 But Soon ⌊the Expected time wil⌋ draw Near,
    When* the Cloud:s: will disperse and the ⌊dawn will⌋ appear,
    Then the ⌊North and the South & the East & the⌋ West
    ⌊Nay all our favour.red I:s:le Shall Be Bless:d:⌋

⌊Nic^s Cowey   Shotton Colliery   june: th 28 1844⌋

> B: *all omitted*, C: Nicholas Cowey, Shotton Colliery

A & B: Manuscript. C: Print. A & B: Picton. C: NCL 1844. A: Hand: Nicholas
Cowey. B: Hand: William Daniells. C: Broadside. Decorative border. No
colophon [Dodds].
    Probably from late June or early July 1844. Cowey also wrote **49**.

13/1 **B&C**: Every ear hath regarded and eyes have beheld,
13/2 **B&C**: The guilt that appears like a Cloud to have Swelled! –
13/3 **B&C**: with joy shall Soon Sing,
13/4 **B&C**: Now; appears; glad

14/1 **C**: *next three verses omitted*; **B**: false hearted {imbecile} ⟨tattling?⟩
14/2 **B**: far
14/3 **B**: Tho'; &; intermingled now
14/4 **B**: The time will arrive when the weeds will lie low!

15/1 **B**: world in a wonder is ⟨anxious⟩ wishful; learn
15/2 **B**: their footsteps to houses are openly borne;
15/3 **B**: For; is certain
15/4 **B**: cover with evils

16/1 **B**: shall the time long expected
16/2 **B**: And; morning
16/3 **B**: ends of the land, {the} North, South, East &
16/4 **B**: Yes! our own favoured Island again shall be blest.

102. THE MINER'S DOOM.

Composed by Henderson Fawcett,
        Miner, South Wingate.

Tune,- "The Mistletoe Bough."

Aroused by the Caller's well-known voice
Near midnight, calling, "'tis time, my boys!"
The old and the young at the sound arise,
And each to his dreary toil quick hies;
But little they thought in descending the mine,
No more they'd see the bright sunshine.

> Chorus,- Oh! the slaves of the mine,
>   The slaves of the mine.

Now, down the deep shaft, far out of sight,
They toil with a dimly burning light;
Far, far, from meadows and rivers clear,
They're breathing a noxious atmosphere;
The dangers they brave, the world seeth not,–
It sighs o'er their doom, but soon 'tis forgot.

O, sudden and sad is the miner's doom;
See the clouds which up yon shaft now come!
The alarm is given – "she's fired!" they cry:
To the shaft, to the shaft, all quickly fly:
The Mother exclaims, in anguish wild,
"My son! my son! my darling child!

"Oh, mother!" yon little mourner doth cry,
"Will not father come to me bye-and-bye?"
"No more he'll return, my only joy!
Thy father is gone, thou'rt an orphan boy;–
No more he'll list to thy prattling tongue,
Or lull thee to sleep with the soothing song."

The aged father, he tore his hair,–
No words he spoke – he looked despair:
His son was slain; like the mighty oak,
When shattered by the lightning's stroke,
Cut off in the flower of youthful bloom,
The deep drear mine was his early tomb.

See yonder maid, in silent grief,
No tears do come to her relief;
She'd fixed the day to form for ever,
That bond which only death can sever:
No more his active limbs now move–
No more he'll smile upon his love!

Now struggles the miner to better his state;
May he triumph in a cause so great!
Though yet he may toil in the darksome mine,–
Away, away, from the bright sunshine;
Yet kind, and just, and equal laws,
Shall happiness bring to the miner's cause.

Print. **A:** Wigan 111. **B:** NCL 1844. **A:** Broadside. Colophon: Williams &
Morrison, Printers. See also Bell 12/256. **B:** Broadside. No colophon [Dodds?].
    The NRO exemplar has a manuscript date of 'July 1844'. No printing
patnership between a Williams and a Morrison is known to Hunt, nor is any
printer named Morrison, though John R. Williams operated as a printer in
Sunderland between 1841 and 1855 (Hunt, *The Book Trade*, p. 96). Henderson
Fawcett also wrote **56**. See also C & R, *The Miners' Association*, p. 202.

103. MR ROBERTS THE PITMEN'S FRIEND
TUNE – *"William and Phillis."*

Ye working-men of collieries attention pay to me,
And when I have done my verses with me you will agree,
That England's long gone down the hill it's time that it should rise,
If we had a few such men as Roberts it soon would then revive.

The gentlemen of England have long kept down the poor,
And bridged down all trades of every kind unto this very hour,
For want of such men as Roberts to look about our rights and dues,
For he's the man that will put them on their P's and Q's.

The Pitmen a few years ago good wages they have got,
Which made them blithe and happy and contented with their lot,
But by degrees they brought them down which caused them to say,
They would rather be transported and sent to Botany Bay.

Their oppression was so great they could not with it stand,
Which made them join in heart and voice likewise in hand and hand;
And meetings rose in different parts their rights for to unfold,
Then O'Connor thought of Roberts and his name unto them told.

Then to the north they brought him down their rights for to maintain,
To stop the tyrants of their tricks which no one could them blame;
For down below they venture where the darkness is enroll'd.
And the treasure they do work for their masters they do hold.

Now as for the New Thornley men it's Roberts has stood true,
He has stood as great a contest as not many more could do,
Four days in Durham he did stand, their trial for to gain,
And for to release these prisoners out of the city Goal.

But their masters would not yield to them nor yet release the men,
So of[f] to London Roberts went the trial to extend;
His men he took along with him the Queen's bench for to see,
And in less than half an hour his men with liberty were free.

Then the trial into chancery straightway did Roberts fling,
And his men to view the city then along with him did bring,
Then to O'Connor he did go, took with him every man,
And he treated them far better than the noblest in the land.

When back to Thornley they arrived their news for to unfold,
The noblest sights that they beheld unto their men they told,
With hearts rejoiced they danced and sung the music kept in tune,
And these men chaired round Thornley Streets all on that afternoon.

Now as for these poor Thornley men no one should on them frown.
For sticking out for their rights which ought to be thei[r] own.
But we hope they will soon return again the time is drawing nigh
And the north coal trade revive again and away all tyranny fly.

Now the blacklegs I must give a rub before that I do end,
They will wish when we do get our rights they had been union men,
It is such as these blacklegs has caused all trades for to go down,
And caused thousands for to beg their bread and the rich on them to frown.

Now here's to Mr. Roberts for he's the Pitmen's friend,
He's worthy of his salary to make the tyrants bend,
Now may he live in unity and his men unto him cling
For to take all tyranny from them and out of them the sting.

Print. NCL 1844. See also Bell 12/259 and Wigan 58 (297). Broadside proof? No colophon [Dodds]. Lloyd, *Come all ye bold miners*, (1978), pp. 240–41, 356, gave a text as from 'a broadside, no imprint, undated (but apparently 1844), printed along with *The Miner's Friend*, a song written by W. Johnson of Framwellgate Moor'. No such double broadside can now be traced, but for Johnson's text see **76**. Lloyd also supplies a tune from the *Journal of the Folk Song Society* collected in London in 1904.

Both NRO and Wigan exemplars are inscribed '4 July 1844' in the same handwriting, though the reference to Thornley encouraged C & R, *The Miners' Association*, p. 109, and Lloyd, *Come all ye bold miners*, (1978), p. 356, to assume that this piece was written in January 1844.

104. WONDERFUL!

A year of wonder now is come,
A viewer's dead, no worse for home.
A year that Union has worked wonder,
A year her cannons roared like thunder;
A year when tyrants all must vanish,
A year that blunders we will banish;
A year that docks the viewers' wages,
A year when frauds must keep their cages;
A year that sets some miners jogging,
A year when masters fear a flogging;
A year that sets some strangers grinning,
A year they find that hewing's pinning;
A year when charity is blended,   *   *last three lines bracketted*
And to good men by right extended,
And thus the year of grace is ended.

Seghill, June 18, 1844.   C. RATCLIFFE.

Print. *Miners' Advocate*, July 27th 1844, p. 148.
    C. Ratcliffe of Seghill also wrote **117**.

105. SONG OF THE OPPRESSOR.

The Coal King sat in his chair of state,
And looked on his slaves with heart elate,
As on things that nature had made to be
Part of his worldly property!
He drains the wine-cup bright and clear,
Tho' mixed with the widow and orphan's tear;
He heeds not the price, no remorse can sting
The flinty heart of the great Coal King!
    Oh misery! that men should be
    Such fettered slaves when their hearts are free.

"More wine! more wine!" shouts this mighty king,
Tho' for it the heart of my slaves I wring;
Tho' every drop in the goblet be
Bought with the blood of slavery.
Let them sweat and toil in the loathsome pit,
Cursing the bonds they cannot quit;
They are *mine*, and death release must bring
Ere they slip from the grasp of the great Coal King.
　　Oh misery! that men should be
　　Such tyrant slaves when their minds are free!

Look! look! the face of the King grows pale,
His mighty heart begins to quail,
For a voice like the roar of the stormy sea
Bursts on his ears – 'tis liberty!
For sufferings long and sufferings sore
Men's hearts oppressed, they could bear no more.
They are free! and that word o'er the land shall ring
A dirge to the might of the great Coal King.
　　Oh liberty! 'tis sweet to be
　　Freed from the Coal King's tyranny!

Behold the fair star that hath risen to shine,*   *asterisk in original – see footnote:*
That cheers the deep gloom of the misty mine,
While a champion goes forth in the Miners' cause,
To teach the oppressors their country's laws;
And united for freedom with heart and hand,
Shame! shame! to the wretch who breaks the band,
Or barters his rights for such base things
As the lords of oppression – the great Coal Kings!
　　Oh liberty! 'tis sweet to be
　　Free from the Coal Kings tyranny!

Southwick, 1844.   JOHN MARTIN.
　　　　　* The "Miners' Advocate."

Print. *Miners' Advocate*, July 27th 1844, p. 148.
　Robert Martin of Percy Main wrote **121**.

106. THE PITMEN DETERMINED TO BE FREE.

Come all good people lend an ear
and listen unto me. *   B&C: *every other line indented*
and of our wrongs you Soon Shall hear
likewise our misery,

We,ve* dragg,d the Chains of Slavery   B&C: *apostrophes raised
for many years you know,   throughout*
and now that we, wish to be free
is the Cause of all our woe,

Our iron hearted* Masters   B&C: iron-hearted
have used us very ill,
and had we thought fit, for* to Submit   B&C: *omitted*
they would oppress,d* us Still.   A: *long 's'*

But now w,'re Joined in union
we brave Sons of the Mine,
and we Soon Shall Conquer the tyrants
of the Tees, Wear, and the Tyne.

They,ve long kept us in Slavery
but now we,ll let them see,
if it Should Cost some of our lives
we,re Determined to be free.

They,ve driven us from our Dwellings
to Camp ⌊all in⌋ the field,   B: in all
but we, will let the Tyrants See
that we,ill* die before we,ll yield,   B&C: we'll

Now fifteen* weeks we,ve been on Strike   B&C: seventeen
and Still we,re Standing true,
but just a handfull* of dislike,   B&C: handful
I mean the blackleg Crew.

But every dog will have his day,
and So will blacklegs too,
we,ll very soon Cry, Hurrah, Hurrah.
at the downfall of that Crew.

W.N.

A: Manuscript. **B** & **C**: Print. **A**: Picton. **B**: NCL 1844. **C**: Wigan 109 (301). **A**: Hand: W.N. **B**: Broadside. Decorative border. No colophon [Dodds]. **C**: Broadside. Decorative border. No colophon [Dodds].

The fifteenth week of the strike ended on July 19th 1844, and the seventeenth on August 2nd. The single typographical difference between **B** and **C** suggests that this may have been corrected after proof stage. The title may have been taken from **54**. See also C & R, *The Miners' Association*, p. 140.

107. A NEW SONG*

B: THE OLD WOMAN AND THE COAL OWNER.

A dialogue I'll tell you as true as my life
Between A coal owener* and A poor pitman's wife. B: Owner, *here and elsewhere*
As she was a traveling* all on the high way* B: travelling; highway
She met A coal owener and this she did say* B: *line omitted*
She met † A coal owener and to him she said B: with
Sir to beg on you ⌊I am not affraid⌋;+* (down hey B: I'm not afraid; A: *cross in*
        derry {(down}* *manuscript;* B: *no chorus or crosses*
Then where do you come from the owener he cries* B: *no stanzas throughout*
I come from h—l the old women* replies B: woman
If you come from h—l come tell me right plain
How you contrived to get out again +

Aye the way ah* [g]at out the truth ah* will tell B: aw; aw
They are turning † the poor folk all* out of h—l B: all; *omitted*
This is † make room for the rich wicked race B: to
For thare* is A great number of them in that place + B: there

And the number's* not known sir that is in B: number is
   that place
And they chiefly consist of the rich wicked race
And the coal oweners is* the next in command B: are
To arrive into h—l as I understand +

How know you the oweners is next in command
How div ah naw ye shall understand
Ah* hard the old* devil say when ah* cam out   B: Aw; awd; aw
The coal oweners all had reciv'd* their rout +   B: received

Then how does the old* devil behave in that place B: awd
O sir he is* cruel to the rich wicked race   B: he's
He's far ⌊more uncrueler⌋ than you can suppose   B: fiercer
Aye even A mad Bull with A ring thro* his nose +   B: through

Good woman say's* he I must bid you fare well*   B: says; farewell
You give me A dismal account about h—l
If this be all true that you say unto me
I'll go home and with my poor men I'll agree +

If you be A coal owener, sir take my advice
Agree with your men &* give them their ful* price B: and; full
For if you do not ah* naw very well   B: aw
You'ill* be in great danger of going to h—l +   B: You'll

For all ye coal oweners great fortunes has* made   B: have
By ⌊those Jovel men⌋ that work's* in the coal trade B: these jovial fellows; works
Now how can ye think for to prosper or thrive
For wanting to starve your poor* workman* alive +   B: omitted; B: workmen

So* all ye gay gentlemen that's got riche* in store B: Now; riches
Take my advice and be good to the poor
And if ye do this all things will gan* well   B: go
Perhaps it will save ye for ganin to h—l +

So now the poor pitman* may join heart &* hand   B: Pitmen; and
For when ⌊their of⌋ work all ⌊trade's⌋ at A stand   B: they're off; trades are
Yon town of Newcastle all cry out amain*   B: a main
O since the pits were at work once again +

Its* now to conclude little more I've to say   B: It's
I was turn'd* out of my house on the 13* of May   B: turned; 13th
But its* now to conclude and I'll* finish my song   B: it's; omitted
I hope you'll relive* me and let me carry on +   B: relieve

A: Manuscript. B: Print. A: Picton. B: Wigan 107 (303 verso). A: Hand: ?William Hornsby. B: Broadside. Decorative border. No colophon [Dodds]. Lloyd, *Come all ye bold miners*, (1952), pp. 93, 137, retitled the piece *The Coal-Owner and the Pitman's Wife*, and published a second stanza not to be found in either of these texts. Moreover, his version did not have half of each of stanzas four and five (while the other halves are forged into one stanza) and stanza nine became stanza seven. J.S.Bell was reported as believing that 'this ballad, which appears to date from the 1844 Durham Strike [sic], was written by William Hornsby, a collier of Shotton Moor', while 'the tune and a fragment of the text was communicated by J.Dennison, of Walker'. The handwriting is indeed similar to 89. Hornsby also wrote 57. Lloyd, *Coal Dust Ballads*, pp. 36–37, 40, referred to Mr Bell as 'a studious Lancashire miner', and gives this song a different tune, 'a variant of the Wearside song, "Spottie"'. Lloyd, *Folk Song*, pp. 344–46, published a version with his own title, crediting Mr Bell ('a miner') with having 'unearthed' it in 1951, excising stanzas nine, ten and twelve, and tinkering with the text in other ways. Lloyd, *Come all ye bold miners*, (1978), pp. 253–55, 357–58, reverted to a twelve-stanza text which corresponded rather more closely to the manuscript version, and he also referred to the 'edited version' published in 1952, but not that published in 1967. In a letter to the Editor dated July 25th 1972, Lloyd indicated that the text had been 'altered to accomodate bits of the incomplete text I got from Jim Dennison'. Harker, *One for the Money*, pp. 166–70, gave an account of the treatment of this song by Lloyd, and supplied an almost accurate transcription. Compare Colls, *The Collier's Rant*, pp. 204–5 note 2. This song has been frequently reprinted, usually from Lloyd's 1952 text. A version was recorded by Tommy Gilfellon on 'The Bonny Pit Laddie' (Topic Stereo 2–12TS 271/2, 1975).

Probably from July 1844.

108. A DIALOGUE BETWEEN PETER FEARLESS* AND DICK FREEMAN   *long 's', here and elsewhere*

Peter - Now Dickey, was thou at Meeting to day,
   Aw look'd – but aw saw nought o' thou by the way,
   Aw hope that thou's not turnin' Cowardly now,
   Or yet thinking a gannin' doon the coal pit to hew.
Dick⟨y⟩- No, Peter, aw hev not been there aw allow,
   Or am aw yet thinking of gan'in doon to hew;
   But the family thou naws – if aw did'not look out,
   Would starve, wey, awve had to put things up the spout.

Peter -   Wey man, such a meeting weve had dis't thou naw,
           Wey the justice was there, and he talked about law;
           He said, if the peace we kept, he would back us,
           And if we did not, wey the police should tack us.

Dick⟨y⟩·   Wey Peter, thou naws aw wad lik'd ta been there,
           What we redcoats & blue coats 't'wad be like a fair
           But now aw will tell thow aw've got somthing to say.
           There is things in wor bond aw think out o' the way

Peter -   Things in wor bond man, thou's nought out o' reason,
           Wey man, aws surpris'd, thou talks nowt but treason.
           Now where's there ought rang, ⟨now⟩ lets hear thou {just} say,
           For aw think aw can prove – there's nowt out o' the way.

Dick⟨y⟩·   Aw wad like for to hear – twad cheer up my poor heart
           If thou only could prove how the ten shilling smart
           Is not far too much for the Masters to pay,
           This is one of the things aw think out o' the way

Peter -   Now {Dickey} aw will let thou see what ⟨all⟩ this is for
           There is bad ventilation ⟨and⟩ what is worse, ⟨?⟩ and
                      wanting a door
           And a great deal more aw will tell before aw do stop
           That the place where we hew it very oft wants a prop.

Dick -   Wey now aw de see, te prevent things like this
           That its {to} hinder⟨ing⟩ the maisters for doin' ought amiss;
           But its to prevent the poor collier from accident heavy
           That we the ten shillings smart on our maisters do levy.

Peter -   Then the same thing applies to the rest that we ask
           That's ⟨?⟩ to hinder our maisters from wearing a mask;
           They say that ⟨?⟩ {its} accidents, when we know its neglect
           Then these things we do ask ourselves to protect

Dick -   Why Peter aw begin ta see things right plain
           For our maisters they care for nought else but gain
           Then its only in reason we ourselves do protect
           And to make them pay smartly for ony neglect.

Peter -   Then lets keep up our hearts Dick we are sure to win
           Our Maisters aw naw before lang will give in;
           Then let us Stand fast never stop by the way
           And victory we'll shout when we win the day

Manuscript. Picton. Hand: ? . Lloyd, *Come all ye bold miners*, (1952), pp. 85–86, 1
published a version not including quatrain 11 and with a number of other differen

from the manuscript text. Lloyd, *Folk Song*, pp. 342–43, published a seven-quatrain version without indicating it was a mediated text, and ascribed the piece, with no evidence, to 'the 1831 Durham Strike'. Lloyd, *Come all ye bold miners*, (1978), pp. 242–43, 356–57, associated what has now become his ten quatrain version – missing quatrains 6 and 11 – with the '1844 Durham Strike', and described it as coming 'From a manuscript copy among papers relating to events in the north-eastern coalfield in the 1830s and 1840s, in the Picton Library, Liverpool', as 'Communicated by J.S.Bell'. There are several other departures from the Picton manuscript text.

Probably from July 1844.

109. FISH BETTYS* ACCOUNT OF HERSELF

A Parody on Billy Oliver

⌊My nyem it's Fish Betty⌋
In Camperdown aw dwell
Now isnt* aw A Clever † Hussy*

⌊Thow aw de⌋ say't mesel*
Sic ⌊An Clever Hussy am aw.⌋⌊am aw. am aw.⌋
    Sic A Clever Hussy am aw*

There's Not A Woman* in the* Town*
Can fight or Scold <like> {with}* me
Nor Not A Widow* in Camperdown
Can suit the Men like me
    Sic ⌊an a Clever <Widow> {Hussy} am⌋ aw.

And when ⌊aw gan's untiv the Chapel⌋
To see if maw* Cuddy's There
Aw dress mysel se* verra fine
Lord how Wur* Neighbours Stare
    Sic A Clever ⌊Hussy am⌋ aw.

An then aw walk with* sic an Air
⌊That if the Folks hev⌋ Eyes
They think ⌊it is⌋ some **great** Woman*
That's ⌊cum in i'⌋ disguise
    Sic a Clever ⌊Hussy am⌋ aw.

Right-column textual notes:

B & C: Betty's

B&C: Fish Betty, is my nyem, you see. C: *every other line indented*; B: aw'
B&C: is'nt; B: lad, *altered to* lass, *then deleted*; B: lass – *long* 's', C: lass
B&C: Altho' aw; B: mysel', C: mysel.
B&C: a Clever wife <u>is,</u> B: aw', C: aw; B&C: *omitted*
B & C: *line omitted*

B&C: wife; B: a', C: aw; B&C: wor toon
B&C: wi'
B&C: lass

B&C: a Clever wife is

B&C: to Chapel aw just, B: gan', C: gan
B&C: *omitted*;
B: se<e>
B&C: wor
B&C: wife is

B&C: wi'
B&C: Aw dazzle folk's
B&C: it's; dowager
B&C: coming in
B&C: wife is

⌊An if the Folks that's in the Chapel⌋   B&C: And when the folks in
⟨Should lyeuk and Stare at me⟩*   Chapel sit
                                                B&C: *line omitted*
Thee* Nasty stinking Varmint †   B&C: The; B: *line bracketted*
Aw ⌊Naw Their {thinking} Mare⌋ o* me   B&C: knaw they're thinkin'
                                                mair
Then* ⌊they are About⌋ the Sarmint   C: Than; B: ought aboot, C:
    Sic A Clever ⌊Hussy am⌋ aw   ought about
                                                B: wife is

An When aw've heaved A Sigh or Two*   C: twe
For my* awn Canny Cuddy   B: *altered from* ma
Aw think Ne mair About* my Mark   B: aboot
For ⟨aw's⟩* aw's baith fair and* Ruddy   B&C: *omitted*; an'
    Sic A Clever ⌊Hussy am⌋ aw.   B&C: wife is

Now* since my lads I've* got to Work*   B&C: But; aw've; wark
Ill* get the Master's Favours*   B&C: I'll; praise;
So ⌊Ill Just think About my Cuddy⌋   B&C: So just about my Cud I'll
                                                think
⌊And Never mind my Neighbours⌋   B&C: Nor mind the
    ⌊Sic An an⟨?⟩ Clever Hussy am⌋ aw   neighbours ways.
                                                B: Since a clever wife is, C: Sic
                                                a clever wife is

A & B: Manuscript. C: Print. A & B: Picton. C: Wigan 107 (303). See also NRO
3410/Wat/1/27. A: Hand: ? B: Hand: William Daniells. C: Broadside.
Decorative border. No colophon [Dodds].
    Probably from late July or early August 1844. For *Billy Oliver*, see Allan,
Tyneside Songs, p. 221.

110. THE MINER'S PRAYER.
Common Metre.

1* Thou, Lord, dost make the meanest soul,   B: *no verse numbers*
        An object of thy care,
    Regard the feeling of my heart,
        And hear the Miner's prayer.

2 The Saviour died upon the cross,
  My sins and grief to bear,
 For his sake, Lord, turn not away,
  But hear the Miner's prayer.

3 Arise my soul from deep distress.
  And banish every fear,
 God calls thee to his throne of grace,
  To spread the Miner's prayer.

4 Ours was a wretched state exposed,
  To men and angels' view,
 A slave to man, a slave to sin,
  A slave to satan too.

5 Father, thy long lost child receive,
  Saviour thy purchase own,
 Blest comforter with peace and joy,
  Thy waiting creature own.

6 Whose God is like the christian's God,
  Who can with him compare,
 He has compassion on my soul
  And hears the Miners* prayer.   **B:** Miner's

7 In heaven the land of glory lies,
  If I should enter there,
 I'll tell the saints and angels too,
  Thou hard'st* the Miner's prayer.   **B:** heard'st

8 This shall be known when we are dead,
  And left on long record,
 That ages yet unborn may read
  And trust and praise the Lord.

Print. **A:** Wigan 112 (298). **B:** Wigan 106 (304). **A:** Broadside. Decorative border. Colophon: Printed by J. Rewcastle, Bookseller, Dean Street. **B:** Broadside. Decorative border. No colophon [Dodds].

 Possibly from late July or early August 1844. For James Rewcastle, see Hunt, *The Book Trade*, p. 77, and above, pp. 61–2, note 167.

111. [THE SAVIOUR'S DEATH]*   B: *title supplied*

4* Darkness prevailing, darkness prevailing,   A: *sic*
        Darkness prevail'd o'er the land
    The solid rocks were rent through Judea's vast
        extent
        We* the Jews crucified the God Man.*   B: While; God-man

5   There is my surety, there is my surety,
        Jesus my Lord do I see;
    On him my sins were laid &* for me the debt   B: and
        he paid
        When he groan'd and expir'd on the tree.

6   When it was finished, when it was finished,
        And the atonement was made;
    He was taken by the great, and embalmed in
        spices sweet
        And in a new sepulchre was laid.

1   Sigh* ye me* Saviour   B: Saw; my
    † Sigh* ye me* Saviour – † Shamefully nail'd to   B: *same line as above*; saw; my;
        the {tree}   *new line*
    He was nail'd to the tree too atone* for you   [B: above
        {and me}
    In a new Sepulcher* was laid.   B: sepulchre

2   Death could not hold him. Death could not
        {hold him}
    See the mighty conqueror <?> arose,
    He assended* up on high there no more to   B: ascended
        plead {and Die}
    But now sits on* glory above   B: in

3   He is now interceeding* he is now interceeding*   B: interceding; interceding
    Pleading that Siners* may live   B: sinners
    Saying Farther* I have Died see me* wounded   B: Father; my; hands
        hand* {and side}
    I have redeemed them I pray the* forgive   B: thee

4 I will forgive them. I will forgive them
   If they repent and beleive,*   **B:** believe
   Let them turn unto me And depend alone on thee
   and Salvation they freely Shall have.

A: Print and manuscript. **B:** Print. **A:** Picton. **B:** Wigan 110 (300). **A:** Hand: ?
Print: Broadside? Decorative border. No colophon (Dodds?). **B:** Broadside.
Decorative border. No colophon [Dodds].
   Possibly from August 1844.

112.   JOB, THE PATIENT MAN.

Come all you worthy Christians,
   That dwell within this happy land,
Who spend your time in piety,
   Remember you're but man;
Be watchful of your latter end –
   And ready for Death's call:
How many changes in this world!
   Some rise and some do fall.

For Job was a most patient man
   The richest in the east;
When he was brought to poverty,
   His sorrows did increase;
He bore them with great patience,
   And never did repine;
But always trusted in the Lord,
   And soon got rich again.

Come all you worthy Christians,
　　That are so very poor,
Remember how poor Lazarus
　　Sat at the rich man's door,
Begging for the crumbs of bread,
　　Which from his table fell,
The Scripture doth inform us,
　　In Heaven he now doth dwell,

Tho' poor, we are contented,
　　No riches we do crave,
For they are only vanity
　　On this side of the grave;
Though we may roll in riches,
　　Our glass is near run out,
We brought no riches in this world,
　　And none can we take out.

Then the time will quickly come,
　　When parted we must be –
The only thing that doth remain,
　　In death or misery;
But as we all account must give,
　　Both great as well as small,
Remember, my good Christians,
　　One God has made us all.

Print. Wigan 110. Broadside. Decorative border. No colophon [Dodds].
　　Probably from August 1844.

113. THE COLLIER'S COMPLAINT.
By Mrs. Mainwaring.

Toil unceasing has been ours,
   Labour's curse bedews our brows,
Wither'd strength and wasted powers
   Slowly steal upon us now.
All our life is one of sorrow,
   All our days are days of pain,
No bright sun reveals our morrow,
   His glad beams to us are vain.

Dark and dreary in yon pit,
   With its noisome pent-up air,
Crouching must the Collier sit,
   Nor the light of heaven share.
The sweet breath of early morning
   Yields no perfume on our way,
No blue sky our world adorning,
   Changing darkness into day.

Yet we shrink not from our task,
   Of our lot we'll scarce complain;
All we seek for – all we ask,
   For our babes is food to gain.
Deem ye not the collier's story
   One of fancied – trifling woe,
There are proud ones in their glory
   Who our sufferings well, well know

Patiently we've strove with fate,
   To stern vicissitudes have bow'd;
See our wretched woe-worn state
   Calling for redress aloud!
Let our labour be rewarded,
   Let us live as men SHOULD live,
Let our sacred rights be guarded,
   Grateful thanks ye shall receive.

   Sheffield, August 4, 1844.

Print. *Miners' Advocate*, August 24th 1844, p. 164.

114. AN ACROSTIC.

M en for themselves now reflect in due season,
A nd the cause of effect they inquire;
T hey use their own reason,
T ho' priests call that treason,
H onest men must the system admire.
E very face beams with hope at the prospect in view,
W hich shall free the great mass from the force of the few.

P oor base creeping things from a hole in the earth,
A ssume to be equal to all by their birth;
S tand and prove their own rights to subsist by their labour,
Q uestioning the might of their noble-born neighbour.
U nless such proceedings be soon put a stop to,
I can see that monop[o]ly is doomed for to drop too:
L ook, here is the plan that will quickly arrest it,
L et there be greater power in the magistrates vested.

Bolton, August 1844.

Print. *Miners' Advocate*, August 24th 1844, p. 164.

115. THE PITMEN'S 'TORNEY-GENERAL.
A New Song to an Old Tune.

Air – "*The King of the Cannibal Islands.*"

Oh have you heard the news of late,
About this "'Torney-General" great,
If you have not I'll tell you straight,
How a Wire-rope hang'd the traitor.
He'd got in gold a goodly store –
Six hundred and forty pounds and more,
To fee a Counsel of great lore,
To fire his gun of wondrous bore.
To rob the poor it was too bad,
Once goodly store and hearts so glad,
Now "hungry guts" he knew they had
This rogue of a Pitman's 'Torney.

    Hokee pokee wankee fum,
    Roberts and Beazeley England's scum,
    The curse of all, the fear of some,
    This rogue of a Pitman's 'Torney.

To sack this blunt was his intent,
Sir Thomas Wilde was all a feint,
But goaded by Veitch he did repent,
And gave ten sovs to Granger.
In Durham Court the case came on,
No Wilde was there, the 'Torney's blown,
The Wire-rope round his neck is thrown,
And hang'd was the Pitman's 'Torney.
Oh dear! it was a shocking sight,
The jury pull'd the rope so tight,
Roberts so black, and Beazeley white,
When scragg'd was this Attorney.

Hokee pokee wankee fum,
Roberts and Beazeley England's scum,
The union-men looked mighty glum,
At the "kick" of their Attorney.

And now that Roberts is fairly dead,
From pit to pit the news soon spread,
Every man now earns his bread,
His wife's no longer a vagrant.
The children too are seen at home,
To beg, or steal, no longer roam,
While pris'ners gnash their teeth and foam,
At losing all – both house and home.
The Union-men all stand aghast,
They've clad in crape the Ponies, fast,
And Beazeley is pack'd off at last
"To Bath," with the Pitman's 'Torney.

Hokee pokee wankee fum,
Roberts and Beazeley England's scum,
Peace and plenty soon will come,
Sin' dead is the Pitman's 'Torney.

Print. NCL 1844. Unidentified newspaper cutting.

This text refers to the Thornley case of January 1844 but seems to date from August 1844 – compare C & R, *The Miners' Association*, pp. 99–109, 149–50, and Challinor, *A Radical Lawyer*, pp. 137–38. This tune and verse-form were popular with conservative writers – see *The Lord of the Allendale Miners* (B/W13).

116. A NEW SONG.
    Tune – "Auld lang syne."

How, Jobson, has the heard the news
    About this d——d wire rope –
That Durham men (they mun be Jews)
    Hev left us nowt to hope.
        Maw wife sal darn and cloot maw claise,
            And brush maw Sunday coat;
        An ne mair unyen* au me days,   onion
            Or thou sal cut me throte.

Our delegats are nowt but theves;
    They've rob'd us au thegether.
We've pan'd our beds, and best sark sleves,
    Wor byuts of guid caff lether
        Maw wife, &c.

Our wives an bains ha nowt to eat,
    This twenty weeks, an mair;
We ha ne tyeble, nor ne meet;
    A man, that's vara sair.
        Maw wife, &c.

This *Rob* we may sa's ful o' *arts*,
    And B——y just as bad;
We now see through their roguish parts;
    Wy man, we've au been mad
        Maw wife, &c.

We thowt him just the king o' harts,
    See clever an see brave;
Now see how he wor cause desarts,
    An hes turned out pick nave.
        Maw wife, &c.

There's only ane thing noo, aw hope,
    An wish it from my heart, –
That R——s was hung in a rope
    And B——y had his part.
        Maw wife, &c.

They've left us bare o' bed and claes –
   De'il brust them every yen –
Wi thare deceitful leein ways
   They've left us siller – nyen.
      Maw wife, &c.

Aw ken what's the furst thing aw dees, –
   Aw'll just gan to maw wark,
To get the bairns some breed an chees
   Aw'll strip inte me sark.
      Maw wife, &c.

May R———s, B———y gan to h—l,
   The unyen to the de'il,
Maw wife an bairns agyen live well
   On wheet and haver meal.
      Maw wife, &c–

Now sharp maw picks, and trim maw lamp,
   Maw hoggars, an pit shun –
Aw'll through the country ne mair tramp
   Until maw life be duin.
      Maw wife, &c.

Now mine me, pit lads, yen an au,
   Ne mair wi hungry guts –
Maw Jack sal to the huin fa,
   An Tommy fills and puts.
      Maw wife sal darn and cloot me claes,
        An brush my Sunday coat;
      And ne mair unyen au me days,
        Or thou sal cut me throte.

Print. B/W2. Broadside. Colophon: Printed by J.Proctor, Hartlepool. Also published in Vicinus, *Broadsides*, p. 51.
   The twentieth week of the strike ended on August 22nd 1844. For John Proctor, see Hunt, *The Book Trade*, p. 74.

117. THE COAL KING AND THE PITMAN.

As late I passed a stately hall
   Midst Seghill's village reared,
And gorgeous seemed the fabric vast
   Which unto me appeared.
Whence came this wealth, I musing said,
   To raise this structure there?
"'Twas wrung from bleeeding hearts," said one,
   "The coal-pits placed it there!"

Its owner's gains have often caused
   The widow's heart to fail;
And infancy hath pined for want
   And manhood's cheek grown pale.
Children have spent their little strength
   Their hard-earned bread to win,
And thousands, innocent before,
   Have learned to slave and sin.

I left the spot and wandered on,
   A peasant's cottage rose,
All nature smiled in beauty there
   And lay in sweet repose.
The corn waved gloriously around,
   The birds made music clear,
Surely the ills of want, I thought,
   Can find no dwelling here.

I entered – and I then beheld
   The father pale in bed;
His wife's wan aspect spoke of want
   And many a tear she shed.
Three weeping children cried for bread
   In such a plaintive tone,
Oh, to have heard their bitter wail
   Had softened hearts of stone.

The sick man said that plenty once
  Had crowned the lowly cot,
And peace and humble comfort then
  Blest England's peasant's lot.
Now tyranny had brought a change,
  And bread he could not buy,
And all his toil could not suffice
  His children to supply.

Meanwhile such wretchedness I viewed
  How could I but inquire,
What is it stints the children's food,
  Puts out the poor man's fire?
A question this of interest deep,
  And import vast and high,
What blight is fall'n upon our land?
  Let greedy wealth reply!

Yet, onward! Britons, one and all!
  And join the bloodless fight;
Arise, and with resistless voice
  Assert the cause of right!
Your pleading sounds shall not be vain,
  For justice shall prevail,
And once again prosperity
  Our native isle shall hail.

Seghill, Aug. 16, 1844.   C. Ratcliffe.

Print. *Miners' Advocate*, September 21st 1844, p. 180.
  Ratcliffe also wrote **104**.

118. THE PIT BOY.

The sun is sinking fast, mother,
   Behind the far Clee hills;
The signal bell has ceased, mother,
   The breeze of evening chills.
They call me to the pit, mother,
   The nightly toil to share;
One kiss before we part, mother,
      For danger lingers there.
         One kiss before we part, mother,
         For danger lingers there.

My father's voice I hear, mother,
   When o'er his grave I tread,
He bids me cherish thee, mother,
   And share with thee my bread.
Then while I see thee smile, mother,
   My labour light shall be;
And should his fate be mine, mother,
      Then heaven will comfort thee.
         And should his fate be mine, mother,
         Then heaven will comfort thee.

Print. *Miners' Advocate*, 19.10.1844, p. 187. Hair, *Sketches*, p. 13 note, quoted
G.P.Codden's 'the Pit-boy's Address to his Mother'. It was also used on a
Barnsley broadside in 1851 (Vicinus, *Broadsides*, p. 79), and together with a
'Parody' in a songbook produced by James Selkirk (*Selkirk's Collection*,
pp. 71–72). The 'Parody' is also in the 1872 edition of Allan, *Tyneside Songs*, p.
369, where authorship is ascribed to Thomas Wilson.
   Topliff evidently set the piece to music.

119. THE COLLIER'S WORTH.
AIR – *"The Woodman's Stroke."*

Ye pamper'd rich ones of this earth
List while I sing the Collier's worth,
Who, when his labour calls him forth,
   He quits the smile of day:
Descends the regions underground,
Where death and danger lurk around,
And cheerful at his work is found,
   He sings his fears away.

Tho' but a woolsey suit he gains,
Tho' one poor meal his bag contains
He never of his lot complains,
   But faithful to his charge.
For labour and for sweat prepared,
His limbs, his joints are never spared,
Content is with his hardship shared;
   He loves mankind at large.

The mighty prince – the pauper mean;
The beggar girl – th' illustrious queen;
And all the various ranks between
   At his coal fire regale.
Oh ye who are on dainties fed,
Think, when your table's richly spread,
What roasts your beef, and bakes your bread,
   And brews your sparkling ale.

The mighty, raging element
By man is taught a due restraint,
And oft its energies are spent
   On projects well designed.
It works the forge – it turns the mill:
It lifts the beam – it moves the wheel;
And art and commerce jointly feel
   Its benefactions kind.

The collier then, who health immures,
Who weary days and nights endures,
And the black sparkling coal procures
　　Which is so precious found.
His person and his trade should be
Regarded in a just degree,
And lauded by society,
　　By every neighbour round.

For me when wintry breezes blow,
When fast descends the driving snow,
At fire my freezing heart shall glow
　　While gratefully I think
How blest to have the coal-house stored
Such daily comforts to afford.
And when the glasses crown my board
　　The collier's health I'll drink.

Normanton, Derbyshire.

Print. *Miners' Advocate*, November 16th 1844, p. 195.

120. GOD HELP THE POOR.

God help the poor, who on this wintry morn
Come forth of alleys dim and courts obscure!
God help yon poor, pale girl, who droops forlorn,
And meekly her affliction doth endure!
God help the outcast lamb! she trembling stands,
All wan her lips, and frozen red her hands;
Her sunken eyes are modestly downcast;
Her night-black hair streams on the fitful blast;
Her bosom, passing fair, is half reveal'd;
And, O! so cold, the snow lies there congeal'd;
Her feet benumb'd, her shoes all rent and worn:
God help thee, outcast lamb, who stand'st forlorn!
　　God help the poor!

God help the poor! An infant's feeble wail
Comes from yon narrow gateway; and, behold,
A female crouching there, so deathly pale,
Huddling her child, to screen it from the cold!
Her vesture scant, her bonnet crush'd and torn;
A thin shawl doth her baby dear enfold:
And there she bides the ruthless gale of morn,
Which almost to her heart hath sent its cold!
And now she sudden darts a ravening look,
As one with new hot bread comes past the nook!
And, as the tempting load is onward borne,
She weeps. God help thee, hapless one forlorn!
    God help the poor!

God help the poor! Behold yon famish'd lad;
No shoes, nor hose his wounded feet protect;
With limping gait, and looks so dreamy sad,
He wanders onward, stopping to inspect
Each window stor'd with articles of food.
He yearns but to enjoy one cheering meal;
O! to his hungry palate, viands rude
Would yield a zest the famish'd only feel!
He now devours a crust of mouldy bread;
With teeth and hands the precious boon is torn,
Unmindful of the storm which round his head
Impetuous sweeps. God help thee, child forlorn!
    God help the poor!

God help the poor! Another have I found,
A bow'd and venerable man is he;
His slouched hat with faded crape is bound;
His coat is grey, and threadbare, too, I see;
"The rude winds" seem to "mock his hoary hair;"
His shirtless bosom to the blast is bare.
Anon he turns, and casts a wistful eye,
And with scant napkin wipes the blinding spray;
And looks again, as if he fain would spy
Friends he hath feasted in his better day
Ah! some are dead, and some have long forborne
To know the poor; and he is left forlorn!
    God help the poor!

God help the poor, who in lone valleys dwell,
Or by far hills, where whin and heather grow!
Theirs is a story sad, indeed, to tell;
Yet little cares the world, and less 'twould know,
About the toil and want they undergo.
The wearying loom must have them up at morn;
They work till worn-out nature will have sleep;
They taste, but are not fed. The snow drifts deep
Around the fireless cot, and blocks the door;
The night-storm howls a dirge across the moor,
And shall they perish thus, oppress'd and lorn?
Shall toil and famine hopeless still be borne?
No! God will yet arise, and HELP THE POOR!

                    Samuel Bamford.

Print. *Miners' Advocate*, December 14th 1844, p. 203
      Samuel Bamford was a veteran of Peterloo and a Lancashire poet.

121. POETRY COMPOSED ON ⌊JOB THE 14 CHAPTER⌋   **B&C:** the 14th
BY ROBERT* MARTIN {MINER} PERCY MAIN   Chapter of Job [C: R. only

Another year is allmost* gone   **B&C:** almost
And we are spared here to day *   **B&C:** *every other line indented*
How shall we our tribute bring   *throughout*
Or how shall we its debts repay

The time to man is short
His days they are but few
Let us not trifle with that time
To which we soon must bid adieu

Man is compared to yon* + flower   **B&C:** yonder
Which doeth* its bloming* nature crave   **B&C:** doth; blooming
And as is* the fall of every leaf   **B:** ⟨is⟩, **C:** *omitted*
So is* his steps toward the grave   **B&C:** are

Tho* short may be our time   B&C: Tho'
Tho* death our steps persue*   B&C: Tho'; pursue
We must not look on neither* side   B&C: either
But keep the prise* in view   B&C: prize

⌊It is god above⌋ that hath the power   B&C: 'Tis God alone
⌊It is⌋ he that hath the fountain made   B&C: 'Tis
⌊It was⌋ on yon* + calverys* cross*   B&C: 'Twas; yonder, *long 's'*
                                              here and elsewhere
His son the ransom paid   B: Calvery, C: Calvary

Thou hast determined ous* our day   B&C: us
From the* we cannot hide   B: thee, *altered from* ?,C: thee
Be with us lord while here on earth
And be our heavenly guide

Turn not from us thou heavenly king
But with us allways* keep   B&C: always
For ⌊we of the have need⌋   B&C: greatest need have
While passing through this watery deep   we of thee

Yonder + is* death with his cold hand   B&C: *omitted*
Appears approaching nigh
When he shall strike his killing dart
May we mount ⌊the upper⌋ sky   B&C: up unto the

Happy slumber to the christian
That doeth* sleep in yonder + shade   B&C: doth
Yea thrice happy are they †   B&C: all
That* in heaven their home hath made   B & C: Who

Friends: look: they are yonder +
Now in white before the throne
Fathers: Mothers: wate* with patience   B & C: wait
We shall soon arive* at home   B & C: arrive

+ A: *conventional hand with the fore-finger pointing rightwards, presumably to indicate a gesture used in public speaking – omitted in* B & C.

A & B: Manuscript. C: Print. A & B: Picton. C: Wigan 116 (294). A: Hand: Robert Martin. B: Hand: ? C: Broadside. Decorative border. Colophon: Newcastle: Printed by T. Dodds, 77 Side.

   Probably from December 1844, given the reference to the end of a year, and the fact that the decorative border seems to have been used by Dodds only after August 1844, as on 60B.

Appendix 1. The Roving Ploughboy

1

You lads and lasses* every where   *long 's', here and elsewhere*
[Un]to my song I pray Draw near
[Beli]eve me it is something queer
Concerning the roving ploughboy
[H]e was so tall genteel with all
[H]e was admired by one and all
And to kiss the girls against the wall
Indeed he was A droll Chap

Chorus
With my ran tan tweedle hi-ge-wo
We are the lads to reap and mow
We are the lads to plough and sow
Hurra for the roving ploughboy

2

When he was sixteen years of age
Indeed he was a roving blade
To kiss the girls he wasnt afraid
What think you of the ploughboy
He kiss-d you Nancy of the green
When she was scarcely turned sixteen
And then to Royton he did go
<?>{And} kissed the P———s daughter O

3

And when he came to Saxondale
He met a maid with a milking pail
She is called fair susan of the Vale
And she loved the roving ploughboy
He says young girl if you ll agree
To take a walk along with me
And thinking then they were not seen
They danced jack upon the green

4

And then he went to stockton town
And kissed the daughter of the crown
From there to sedgefield he did go
And took his lodgings at the plough
The landlady she loved him well
She treated him with gin and [ale]
What he did to her I will not tell
But she loved the roving ploughboy

5

And then to Durham he did stray
And found his way into the Bay
And there they had jovial spree
With the roving ploughboy
But soon from there he did retire
For fear his pistol should get fire
And to travel the country was his desire
So of went the roving ploughboy

6

Then for Newcastle he did start
And found his way into sandgate
Where he did meet A girl so smart
And she loved the roving ploughboy
He said young girl if you think it right
I ll lay with you this <?> very night
And when they had made all things right
Of went the roving ploughboy

7

And then to sunderland he did go
To view the bridge and see the shows
And to see them dncing* on their toes   *sic, ie* dancing
It surprised the roving ploughboy
He got a girl behind a show
And there they played at hi-ge-wo
But her name I do not know
But she loved the roving ploughboy

8

Then unto sheilds this youth did go
And stright into the steam mill now
And then to view the country round
He took a walk to morpeth town
And when he came to the Boars head
He went and called for A Bed
He laid with the maid as it is said
Then of went the roving ploughboy

9

And when to Alnwick town he came
He found his way into church lane
And among the lasses of the game
A sporting whent the ploughboy
They said young man can you use a flail
He told them many a pretty tale
But for fear that he should burn his tail
Of whent the roving ploughboy

10

Then through the country he did run
And stright away to stanerton
And when he came to Bellingham town
He took his lodgings at the crown
A gipsy girl was drinking there
She treated him with gin and beer
He pleased her well you need not fear
Then of went the roving ploughboy

11

So now for to finish my tale
He took a walk into the Vale
There he got married without fail
So success to the roving ploughboy
His wife and him they well agree
He has Been a roving blade you see
And may he ever happy be
So farewell to the roving ploughboy

Manuscript. Picton. Hand: ?
    This apparently anomalous piece is the first-placed of the manuscript texts
in the Picton Library collection, but its date is uncertain. It had been spiked.
There are some apparent echoes of *The Blacklegs* (90), and both Fordyce and
Ross published a piece called *The Roving Bachelor*.

Appendix 2. The Blackleg Miners [A & C]

Oh, early in the evening,* just after dark,
The blackleg miners creep ⌊out and go to work,⌋
With* their moleskin trousers ⌊and dirty old shirt⌋
    * ⌊Go the dirty⌋ blackleg miners.

B: evenin'
B: te wark
B: Wi'; an' dorty short,
B: *no indentations throughout;*
There go the

They take their picks ⌊and down⌋ they go,
⌊To dig out the coal that's lying down below,⌋
⌊And there isn't⌋ a woman in this town row**
    Will look at a blackleg miner.

B: an' doon
B: Te dig the coal that lies belaw,
B: An' there's not; toon-raw

Oh, Delaval is a terrible place,
They rub wet clay in the* blackleg's face,
⌊And round⌋ the pit-heaps they run a foot-race
    ⌊With the dirty⌋ blackleg miners.

B: a
B: An' roond
B: Wi' the dorty

Oh,* don't go near the Seghill mine,
For* across the mainway* they hang* a line,
To* catch the throat and* break the spine
    ⌊Of the dirty⌋ blackleg miners.

B: Now
B: *omitted;* way; stretch
B: Te; an'
B: O' the dorty

They'll take your tools and* your* duds as well,
⌊And throw them down in the pit of⌋ hell,
It's ⌊down you⌋ go and* fare you* well,
    ⌊You dirty⌋ blackleg miners.

B: an'; *omitted*
B: An' hoy them doon the pit o'
B: doon ye; an'; ye
B: Ye dorty

So* join the union while you* may,
Don't wait till your dying* day
For that may not be far away,
    ⌊You dirty⌋ blackleg miners.

B: Se; ye
B: dyin'

B: Ye dorty

Print. A: Lloyd, *Come all ye bold miners*, (1952), pp. 99–100. B: Lloyd, *Folk Song*, pp. 385–86. C: Lloyd, *Come all ye bold miners*, (1978), pp. 263–64.

Lloyd, *Come all ye bold miners*, (1952), p. 137, gave a text 'As sung by W.Sampey of Bishop Auckland, Co. Durham (1949). Cf. Korson, *Coal Dust on the Fiddle*, p. 334'. Lloyd, *Coaldust Ballads*, pp. 28–29, contained arrangements of material found in *Come all ye bold miners*, including this one, evidently adapted to (largely, male-voice) choirs. Oddly, this version was said to have been 'Collected in 1951':

The song dates from the period of the great Northumberland and Durham strikes of the 19th century when Cornish, Irish and Welsh labourers were imported as blacklegs. Some still worked on after the strikes were settled, and were often roughly treated in the darkness of the pit, particularly in the mines of Cramlington, Delavel and Seghill (Lloyd, *Coaldust Ballads*, p. 40).

Those were the pits named by Fynes, *The Miners*, p. 107–11, and mentioned by Burt, *An Autobiography*, pp. 37–38 and Douglass, *Pit Life*, pp. 66–70.

In 1962, the piece was recorded on *Along the Coally Tyne* (12T189), and the author of the sleeve notes, Frank Rutherford, dated the song's collection to 1949 but suggested it 'was born perhaps a hundred years earlier', noted 'savagery towards enemies' (one of 'the characteristics of the miner') and surmised that

Line three of verse two may be "But there's ne'er a woman in the Lang Row". The Lang Row at Seaton Delavel was one in which many miners were evicted, to provide homes for blackleg Cornishmen. There are people at Delavel who can remember their grandfather saying "There's nae gud luck in a Cornishman."

The Blackleg Miners was issued by Topic Records as part of *The Iron Muse* (12T86) in 1963 – though one side of this album is dated 1956. Lloyd (who wrote the sleeve-notes) had no doubt the piece was one of those which, 'without exception', were 'created by industrial workers out of their own daily experience and were circulated, mainly by word of mouth, to be used by the songwriters' workmates in mines, mills and foundries'. However, his ideas about dating had changed:

At the height of the miners' struggles of the 1880s and 1890s, labourers were brought in from other areas to act as strikebreakers. Ballads of the time describe how the colliers hunted the strikebreakers 'like hares upon the mountain O' [cf *First Drest Man of Seghill*, (17) published in 1831]. When caught, the blacklegs might be stripped and the clothes and tools thrown down the pit shaft. In the dark, a rope might be stretched across the way, to catch the non-union man by the throat and fling him down. The song, recorded in the 'amateur football belt' around Bishop Auckland, is one of several that crossed the sea from Durham to Glace Bay, Nova Scotia, where the American mining-song specialist George Korson found a variant, substantially different but nevertheless related.

Lloyd offered no evidence that his text came from the 1880s or 1890s, or that Korson's text had ever crossed the Atlantic. However, Lloyd's prestige amongst performers was such that when Johnny Handle produced a series of three articles (remarkably similar to Rutherford's earlier sleeve-notes) for *English Dance and Song* in 1965–1966, he completely accepted Lloyd's earlier notion that *The Blackleg Miners* came from the period of 'formation of unions within the coalfield', which took place before 1844:

Villages, towns and large parts of the county were torn by the struggle; in a typical strike in south Northumberland where Cornish labour was recruited to break the strike, the fine song, printed below, was born (Handle, *Industrial Folk Music*, p. 7).

The Blackleg Miners does not mention Cornish blacklegs specifically, though such men are known to have been recruited to break the strike of 1844, yet by the time of Ray and Archie Fisher's 1966 recording for the compilation album, *Folk Favourites* (ZLP 2067), this song had received the ultimate 'folk' accolade by being labelled 'Trad.', though the title was now *The Blackleg Miner* and the text (apparently deriving from Lloyd's) had been significantly Scotticised.

Confusion is worse confounded by the appearance in Lloyd's 1967 *Folk Song in England* of another version of the song, said to have been collected by the author in Durham in 1952 and first published in the 1952 edition of *Come all ye bold miners*. The text, which differs notably from that printed in 1952, appears towards the end of a long and polemical chapter on what Lloyd wished to be understood as a transitional form of English 'folksong', called 'Industrial song', which was a continuation of 'traditional' 'folksong' and a development of it. In this argument *The Blackleg Miners* was strategically important:

> One remarkable song that roamed far from its native Durham and became much altered on its travels is "The blackleg miners", a later and fiercer reflection of the kind of emotion that lay behind, for instance, the ballad of "The best-dressed man of Seghill", in which the strike-breaker is hunted like a hare on the moor and stripped of his clothes and his tools thrown down the pit shaft. Old miners still recall the dangerous practice referred to in the song, of stretching a rope across the pit-way so that, as the non-union man hurried along with his tubs of coal, he might be caught by the throat and flung backward. The great pioneer collector of American coalfields balladry, George Korson, reports a version of "The blackleg miners" from Glace Bay, Nova Scotia. There, the ballad still blazes, but not so fiercely as in its English birth-place. The hard taut entirely unliterary manner of the song (first recorded in Bishop Auckland, Durham in 1949) is in strong contrast to the rhetorical style of most official Labour anthems of the time. By a nice irony, the fierce text is set to a variant of the tune called in the North-East "The mode o' wooing" (Lloyd, *Folk Song*, p. 385).

There are some problems here. Firstly, what happened to the texts supposedly collected in 1951 and 1952? Secondly, why does Korson make no reference to *The Blackleg Miners* in relation to his song, *The Yahie Miners* (Korson, *Coal Dust*, pp. 334–35)? Thirdly, why is there no empirical evidence that Lloyd's text pre-dated 1850, 1900 or even 1949, since Korson's source, Stuart McCawley, believed the piece he sent in was 'sixty years old' in 1943, taking it back only to the 1880s? In fact, whatever 'blaze' had been caused by the song took light after *Come all ye bold miners* in 1952. (See also C & R, *The Miners' Association*, p. 149; Challinor, *A Radical Lawyer*, p. 133).

Lloyd wrote in a letter to the Editor, dated June 3rd 1971, that 'I only know *Blackleg Miners* from oral sources; I've not see a broadside of it'. Then, in 1978, he reissued a revised edition of *Come all ye bold miners*, though now with a rather more circumspect note about *The Blackleg Miners*:

> As sung by W.Sampey of Bishop Auckland, Co. Durham, 18 November 1949. George Korson, in *Coal Dust on the Fiddle* (Philadelphia, 1943) prints what looks like a parody of this song, called *The Yahie Miners*. Korson's version comes from Glace Bay, Nova Scotia, a well-known changing-post for British and American miners' songs. The Durham song has become quite widespread since its appearance in the first

edition of the present work, and the tune in particular has taken on variant shapes (Lloyd, *Come all ye bold miners*, (1978), p. 359).

Even then, Lloyd offers no evidence that his text pre-dates the 1880s, or even 1943, and so we are free to choose almost anywhere between 1844 and 1952 for its date of composition.

INDEX OF PLACES, PERSONS AND INSTITUTIONS

References to Durham City, County Durham, Newcastle and Northumberland are too frequent to be usefully listed. All collieries are listed together. References to textual sources are to be found in the appropriate footnote.

A., G., 54, 271
Accrington (Lancashire), 25, 66, 270
Adley, John, 6, 10, 105
Africa, 279
Ainsley, William, 43, 231
Albert, Prince, 21
Allan, Thomas, 74, 76, 87, 89, 105
Allendale, 142, 306
Alnwick, 319
Anderson, Kenneth, 100
Angus, George, 16, 86–87
Angus, Margaret, 4, 86–87, 92
Angus, Thomas, 4, 16, 86–87
Arbuthnot, General, 42
Ashton, Owen, 11, 35, 281
Atkinson, John, 48, 243
Australia, 23, 148, 167, 288
Baird, 23, 167
Bamford, Samuel, 65, 315
Baptists, 5, 170
Barkhouse, John, 30
Barnard Castle, 75
Barnsley (Yorkshire), 311
Bates, 183
Bath (Somerset), 25, 306
Bath Working Men's Association, 25
Beaumont, Augustus Hardin, 18
Beaumont, Thomas, 142
Beckwith, James, 10, 125
Bedlington, 208
Beehive, 208
Beesley, William, 25, 27–28, 31–32, 34, 37, 40–41, 54, 66, 69, 239, 270, 305–308
Bell, John *junior*, 11, 22, 70, 72–73, 76, 83, 86–87
Bell, John Gray, 68, 70, 73, 75, 216

Bell, John Spalding, 120, 215–216, 225, 235, 243, 268, 295, 297
Bell, Thomas, 70, 72–73
Bell, William, 70
Bellingham, 319
Benson, Michael, 40
Bewick, Thomas, 12
Binney, Thomas, 42
Binns, George, 18–19, 21
Birmingham (Warwickshire), 158
Birtley, 9
Bishop Auckland, 24, 64, 320–322
Black Dwarf, 6
Black Fell, 9, 121–122, 138, 140
Blyth, 74, 208
Boag, William, 40
Bolam, 183
Bolden Fell, 134
Bolton (Lancashire), 63, 304
Bond, Douglas, 74
Bo'ness (Scotland), 45, 47, 237
Botany Bay (Australia), 23, 148, 167, 288
Bouverie, General Henry, 10, 14
Brandling, Reverend, 14
Brazil, 208
Bridgton (Scotland), 168
British Museum (London), 76
Brockie, William, 3
Brown, C., 29, 181
Brown, Captain, 265
Buddle, John, 6, 9, 16–17, 74, 223, 225
Burdis, 183
Burt, Peter, 20, 50
Burt, Thomas, 2, 16, 42
Bury (Lancashire), 58
Butes ('plain face'), 257

Callinicos, Alex, 2, 58
Calton (Scotland), 168
Calvinists, 170
Cambridge University, 120
Cambridge University Library, 75–76
Camlachie (Scotland), 168
Camperdown, 297
Canada, 321–322
Carlisle (Cumberland), 16, 52
Cappy – see Ernshaw
Carr, Robert, 48–49, 244
Carr, Willie, 74
Castle Eden, 26, 172–174
Catchside-Warrington, C.E., 100, 103, 189
Catholics, 157
Challinor, Raymond, 2
Charnley, Emerson, 9
Charterhouse School, 25
Chartists, 1, 11, 16, 18–21, 23–32, 34–35, 37–38, 40–43, 45, 54, 60, 64–67, 76, 157–159, 281
Cheshire, 74
Chester-le-Street, 21, 41
Chicken, Edward, 3
Chirton, 101
Church of England, 14, 20, 25
Clark, Joseph, 7
Clarke, John, 12
Clasper, 64, 161
Cleadon, 208
Cockfield, 256
Cockrine, ('Master'), 108
Codden, G.P., 65, 311
Collieries:
    Backworth, 9, 106
    Bella Pit, 91
    Biggesmain, 258
    Bishop Auckland, 24
    Byker Hill, 21, 37
    Cassop, 37
    Coxlodge, 14, 141
    Cramlington, 52, 321
    Derwent, 226
    Earsdon, 60, 117, 119
    East Cramlington, 52
    East Holywell, 33, 37–38, 210, 236
    Ellison Main, 91
    Elswick, 56
    Fatfield, 121
    Framwellgate Moor, 44, 48, 53, 213, 232, 235, 244, 263–264, 289
    Greencroft, 54, 266
    Harrington, 121

Haswell, 17, 33, 147–149, 155–157
Hebburn, 53
Hetton, 7, 9, 12, 108–109, 121, 123
Hilda Pit, 7
Horton, 67
Isabella Pit, 91
Kenton, 14, 141
Killingworth, 216
Lambton, 121
Lumley, 125
Monkwearmouth, 54, 264–265
Nesham, 109
Newbottle, 10, 105, 123
New Trimdon, 45
North Elswick, 25–26
Ouston, 49, 121
Percy Main, 6, 68, 87, 291, 315
Pidddington, 121
Pittington, 125
Ravensworth, 63
Renton, 121
Russell, 121
Seaton Delavel, 38, 320–322
Seghill, 9, 53, 59, 65, 117–120, 290, 320–321
Sheffield Colliery (Yorkshire), 58
Sherriff Hill, 10, 120
Shiny Row, 37, 121
Shotton, 57, 285
Shotton Moor, 29, 34, 149, 181–184, 199, 255–257, 295
South Wingate, 58, 197, 286
Southwick, 291
Spital Tongues, 52, 255
Staw Pit, 110–113
Stevenson (Scotland), 53, 183
Thornley, 17, 21, 24, 31, 34, 36–37, 43, 45, 48, 63–64, 148, 206–209, 250, 288–289, 306
Townly Main, 110–113
Trimdon, 55, 277
Wallsend, 17, 225
West Moor, 38, 213, 215–216
West Rainton, 57, 280–281
Willington, 17, 151–152
Wingate, 28, 30, 55, 179, 187, 241, 277
Winlaton, 239
Collingwood, Admiral, 161
Colls, Robert, 2, 92
Combination Acts, 7, 47
Communist Manifesto, 27

Coombes, 64, 161
Cornwall, 321
Cowen, Joseph, 67
Cowey, Nicholas, 29–30, 57, 184, 285
Cowie, George, 47, 237
Cramlington, 158
Cranky, Bob, 4, 84–87, 90–92
Craw Hall, Christy, 81
Crooks, ('Noble' and 'little'), 182, 256
Cumberland, 16, 52
Dalkeith (Scotland), 52, 253
Daniells, William, 28–42, 44–49, 52–53, 55–57, 59–62, 64, 69–70, 176, 179, 184, 189, 192, 201, 206, 225, 229, 235, 240, 243, 255, 268, 273, 275, 277, 285, 298
Darlington, 3, 66
Davis' Straits, 103
Dawson, Willy, 9–10, 122–123
Deans, ('friend'), 253
Dee, ('Admiral'), 140
Dennison, Jim, 295
Dent, Mark, 16, 60
Dent, Roger, 26
Derbyshire, 65, 313
Dixon, William, 32
Dobson (Chirton), 101
Dobson (Willington), 51
Dodds, Henry, 18, 127, 159
Dodds, Matthew Stephenson, 18
Dodds, Thomas, 17–23, 25–27, 29–32, 36–37, 39–40, 42–43, 45–46, 49, 52–56, 59–60, 62, 64, 68–73, 75, 127, 144, 154, 159–160, 162, 164–166, 168, 171, 179–180, 186, 188–189, 206–207, 209, 215, 218–220, 227, 231–232, 235, 240–241, 243, 249–250, 261, 264–265, 268, 270–271, 277, 280–281, 285, 287, 289, 293, 295, 298–301, 316
Dodds, Mrs. T., 46
Doncaster (Yorkshire), 22
Dorset, 25
Douglas, William, 10, 16, 122, 131, 133, 142, 157
Dublin (Ireland), 59
Durham Advertiser, 34
Durham, Bishop of, 4
Durham Chronicle, 13, 37, 47
Durham Goal, 14, 15, 144, 172, 288
Edgar, James, 32
Edinburgh (Scotland), 32

Egypt, 248
Embleton, Benjamin, 4, 9, 21, 24, 66
Emery, Robert, 8, 116
Encyclopaedia Britannica, 11
English Dance & Song, 321
Engels, Frederick, 66–67
Erington, 182
Ernshaw ('Cappy'), 5, 89, 98–100, 103
Fairles, Nicholas, 15, 144
Fatfield, 102
Fawcett, Joseph, 35, 63, 206
Fawcett, R. Henderson, 33–34, 58, 197, 280, 286–287
Fawdon, 6
Fearless, Peter, 61, 295–297
Fenwick, Jack, 82
Fenwick, Peg, 82
Fife, John, 18
Fifeshire, 32
Fish Betty, 61, 297–298
Fisher, Archie, 322
Fisher, Ray, 322
Fletcher, 183
Fordyce, Thomas, 16–17, 21, 26, 83, 92, 105, 127, 152, 164, 319
Fordyce, William, 11, 16–17, 21, 26, 83, 92, 105, 127, 150, 152, 164, 319
Foreman's Row, 158
Forrest, John, 135
Forster, T., 184
Forster, Thomas, 62
Foster, Mr. (Haswell), 148–149
Foster, Mr., (Shotton Moor), 29, 149
France, 5, 105–106, 153
France, David, 32,
Freeman, Dick, 61, 295–297
Frost, John, 23, 41, 167, 185, 227, 229
Fynes, Richard, 2, 60
Gair, Elizabeth, 54, 268
Gape, Willy, 256
Garibaldi, Giuseppe, 67
Gateshead, 5, 14, 16, 22, 75, 105, 113, 135
Gateshead Observer, 16
General and Municipal Workers' Union, 120
General Strike (1842), 23
George IV, King, 5
Germany, 19, 66, 159
Gilbert, John, 100
Gilfellon, Tommy, 295

Glace Bay (Nova Scotia), 321–322
Glasgow (Scotland), 39–40, 167
Glasgow University Library, 76
Goldstein, Kenneth S., 75
Gordon, James, 52, 255
Gosforth, 72
Granger, 305
Gray, John, 216
Greenland, 103
Greenwell, George Clementson, 74
Hall, John, 21, 25, 37, 64, 210–211
Hall, Joseph, 10, 120
Hall, R., 216
Hall, Thomas, 21
Hall, T.Y., 156
Halliday, Mr., 64
Hallowell, 119
Hammond, William, 9, 33–34, 39, 193, 195, 225
Handle, Johnny, 321
Hardie, 23, 167
Harker, Dave, 82, 87, 92, 295
Harney, Julian, 27
Hartlepool, 208, 308
Haswell, Christopher, 9, 66
Haswell, Robert, 9
Heartless, Harry, 53, 261–263
Hebburn, 260
Henderson, John, 53, 261
Henderson, Robert, 54, 270
Hepburn, Thomas, 9–11, 13, 15, 18–19, 33, 38, 42, 54, 121, 134, 144
Hernaman, John, 142–143
Hetherington, 184
High Level Ranters, 83
Hill, William, 45
Hindmarsh, John, 216
Hodge, John Barlow, 164
Hodge, Thomas, 164, 174
Hodgson Family 40
Hogg, 184
Holder, Robert, 43, 49, 245
Holliday, Henry, 54, 266, 268
Hollis, William, 164, 174
Home Office (London), 14, 28, 50
Hone, William, 5
Hopper, 109
Horn, Thomas, 32
Hornby, 29, 34, 183
Hornsby, William, 29, 33–34, 53, 60, 72, 199, 255, 257, 295
Houghton-le-Spring, 10, 102, 125
House of Commons – see Parliament
Hull (Yorkshire), 16

Hunt, Henry, 5
Hunt, Michael, 100, 103
Hunter, W.M., 53, 149, 189
Indian slaves, 126, 247
Ireland, 20, 23, 59, 67, 121, 168, 180, 199, 269, 321
Isle of Man, 64
Israelites, 248
Italy, 67
Jackson, 183
Jarrow Slake, 15, 144–145
Jefferson, 183
Jerusalemites, 170
Jews, 171, 300, 307
Jobling, William, 15, 144
Jobson, 307
Johnson, Alfred, 18
Johnson, ('Brave'), 151–152
Johnson, William, 44, 48, 232, 235, 264, 289
Jones, William, 23, 167, 185
Journal of the Folk Song Society, 289
Jowsey, 7, 109
Jude, Martin, 21, 26, 35, 37, 46, 64, 66–67
Kent, William, 10, 16, 122, 131, 133, 142
Kimbley (Nottinghamshire), 38
Knight, Jane, 48, 240
Knox, Jeremiah, 11–12, 128–129, 131
Knox, Robert, 11
Korson, George, 321–322
Lambton, 102
Lancashire, 6, 21, 23, 25, 29, 40, 58, 63–64, 66, 68–73, 75–76, 120, 215, 225, 235, 243, 257, 261, 268, 270, 295, 297, 304, 315, 319
Lasswade (Scotland), 32
Latter-Day Saints, 51, 170
Leeds (Yorkshire), 18, 25, 158
Leigh (Lancashire), 71
Liberals, 67
Liverpool (Lancashire), 68–73, 76, 225, 235, 243, 257, 261, 268, 270, 297, 315
Lloyd, Albert Lancaster, 82–84, 108, 120, 122, 127, 131, 133, 135, 138, 144, 147, 156–157, 164, 215–216, 225, 235, 241, 243, 255, 261, 268, 270, 273, 275, 277, 281, 289, 295, 297–298, 320–323
Lockey, Liz, 72
London, 3, 7, 11, 14–15, 17, 19, 21–22, 25, 28, 40, 44, 50, 58, 68,

70, 75–76, 127, 135, 153, 158, 161–162, 225, 243, 288–289
Londonderry, Lord, 24, 42, 50, 52, 56–58, 60, 63, 81
Lowery, Robert, 220
Lumley, 102
Lumsdon, ('poor'), 207
McCawley, Stuart, 322
Mc.Clashin, Arthur, 115
Macfarlane, Helen, 27
Mackenzie, Eneas,12–13, 16, 26, 116, 137
Mackenzie, Peter, 42
Madden, Sir Frederick, 75–76
Mainwaring, Mrs., 63, 303
Manchester (Lancashire), 6, 40, 66, 70, 315
Marat, Jean-Paul, 41, 60
Marshall, Betty, 5
Marshall, John, 5–12, 16, 25, 83–84, 86, 89, 92, 98, 100, 105–106, 116, 120, 129
Martin, John, 59, 291
Martin, Robert, 18, 35, 65, 291, 315–316
Matthews, J., 28, 55–56, 179, 277
Marx, Karl, 66
Mental Improvement Society, 32
Methodists, 4, 6, 41–43, 51, 60, 66, 213 – see also Primitive and Wesleyan
Miles, 12
Miners' Advocate, 19, 31–41, 44–49, 52–53, 55–56, 59, 63–66, 69–72, 76, 202, 209, 213, 235–236, 244, 291
Miners' Association, 24–27, 30–56, 58–64, 69–72, 76, 200
Miners' Benefit Society, 71
Miners' Friendly Protection Society, 37, 71
Miners' Journal, 26–28, 31–33, 69, 190–192
Miners' Monthly Magazine, 40, 45, 49, 64
Miners' Philanthropical Society, 21, 23–24, 29, 174–180
Mitchell, William, 49
Mitford, William, 4–5, 89, 92, 98, 100, 103
Moffat, David, 52, 253
Molyneux ('Molinox'), 88
Monmouthshire, 23, 30
Morpeth, 319

Morrison, David, 287
Mouter, 216
Murray, Adam, 55, 68, 277
Murton, 118–119
N., I., 31, 190–192
N., W., 60, 293
N., W.S., 33, 37, 210
Napoleon Bonaparte, 91
New Painshaw, 102
New Zealand, 19
Newbottle, 102
Newcastle Central Reference Library, 74–76, 144, 273, 281
Newcastle Chartist Hall, 24
Newcastle Coal Trade Committee (and Office), 11, 56, 60, 226
Newcastle Corporation, 13
Newcastle Freemen, 8, 18, 114–116
Newcastle Journal, 47, 142
Newcastle Literary and Philosophical Society, 5
Newcastle Music Hall, 59
Newcastle Temperance Society, 62
Newcastle Town Moor, 6, 9, 60, 63, 87, 114–116
Newcastle University Library, 74–76
Newcastle Working Men's Association, 18
Newell, 161
Newerwrick, 182
Newport (Monmouthshire), 23, 30
Newton, William Malcolm, 74
Nicholson, Thomas, 33, 37–38, 45, 210, 236
Normanton (Derbyshire), 65, 313
North of England Institute of Mining and Mechanical Engineers (NEIMME), 72–75
North Shields, 54, 66–67, 70, 98, 103–104, 108, 158, 208, 270 319
North Shields Sailors' Association, 67
Northern District Temperance Record, 16
Northern Liberator, 18
Northern Political Union, 13
Northern Star, 18, 21, 22, 24–25, 32, 37, 45, 51
Northumberland Record Office, 72–73, 76
Norwell, Margaret, 72
Nottinghamshire, 38
Nova Scotia (Canada), 321–322
O'Connor, Feargus, 18–19, 24, 41, 157–159, 227, 229, 288–289
Oddfellows, 35, 89

Ouseburn, 18
Paisley (Scotland), 168
Paradise, 119
Parkhead (Scotland), 168
Parkinson, Charles, 9
Parliament (London), 11–13, 15, 17, 22, 40, 44, 58, 127, 135, 225
Parish, 161
Pasquill, Matthew, 63, 304
Patten, 184
Patterson, George, 48, 244, 264
Pearson, Margaret, 26, 172
Pearson, Robert, 26, 172–174
Peel, Sir Robert, 22
Perring (Printer), 142–143
Peterloo (Manchester, Lancashire), 6, 315
Philadelphia (Durham), 102
Philadelphia (Pennsylvania, USA), 75
Picton Library Liverpool (Lancashire), 68–73, 76, 225, 235, 243, 257, 261, 268, 297, 319
Pluck, Peter, 53, 261–263
Pollock, James Kelly, 5, 7, 98, 100, 103, 108
Potter, ('aud'), 116
Powell, John, 156
Poynton (Cheshire), 74
Preston (Lancashire), 64
Primitive Methodists ('Ranters'), 6–7, 9, 13, 15–16, 21, 24, 27, 33, 38, 42–43, 51–52, 60, 65–66, 170, 213, 218–219
Proctor, John, 308
Purdy, James, 48, 239–240
Pyle, Benjamin, 37–38, 212
R., ('Black') J., 117–119
Radcliffe (Lancashire), 58
Rainton, 102
Ranters – see Primitive Methodists
Ratcliffe, C., 59, 65, 290, 310
Rathcormack (Ireland), 168
Raven, Michael, 164
Reay, Samuel, 87, 89, 105
Rechabites, 20, 53, 258–261
Red Republican, 27
Red Sea, 248
Redford, Bill, 265
Reform Act, 15, 30
Reform Bill, 19, 127, 186
Rewcastle, James, 16, 62, 299
Richardson, 184
Richardson, Edward, 66
Richardson, Thomas, 36, 207–209

Ripley, Brian, 2
Ritson, Joseph, 22, 83–84
Roberts, Stephen, 45
Roberts, William Prowting, 25, 27–28, 31–32, 34–37, 40–41, 43, 45, 48–51, 54–55, 58, 60, 62, 64, 66–67, 144, 206–207, 228–229, 231, 239–243, 250–251, 266, 268–270, 273–275, 281, 288–289, 305–308
Robertson, 39
Robson, Joseph Philip, 35–38, 45, 49, 56, 58, 69, 83, 157, 206, 211–212, 215–216, 245, 280
Robson, Thomas, 63
Ross, John, 100, 157, 245, 319
Roxburghe Collection, 76
Roxby, William, 28, 54–55, 175–176, 229, 272–273
Royal Navy, 17, 20–22
Royton, 317
Rutherford, Frank, 87, 321
Ryan, ('Widow'), 168
Sadler, Mr., 5, 90–92, 147
St. Agnes, 161
Sampey, W., 320, 322
Saxondale, 317
Scaffold Hill, 24
Scargill, Arthur, 58
Scotland, 32–33, 38–40, 45, 47, 52–53, 76, 121, 167–168, 174–175, 180, 183, 193, 199, 209, 230, 237, 253, 269, 272, 322
Seaham, 58, 208
Seaton Delaval, 65
Sedgefield, 318
Seghill, 158, 309–310
Selkirk, James, 311
Selkirk, John, 4, 87
Sern, G., 118
Sessford, Jack, 35
Setter, Mrs., 75
Shadons Hill, 24, 41–42, 50, 64, 120, 123
Sharp, Cuthbert, 83
Sharp, John, 216
Sharp, William, 216
Sheffield (Yorkshire), 63, 303
Sheffield University Library, 120
Shiels, Tom, 265
Shiny Row, 102, 264
Sinclair, James, 32
Smith, ('brother'), 25
Smith, James, 34, 200
Smith, W., 89

Somerset, 25, 306
South Shields, 7, 15, 18, 24–25, 52, 66, 103–104, 144, 158–159, 208, 319
Spoor, Reverend, 51
Staffordshire, 32
Stanerton, 319
Stanhope, 12
Stella, 110–113
Stephenson, (Miner), 109
Stephenson, William, 6–8, 10, 12, 16, 105, 109, 113, 135, 140, 145
Steward, Lord, 109
Stewart, T., 216
Stobhill (Scotland), 52, 253
Stockport (Cheshire), 74
Stockton, 318
Stokoe, John, 87, 89, 105
Stoneyhurst College, 157
Story, William Walker, 57, 272, 280–281
Stove, Anthony, 36
Suffolk, 53
Sunday School Union, 61
Sunderland, 3, 10, 16, 18, 21, 32–33, 103–104, 164, 172, 174, 208, 287
Swallow, David, 24
Tanfield, 50
Tantobie, 50
Tayleure, Mr., 86
Taylor, Dorothy, 70
Taylor, Thomas John, 72
Teetotalism, 16, 19–20, 61–62
Thomason, William, 32, 35, 201
Thompson, Matthew, 216
Thompson, Thomas, 216
Thompson, ('Valiant'), 182
Thornley, 289
Tolpuddle Martyrs (Dorset), 25
Topliff, Robert, 3, 84, 311
Tories, 16, 19, 25, 158–159
Tremenheere, Commissioner Seymour, 32, 43, 51, 66–67
Tulip, John, 50
Turkey, 166
Turton, John, 58–60, 63, 75
Tweedie, P., 216
Twizell, 156
Tynemouth, 74
United Association of Colliers, 7–8
U-[nthan]-k, Tommy, 122
Unitarians, 5
United States of America, 75, 121
Van Dieman's Land (Australia), 148
Veitch, 305

Victoria, Queen, 28, 134, 152, 160, 176, 185
Wade, ('Noble'), 265
Wails, 149
Wakefield (Yorkshire), 24
Wales, 35, 174–175, 199, 210, 230, 321
Wales, Prince of, 22
Walker, George, 17, 21, 75, 147, 149, 154, 156–157, 219
Walker, William, 100
Wall, John, 38, 213, 264
Wappen, 102
Wardhaugh, James, 29, 179–180
Wardle, 183
Wardle, Samuel, 9,
Wardle, Tom, 256
Warrenites, 170
Warwickshire, 158
Watson Family, 75
Watson, George, 57, 280–281
Watson, William, 281
Wearmouth, Kate, 172
Wearmouth, Robert, 60
Wesleyan Methodists, 9, 33, 51, 65, 170
West Houghton, 24
Whigs, 19, 158–159
Whiston, 120, 215, 225
White, Robert, 75–76
Whittle, W., 182
Wigan Archives (Leigh, Lancashire), 69, 71–73, 75–76, 235
Wilde, Sir Thomas, 305
William IV, King, 13
Williams, James, 32
Williams, John, 18, 23
Williams, John R., 10, 287
Williams, Zepheniah, 167, 185
Willington, 51, 75, 101–102
Willis, N.E., 71
Wilson, 23, 107
Wilson, Joseph, 67
Wilson, Thomas, 8, 75, 311
Wingate, 48, 51
Wingate Grange, 30, 188
Winlaton, 11
Wiseacre, Tommy, 49
Wishit, Dick, 115
Wooler, Thomas, 6
Yarrow, Margaret, 172
Yorkshire, 16, 18, 22, 24–25, 29, 58, 63–64, 120, 158, 179–180, 303, 311

INDEX OF TITLES AND FIRST LINES

Titles are given in italic, and are listed alphabetically with any initial definite or indefinite article placed last, after a comma. Titles supplied by the current editor or by a previous one are given in square brackets. Where a title begins with the same phrase (eg, *A New Song*), each entry is followed by the subtitle or all or part of the first line (in brackets). Where differing versions of a piece have notably different titles or first lines each is given, but where they are similar only that of the A text is listed. First lines are given verbatim, including any initial articles, except that potentially confusing punctuation is sometimes omitted. Numbers refer to items, not pages.

A dialogue I'll tell you as true as my life, 107
A Song I,ll sing if you,l attend, and pay attention to my ditty, 89
A voice it hath gone through the breadth of the land, 77
A year of wonder now is come, 104
Address to the Miners, An, 87
Address to the Miners of Britain, An, 57
Address to the Miners of Scotland, An, 54
Alas! what will become of me, 56
All you distress'd tradesmen in country and town, 43
Another year is allmost gone, 121
Aroused by the Caller's well-known voice, 102
As I walked forth one summer's morn, all in the month of June, 40
As late I passed a stately hall, 117
As me and my Marrow was ganning to wark, 2
Auld Lang Syne, 98
Aw wrought in a Pit by the side o' the Moor, 16
Awake, ye sons that work the mine, 87
Away wi' the knave, the lying knave, 86
Away with the king of the bright black coal, 65
Before the rulers of his Fate, 88
Blackleg Miners, The, Appendix 2
[Blacklegs, The], 90
Bob Cranky's Account of the Ascent of Mr Sadler's Balloon, 3
Bob Cranky's 'Size Sunday, 5
Bold Collier, The, 10
Bonnie Pit Lads, The, 40
Britains, Where your once boasted bravery, 74
Call the Horse, Marrow, 1
Call the horse, marrow, 1
Call to the Miners of Great Britain, A, 74
Cappy; or the Pitman's Dog, 5
Cheer up, cheer up, my fellow men, don't let your spirits fail, 75
Coal King!, The, 65
Coal King and the Pitman, The, 117

Coal Owners' Vend, and the Miners' Union, The, 75
Coal Trade, The, 9
Collier Boy, The, 71
Collier Swell, The, 35A
Collier's Complaint, The, 113
Collier's Worth, The, 119
Colliers' Appeal to the Country, The, 85
Colliers Rant, The, 2
Colliers: where's Your once boasted Glory, 96
Colliery Union, The, 94
Come all good people lend an ear, 106
Come all kind-hearted Christians, 81
Come all my friends and neighbours and listen unto me, 25
Come all ye bold miners wherever you be, 93B
Come all ye good people that live in this village, 97
Come all ye brave Miners and listen, 57
Come, all ye Miners, far and near, 17
Come all ye noble Colliery Lads, 94
Come all yea miners of wear and tyne, 49
Come all you bold miners where-ever you be, 93A
Come all you canny pitmen here come listen to my song, 31
Come all you Colliers in this place, 82
Come all you good people and listen a while, 36
Come all you good people and listen to my song, 62
Come all you honest pitmen lads, 22
Come all you jolly fellows and listen unto me, 48
Come all you philanthropists attend a while to me, 44
Come all you working people what shall we do now, 38
Come all you worthy Christians, 112
Come Hither all Miners Kind, Honoust Social and free, 46
Come, Lay Down Yor Picks, 15
Come, lay down yor picks and awa', marrows, 15
Come, let us make a Union Knot, 63
Come sit ye down and hear the news, 90
Copy of Verses on the Castle Eden Tragedy, 45
Copy of Verses Referring to the Preasant State of Things, A, 101A
Copy of Verses. Written on the Pitmen being turned out from their Houses and Homes..., A, 28
Cries of the Poor, The, 43
Curious Dialogue...between a Pitman and his Wife, A, 6
Darkness prevailing, darkness prevailing, 111
Dear shades of my Fathers! sad thoughts now oppress me, 76
Dialogue between Harry Heartless and Peter Pluck, A, 91
Dialogue between Peter Fearless and Dick Freeman, A, 108
Each feeling heart I pray attend, 28
Eighteen hundred and thirty-one, as I have heard them say, 18
[Explosion, The], 72
Famishing Miner, The, 88
First Drest Man of Seghill, 17
Fish Betty, is my nyem, you see, 109B-C
Fish Bettys Account of Herself, 109
God Help the Poor, 120
God help the poor, who on this wintry morn, 120
Good christians all to me draw near before I go away, 85

Good mornin Harry, how dis things luk now, 91
Good people all give ear we pray, 14
Good people all I pray draw near and listen unto me, 30
Good people listen while I sing, 9
Great George cam ridin' in his gig, 92
Grievances of the Pitmen, 19
Grim Tyrant! when will thy envenom'd darts, 66
Hail union let the echo fly, 53B-D
Hark the noble Pitmen's cause, 95
Haswell Cages, 36
Hetton Coals, 12
Hetton-Main coal now is won, 12
How, Jobson, has the heard the news, 116
Howay a' my marrows, big, little, and drest, 5
Ho'way and aw'll sing thee a tune, mun, 3
I used to be a vulgar clown, with cash and money short in, 35
In a Town near Newcassel a Pitman did dwell, 7
In eighteen hundred and thirty one as I have heard them say, 19
In eighteen hundred and thirty two, 27
In the Year Eighteen hundred, & forty & four, 101
It happen'd on March the twenty-third day, 11
It's on the 5th of April, the days were long and clear, 26
It was on the seventeenth day of March, 34
James Smith, 58
Job, the Patient Man, 112
John Hall, 64
Joy lifts the dancer's merry feet, 64
Just is the cause which in union we are combined, 58
Keep up your hearts, ye noble boys, 100
Lamentation of William Jobling..., 30
Lamented Carr! how sudden was your death, 83
Let canny Newcastle once more raise her head, 39
Let us live by our Labour – and never forget, 84
Lines on the Death of Robert Carr, 83
Lines to the Memory of Mr. B. Pyle, 66
Lines, written on seeing the West Moor Explosion in the 'Miners' Advocate', 67
Lo! What is this that strikes my ear, 72B
Madman of Wingate, The, 51
Matthew Pasquill, 114
Men for themselves now reflect in due season, 114
Men of Britain! now before you, 99
Miner's Binding, The, 11
Miner's Complaint, The, ('Alas! what will become of me'), 56
Miner's Doom, The, ('Aroused by the Caller's well-known voice'), 102
Miner's Doom, The, (' 'Twas evening, and a sweeter balm...'), 60
Miner's Prayer, The, 110
Miner's Right, The, 80B
Miners Advocate, The, 78
Miners' Complaint, The, ('On the twenty fifth of November last'), 61
Miners' Friend, The, 76
[Miners' Grievances, The], 77
Miners' Motto, The, 84
Miners' Philanthropical Society, The, 48
Miners Rights, The, 80A

Mr Roberts the Pitmen's Friend, 103
Munkwaremouth Turn-out, 92
My hearty cocks come join with me, 32
My nyem it's Fish Betty, 109A
Neighbours, countrymen, and friends, 42
Newcastle & London Boat Match..., 39
New Song, A, ('A dialogue I'll tell you as true as my life'), 107A
New Song, A, ('A Song I,ll sing if you,l attend...'), 89
New Song, A, ('Come all ye bold miners wherever you be'), 93B
[New Song, A], ('Come all ye good people that live in this village'), 97
New Song, A, ('Come all you bold miners where ever you be'), 93A
New Song, A, ('Come all you canny pitmen...'), 31
New Song, A, ('Come all you Colliers in this place'), 82
New Song, A, ('How, Jobson, has the heard the news'), 116
New Song, A, ('In eighteen hundred and thirty-two'), 27
New Song, called, the Haswell Binding, A, 32
New Song, called the Wonderful Shaver, or Tom R-d-n's Life, A, 62
New Song composed and writen for the Miners Philanthropic Society..., A, 46
New Song composed for the Miners' Philanthropic Society, A , 47A-C
New Song in praise of Willington Colliery, A, 34
New Song on the Pitmen's Grievances, A, 81
New Song on XYZ: or, Pitmen's Luck, A, 4
Now Dicky, was thou at Meeting to day, 108
Now let the colliers' hearts be glad, 24
O'Conner's Visit to Newcastle, 37
O! how can a mortal or his pen describe, 13
O listen to our mournful tale, 41
O Lord hear the poor pitmen's cry, 20
Oh, early in the evening, just after dark, Appendix 2
Oh have you heard the news of late, 115
Old Woman and the Coal Owner, The, 107B
On the eighteenth of march eighteen hundred forty three, 80
On the Sufferings of the Pitmen in the dreadful explosion, in Staw Pit..., 13
On the twenty fifth of November last, 61
Once compensations bounteous hand, 98
One night as I came home from work, 8
Oppressions of the Pitmen, The, 18
Patriotism, 79
Pit Boy, The, 118
Pitman's Complaint, The, 20A
Pitman's Courtship, The, 8
Pitman's Hymn, The, 69
Pitman's Surprise, The, 16
Pitman's Union, The, ('It's on the 5th of April...'), 26
Pitman's Union, The, ('You Britons all where'er you be'), 50
Pitman Turned Swell, The, 35B
Pitmen Determined to be Free, The, 106
Pitmen's Agreement, The, 22
Pitmen's Complaint, The, 21
Pitmen's Disgust to the Monthly Bond, The, 73
Pitmen's Stick, The, 23
Pitmen's 'Torney-General, The, 115
Pitmen's Union, The, ('Keep up your hearts, ye noble boys'), 100
Pitmen's Union, The, ('To our camplaints give ear'), 29

Pitmen's Union, The, ('Ye Pitmen who dwell near the Wear and the Tyne'), 33
Pitmen's Union: or the Lads of the Wear and Tyne, The, 24
Poetry Composed on Job the 14 Chapter, 121
Poor Tradesmen's Lamentation, The, 42
Ranters' Ship, The, 70
Reason's Claim, or, the Miners' Plea to the Owners, 99
Relentless death, untimely to destroy, 67
Roving Ploughboy, The, Appendix 1
[Saviour's Death, The], 111
Silence was in the lowly cot – the Trapper-boy reclined, 68
Smash, Jenny, let us buss, we'll off and see Newcastle races, 4
Song, ('Away wi' the knave, the lying knave'), 86
Song of the Oppressed, 95
Song of the Oppressor, 105
Song to the Blacklegs and all thats not in the Union, A, 96
Sons of slavery come with me, 55
State of the Times, 38
State of the Times and their Causes, The, 44
Sweat union let the echo fly, 53A
Sweet, dear and loving Wife, 6
The christian collier rises soon, 69
The Coal King sat in his chair of state, 105
The light of day had scarcely dawn'd, 59
The man who's got so strong an arm, 51
The noble patriot scorns to plant a root, 79
The Ranters's ship along is sailing, 70
The sun is sinking fast, mother, 118
Thou, Lord, dost make the meanest soul, 110
Thou tyrant, see the Miners' glass displayed, 78
Tis of a fox hunting which latley took Place, 52
To our camplaints give ear, 29
Toil unceasing has been ours, 113
Total Banishment of Self-Tyranny & Oppression, The, 25
Trapper-Boy's Dream, The, 68
'Twas evening, and a sweeter balm on earth was never shed, 60
Union, ('Hail, Union! let the echo fly'), 53B-D
Union, ('Sweat union let the echo fly'), 53A
Union!, ('Sons of slavery come with me'), 55
Union and Liberty, 47D
Union Knot, The, 63
[Ventilation], 49
Verses on the Cruelty of the Masters to the Pitmen, 20B-C
Verses on the Present State of Things, 101B-C
Weaver's Lamentation, The, 41
What is this which strikes my ear, 72A
Widows' Lamentation, The, 14
Wingate Grange Blue Hounds in Pursuit of a Fox, The, 52
Wonderful!, 104
Workhouse Boy, The, 59
Ye Collier Lads, I pray attend, 21
Ye collier lads I pray attend, 23
Ye Miners all both great and small, 73
Ye pamper'd rich ones of this earth, 119
Ye pitmen who dwell near the Wear and the Tyne, 33

Ye Scottish sons who daily toil, 54
Ye true Sons of union, like Britons, be bold, 47A
Ye Working men of Briton's Isle, 45
Ye working-men of collieries attention pay to me, 103
Yea true Sons of union like Britons be bold, 47D
Yon starry light that rules the night, 71
You Britons all, where'er you be, 50
You Chartists all both far and near, 37
You gallants of England, come listen awhile, 10
You lads and lasses every where, Appendix 1